COLLECTORS' CARS

COLLECTORS' CARS

Lee Culpepper

Foreword by
Albert R. Bochroch

CRESCENT BOOKS

© MCMLXXIX Octopus Books Limited

First English edition published by
Octopus Books Limited
59 Grosvenor Street
London W1

Library of Congress Catalog Card Number 78-21133
All rights reserved
This edition is published by Crescent Books
a division of Crown Publishers, Inc.
One Park Avenue, New York, N.Y. 10016

Printed in Singapore.

Contents

Foreword

To the collector of old cars and to the thousands who follow car collecting, Classic as well as Antique, Veteran, Edwardian, Vintage and Pioneer, have come to mean cars of a certain age. However, age is not necessarily a universal criteria. The newest of America's national car collecting groups, the Milestone Club, is a multi-marque society that uses distinction rather than age as its criterion, with all types of car from the two decades following World War II receiving its attention.

In the United States and Canada, the Antique Automobile Club of America designates any car made before January 1930 as an antique. Founded in 1935, the AACA is the nation's largest car club, and its more than 300 regions have a world-wide membership of over 35,000. In 1975, the AACA expanded its car classifications to 54. Antique cars remain those made before 1930; Classic cars are described by the AACA as 'exceptionally fine cars of specific makes . . . dating from 1930 until 1942,' while vehicles more than 25 years old fall into the Production category.

The Classic Car Club of America takes several hundred words to spell out its definition of a classic, which, boiled down, is largely any automobile made between 1925 and 1942. Cars built before November 15, 1915 are neatly catalogued as Horseless Carriages by the Horseless Carriage Club of America. To certain American enthusiasts, machines manufactured prior to 1905 belong to a hardy group known as Pioneers.

Although Veteran and Vintage are universal terms, in the car collecting worlds of Great Britain and America they stand for quite different motor cars. In the United States, Veteran cars are those cars produced from 1906 to 1912, Vintage *usually* refers to cars made between 1912 and 1929. Great Britain's Veteran Car Club classifies all cars made before the last day of 1904 as Veteran, and it brackets those machines produced from January 1905 until the end of 1918, a period graced by some splendidly baroque coachwork, as proper Edwardians. In England, the Vintage car period runs from the beginning of 1919 up to the last day of 1930.

This volume is not concerned with antiquity as such. Neither is it preoccupied with rarity. What the author and the artists have so admirably presented is a cross section of established classics as well as a large number of more recent makes that collectors may have overlooked.

Since the first marketable automobile was made 90 years ago it has transformed society. That our society now shows an ever increasing interest in collecting cars is appropriate. For every actual old-car owner there are scores who read about them and who visit the hundreds of motor shows and car museums. Old cars appeal to almost everyone. The connoisseur of fine arts sees the classics as moving sculpture, and engineers are amazed at the inventiveness shown by the pioneer builders. Not too many people can aspire to owning a classic, but for most of us, the simple pleasure of being around these gleaming examples of an earlier age is reward enough.

Albert R. Bochroch

Early makes

The automobile, in shaping the 20th century, has significantly shaped the way we live. Yet little more than 90 years have passed since Karl Benz built the first practical internal combustion powered car. Before the internal combustion engine, steam-propelled vehicles were in use. In 1769, Nicolas Cugnot, who is generally credited with inventing the first self-propelled road vehicle, tried to interest a French army purchasing commission in his steam-driven gun carrier. In England, a number of experimenters built quite viable road carriages powered by steam between 1800 and 1840, but vested road interests and the coming of the railways drove them into oblivion. Amédée Bollée of Le Mans, whose son Leon was to influence the future of aircraft and calculators, as well as motoring, began making steam-driven tractors and carriages in 1873.

For many years steam and battery powered cars rivalled internal combustion machines. Motor races, the means used by almost all the early manufacturers to advertise, were frequently won by electric and steam cars. Eight of the 21 machines than ran in the first of all motoring contests, the July 22, 1894 Paris-Rouen Trials, were steam powered.

The first recorded Land Speed Record was the result of an international duel contested during 1898 and 1899 between Count Chasseloup-Laubat of France and the Belgian,

Camille Jenatzy. Both drove electric cars, Jenatzy finally winning when his streamlined 'La Jamais Contente' averaged 65.79mph for a kilometre.

The best known and longest lived steam car was the Stanley, which remained in production until 1927. A Stanley Special, the streamlined Rocket, exceeded 127mph over the measured mile on the sands of Ormond Beach, Florida, in January 1906.

By 1900, petrol powered cars were clearly in the ascendancy, and by the end of World War I electric and steam propelled cars had become a novelty.

To Karl Benz of Mannheim went the honour of inventing the first successful car driven by an internal combustion engine. Evidence points to others, Siegfried Marcus and Etienne Lenoir for example, as having built earlier internal combustion engines. Marcus, a German mechanical engineer who became an Austrian citizen, started with an engine in a hand cart that lacked both brakes and any arrangement for steering and subsequently built a couple of cars, one of which, believed to date from the 1880s, survives. Lenoir obtained patents in 1860 for an internal combustion engine that was designed to operate on household gas ignited by electricity, and installed it in a carriage that was running in 1863. In 1864 Nikolas Otto and Eugen

A Bollée steam carriage of 1878.

Nicolas Cugnot's steam-driven artillery tractor of 1769.

Langen began work on an internal combustion engine in Cologne. An Otto engine which ran on coal gas, was displayed at the 1867 Paris Exposition, and another Otto engine was shown at the Philadelphia Centennial in 1876. By then, Otto was running a four stroke engine, and by 1885, he was using liquid fuel. But Otto was primarily interested in supplying power for stationary engines.

From the beginning, Benz thought in terms of a complete unit. Unlike the majority of pioneers who placed their contrivances in carriages and wagons, Benz designed a special chassis and a neat, three-wheeled two seater to take his single cylinder engine in 1885. Benz showed his car at the Munich Exhibition in 1888, but made only a few sales until he exhibited at the Paris Universal Exhibition the following year. The French representative for Benz stationary engines, Emile Roger, then took on the Benz car. Benz stayed with his original design until 1901 when, after selling

over 600 cars in 1900, sales began to fall as other makers offered more advanced designs.

Among his competitors were Gottlieb Daimler and Wilhelm Maybach; Daimler established his own firm in 1883, and Maybach soon joined him. Daimler originally directed his efforts at finding an engine suitable to power boats and rail and road transport. In 1885 Daimler built the first internal combustion engine powered motorcycle, and in 1886, he fitted an engine into a carriage.

With Maybach's encouragement, some say his insistence, Daimler built a complete car in 1889. This was the Stahlradwagen, a two seater, four wheeler with a tubular steel frame and wire wheels.

When Daimler was still with Gasmotorenfabrik-Deutz, the Cologne firm retained Edouard Sarazin, a Paris lawyer, to handle a patent infringement case in France. On one of his trips to see Nikolas Otto, the head of Deutz, Sarazin met Daimler, and they became friends. After Daimler opened his own plant, the lawyer became his French representative and, in October 1886, Sarazin obtained the French patents to the Daimler engine.

Sarazin was also friendly with Emile Levassor of Panhard et Levassor, Paris based manufacturers of wood working machinery. Sarazin commissioned Levassor to build a Daimler engine, but the lawyer died suddenly in December of 1887. Sarazin's widow, Louise, then went to Stuttgart to receive assurance from Daimler that she could represent him in France. Levassor began to see a good deal of the new widow, and he accompanied her to Germany to visit Daimler. There Levassor saw the Daimler engine applied to boats, street cars and a horseless carriage. In May of 1890, Louise Sarazin and Emile Levassor were married.

Daimler and Levassor also became good

A model of the vehicle, said to have been built in 1875, by Siegfried Marcus.

friends. In 1889 they had travelled to Valentigny to see Armand Peugeot of the well established firm of Peugeot Frères, manufacturers of hardware and bicycles. With Leon Serpollet, Peugeot also made a steam

Camille Jenatzy in the electric La Jamais Contente *(Never Satisfied).*

car. Levassor and Daimler made the sale, and in 1890, Peugeot began French manufacture of Daimler engined automobiles.

There was never a written contract between Daimler and Panhard et Levassor. Daimler and Levassor wrote to each other weekly, and they freely exchanged ideas, and each was to credit the other with improvements to their cars. Unfortunately, Madame Levassor was to be widowed again when Emile Levassor died in April 1897.

Daimler of Great Britain was founded in January 1896, though an agency for German Daimler engines had existed earlier. Gottlieb Daimler remained a director there until 1898. By this time, the British Daimler was one of H. J. Lawson's many holdings.

The wealthy Consul-General of Austria, Emile Jellinek was responsible for another historic development in the Daimler line. A car enthusiast and, unofficially, an agent for

Karl Benz's single-cylinder three-wheeler, built in 1885.

A similar Benz vehicle of 1888.

11

Daimler cars, Jellinek named his entry in the 1899 Nice Week Concours, Mercedes, after his eldest daughter. Jellinek became a director of Daimler in 1900 and was soon given the sales rights for Belgium, Austria-Hungary, the United States and France. As Panhard et Levassor still owned the Daimler name in France Jellinek used the Mercedes name on all Daimlers sold in his territory. Also called Mercedes were the first high performance Daimlers, which Jellinek is credited with having pushed the firm into making. In 1902, Daimler began calling all of its passenger cars Mercedes, retaining the Daimler name for commercial vehicles. The name Benz was added to Mercedes years later following the 1926 merger of Daimler and Benz. The two German giants

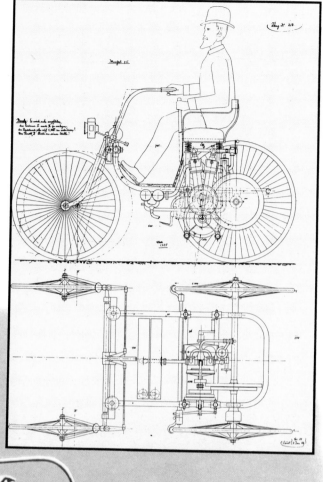

Above: A diagram and a photograph of Daimler's Stahlradwagen, built in 1889.

never met.

Ettore Bugatti and Ferdinand Porsche were innovators whose ideas would live far beyond their lifetimes. Bugatti was the child of artistic parents. His father was a furniture designer and his brother, Rembrandt, an accomplished sculptor. An Italian who spent most of his life in Alsace, Bugatti began making his jewel-like machines after he had worked, among others, for De Dietrich, Mathis and Deutz. From 1909 the Bugatti factory at Molsheim, in Alsace produced dashing sports cars and some of the most lavish luxury cars of all time. One of the first to make smaller, better handling Grand Prix cars, French blue Bugattis became European favourites during the 1920s and 1930s.

Ferdinand Porsche was born in 1875 in Bohemia, then a part of Austria, now in

The Hon. C. S. Rolls in an 8hp Panhard-Levassor of 1895.

A Panhard-Levassor with a Daimler engine, 1893.

A Daimler-engined Peugeot vis-à-vis of 1894.

Czechoslovakia. He attended classes at several technical colleges and first worked in the automobile industry for Ludwig Lohner, in Lohner's then new coachbuilding department. Porsche's first design was the Lohner-Porsche of 1900 which featured an electric motor built into the hub of each of its front wheels.

He joined Austro-Daimler in 1906, and in 1907 designed the Maja, named after Emile Jellinek's second daughter. Dr. Porsche became managing director of Austro-Daimler but resigned in 1923 to become technical director of Daimler at Unterturkheim. Porsche joined the Austrian firm of Steyr in 1929 and in 1930 opened his own consulting firm in Stuttgart.

Dr. Porsche (he was awarded honorary degrees in engineering in 1917 and 1924) conceived the rear engined Auto Unions and

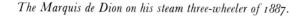

The Marquis de Dion on his steam three-wheeler of 1887.

the Volkswagen Beetle in the early 1930s. In 1934 the Volkswagen became a Nazi government project. That involvement led to a jail sentence by the French following World War II, but Porsche was released when Piero Dusio of Cisitalia interceded on his behalf. Although the post war Porsche sports car was the work of Ferry, Ferdinand's son, it obviously incorporated many of the senior Porsche's ideas.

Germany and France were working on the internal combustion engined car before other nations, but not for long. The 1890s was a time when new makes came into being, and faded away, almost overnight. It seemed that every machine shop, builder of bicycles and wagon maker had plans to manufacture automobiles.

The Lambert 3-Wheeler, made in Anderson, Indiana in 1891 and spasmodically for a few years thereafter, probably was the first petrol engined automobile made in the United States. Another early US make was the San Francisco made 'Golden Gate' of 1894-1895. Henry Ford finished his first engine in 1893 and, on June 4, 1896, ran a successful test on his first complete car, the Quadricycle. Another American pioneer whose name graces a current

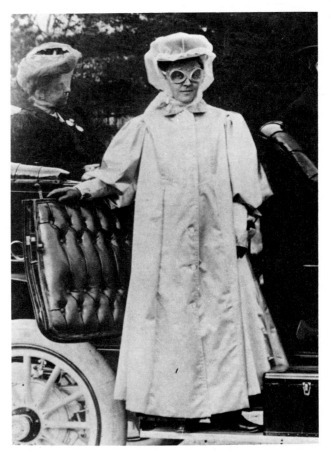

Protective clothing as worn by Edwardian lady motorists.

The four-cylinder Daimler of 1901 was the first to bear the name of Mercedes.

automobile is Ransom E. Olds. Olds produced a steam car in 1891 and five years later, in 1896, made his first internal combustion engine.

Olds also manufactured electric cars, but it was his 1901 Curved Dash Runabout, one of America's first mass produced automobiles, that became the best seller of its time. It had earned an overwhelmingly large share of the early automobile market—425 units in 1901; 2,500 in 1902 (when total US sales were under 9,000) and, in 1903, 4,000 units out of a total national production figure of 11,235.

In November 1904 Ransom E. Olds was persuaded to leave his flourishing firm to form Reo. Business had remained good, but S. L. Smith, a retired timber and copper dealer who had originally backed Olds with $200,000, wanted him to stop making lower priced cars. Olds disagreed as he saw no reason to change so successful a model.

A rear-engined Auto Union driven by Berndt Rosemeyer at Nurburgring.

In 1888 the New York piano manufacturer, William Steinway, visited Gottlieb Daimler in Cannstatt and was given a ride in one of Daimler's motorised Quadricycles. Steinway

Dillon and Cavanagh in a Bugatti at Le Mans, 1912.

16

arranged for the American rights for Daimler engines and, in 1890, the first American Daimler was built in Hartford. Following Steinway's death in 1896, the company was reorganised as the Daimler Manufacturing Co., and by 1906, the American Mercedes was being assembled in Long Island City, New York.

Two of America's most important early automobile builders were the Duryea brothers and a Scottish engineer working in Cleveland, Ohio, Alexander Winton. During 1892-93, Charles and Frank Duryea built a 4hp single cylinder powered carriage. Frank drove the second Duryea to victory in the Chicago *Times-Herald* race of November 1895. Two Duryeas participated in the London-Brighton Emancipation Run in November with considerable swank. Starting in 1902, Frank helped develop the Stevens-Duryea car while Charles continued making Duryeas until 1913.

From the inception of his firm in 1897,

Alexander Winton competed aggressively to promote his cars. Winton himself lowered the running time from Cleveland to New York to 10 days in 1897 and two years later made the same journey in 47 hours and 37 minutes. In 1899 Winton brashly challenged Fernand Charron's Panhard to a 1,000 mile race. The winner a short time before of the Marseilles-Nice and Paris-Amsterdam-Paris races, Charron immediately accepted and posted 20,000 francs with the Paris office of the *New York Herald*. Winton changed his mind but the gesture inspired the publisher of the *Paris Herald*, James Gordon Bennett, to establish the Gordon Bennett Cup series, the first international motor races.

When Henry Ford won a race over Alexander Winton at Grosse Pointe, Michigan in October 1901, he won $1,000, a cut glass bowl and considerable fame. The next year, convinced that his cars needed to win more

Henry Ford's first automobile, built in 1896.

A 1902 Oldsmobile Curved Dash Runabout, a great commercial success.

races to sell more automobiles, Ford built two giant racing cars, one called the 'Arrow' the other, '999', which was named after a famous New York Central train. Crude in the extreme—they had no rear suspension, and the final drive bevels were exposed and unlubricated—Ford's racers were powered by enormous 19,000cc four cylinder engines.

Barney Oldfield drove '999' in October 1902 at the beginning of his career, when the Ford beat a Winton Bullet, but Oldfield was soon to switch to a Bullet, then to the Peerless Green Dragon, the Blitzen-Benz and many more. When Henry Ford and Oldfield met again many years later, Ford is reported to have said, 'Barney, you made me and I made

Charles Duryea in his first powered horse-buggy, 1895.

you,' to which Oldfield replied, 'I did a damn sight better for you than you did for me.' But Henry Ford himself was behind the Arrow's steering-bar when it set a short lived unofficial mile record of 39⅖th seconds over the ice of Lake St Clair on January 12, 1904. One of the last races entered officially by the Ford Motor Company for many years occurred in June, 1909, when a Model T won the New York to Seattle race in 22 days.

Henry Ford also figured in the news in a way that was to affect the course of the American automobile industry. Basing its case on patents granted the American inventor, George Selden, in 1895, the Association of Licensed Automobile Manufacturers, which had acquired Selden's rights, sued Ford for infringement. In 1907, the court required Selden to build a car, based on his patents, to prove them workable. Selden did, and the court ruled that Selden's patents covered the two stroke engine only. As Ford and almost every other engine maker used the four stroke principle, Ford won the case, and the entire industry was freed from paying royalties.

The turn of the century was the time of new dynasties in the automobile business. Three makers, Benz, Daimler and Lutzmann of Dessau, exhibited in the 1897 Berlin Motor Show, the first in Germany. The following year Adam Opel and his five sons, makers of sewing machines and bicycles, began to manufacture one of Europe's longest lived cars. After first using Lutzmann and French Darracq engines, Opel developed their own. General Motors acquired control of Opel in 1928 and full ownership in 1931.

Another European giant that has survived and flourished is Renault. In 1898, Louis Renault, the fourth of six children of a well-to-do button and drapery manufacturer, used the shed behind his father's Billancourt home to install a 1¾hp De Dion engine in a tricycle that he had converted into a four wheeler. Louis and his brothers Marcel and Fernand had orders for 60 of their solidly made voiturettes within six months. Like their competitors, Louis and Marcel went into motor racing to publicise Renault Frères. By 1900 they had won a score of races. Using the De Dion engine, which they increased to 3¾hp, they concentrated on the small car class, which they dominated. When French cars won all three classes in the June 1901 Paris-Berlin race (Mors in the heavy class, Panhard in the Light and Renault the Voiturettes) Paris celebrated for three days.

The last great city-to-city race was the

Henry Ford's 1902 racer, 999.

Paris-Madrid of May 1903. Marcel Renault was seriously injured during the accident-filled first stage. Louis was leading his class and was second overall only to Fernand Gabriel's Mors, but Marcel Renault succumbed to his injuries the following day and Louis never raced again.

In 1903 France led the world in production with 30,000 cars, of which Renault made slightly more than 1,000. The firm continued racing as Ferenc Szisz won the first Grand Prix in 1906, held over a 64 mile triangle of roads outside Le Mans.

Largest of the European automobile dynasties is Fiat of Italy. Fabbrica Italiana Automobili Torino was founded in July 1899 by Giovanni Agnelli, Emanuele di Bricherasio, Roberto Biscaretti and Count di Ruffia. The young Piedmontese were friends, and all four

reportedly held unusually advanced views for wealthy Italians of their time. The 33-year-old Agnelli, a former officer in the Italian cavalry, soon became the driving force in the new firm. For the next 77 years the Italian company was managed by Giovanni Agnelli, his sons and grandson, Gianni.

In its first year, Fiat absorbed the recently established Ceirano works and with that acquisition, though not by design, they secured the services of Vincenzo Lancia and Felice Nazzaro. Lancia, the son of a prosperous manufacturer of soups, had been in charge of the Ceirano stores; Nazzaro was a young handyman. In an age when success in racing could determine a car maker's future, Fiat had stumbled on two men, the reserved Nazzaro and ebullient Lancia, who would be

The Ford Model A had a flat-twin 8hp engine mounted under the driving seat.

numbered among the greatest of all racing
drivers. Before Fiat retired from automobile
competition in the mid-twenties they had
captured almost every important event in the
racing world.

By the beginning of World War I Fiat
was manufacturing aircraft, marine engines
and railway rolling stock as well as cars and
lorries. They had built a substantial export
business and had plants in many countries,
including America, where, prior to World War
I, their Poughkeepsie, New York factory
accounted for 200 to 400 luxury models
annually. More significantly, by this time
Fiat was responsible for 60 to 80 per cent
of all cars sold in Italy. Fiat's record between
the wars was one of steady growth, assuming
more and more civic and social responsibilities.

*The first Renault, with a one-cylinder engine of 273cc,
appeared in 1898. It had a top speed of 36km/h.*

A 1914 Model T Ford Speedster.

The company now makes cars in 25 countries, yet its near monopoly of the Italian market shows no sign of lessening, and Fiat's goal of 10 per cent of the world car market seems within reach.

Handicapped by the archaic 'Locomotives Act' of 1836, Great Britain was the last industrialised nation to develop a motor industry. After she did get started, almost a decade behind Germany and France, British-built cars soon took their place among the world's finest, and Britain's car industry flourished.

Britain's use of steam propelled road carriages, which she had pioneered early in the 19th century, worked against her development of the car. Supported by farmers and landowners, the railways and established horse-drawn stage coach lines convinced Parliament that it should pass the Locomotives Act. Among its many restrictions, the Act called for a man with a red flag to walk in front of all self-propelled vehicles. It also required steam coaches to pay greatly increased tolls, about 10 times those of horse drawn stage coaches. Tolls were made more nearly

Marcel Renault, first home in the Paris-Vienna race of 1902, stands beside his car.

equal during the 1860s, but not until 1896, with the passage of the more liberal Locomotives on Highways Act, were speed limits raised from 4mph to 12mph: the red flag had officially been lowered in 1878.

In celebration of the new act, on November 14, 1896, 17 automobiles, including distinguished participants such as Leon Bollée and Gottlieb Daimler made the 50 mile run from London's Hotel Metropole to the Metropole in Brighton. A nasty bit of gossip claims that the first and third cars to arrive in Brighton, the American Duryeas driven by Frank Duryea and Herb Lytle, were carried at least part of the way by train.

Revived by a London newspaper in 1927, the London to Brighton Run is today a fixture on England's social calendar and affectionately known as 'the old crocks' race'. The event is restricted to cars made prior to the end of 1904. Twenty years ago the film 'Genevieve' (its heroine was a 1905 Darracq!) did much to popularise the Brighton Run, and entries now come from enthusiasts around the world.

Britain's early car builders had found it difficult to find backers as they had been so restricted by law that their machines could not be fairly tested. But several years after the emancipation of 1896, a stroke of good fortune helped to call world wide attention to the British industry.

Having captured the first two Gordon Bennett Cup races, the Automobile Club of France was again the host in 1902. The Cup was run as part of the Paris-Vienna race, one of the classic city-to-city races of the time, and the

The first Fiat, a two-cylinder that developed 3½hp, appeared in 1899.

Cup challangers—there were only five—were to finish their race at Innsbruck. France was represented by Leonce Giradot on a CGV; Henri Fournier on a Mors and the Baron Rene de Knyff on a Panhard. Herbert Austin, who was to leave Wolseley in 1905 to form his own company, drove a Wolseley, and Francis Selwyn Edge, a well-known bicycle racer, brought Great Britain the honour and problems of staging an international motor race.

With the 1903 Cup race, the Gordon Bennett series came of age. So many makers wanted to enter that several nations were forced to conduct elimination trials. Parliament passed special legislation permitting the race to be held. Two suitable circuits of 52 and 40 miles were linked to form a course at Athy near Dublin.

America sent two Wintons and a Peerless. The German Daimler plant was swept by fire and their special 80hp Gordon Bennett cars were destroyed. But private entrants substituted their own 60hp Mercedes. France entered two Panhards and a Mors, and Britain, three Napiers. All three American cars retired early, and the Belgian driver, Camille Jenatzy, won in a Mercedes.

Two of Britain's foremost motoring pioneers were Harry J. Lawson, an entrepreneur, and Fred Lanchester, a gifted engineer whose accomplishments class him alongside the greatest of early motoring innovators. Lawson already owned several bicycle and tyre companies when he began buying British rights and companies in an attempt to corner the British market. He obtained Daimler's British rights from F. R. Simms in 1896, acquired De Dion, Bollée and other French cars for Great Britain and took over the established Humber works. Through his British Motor Syndicate, Lawson was in constant litigation trying to maintain his monopoly.

Lawson also had the misfortune to pay an American swindler, E. J. Pennington, £100,000 for the privilege of building cars under Pennington patents. Pennington was exposed, went bankrupt, and returned to America in 1901 to sell non-existent airships. In 1907 Montague Napier was able to buy what remained of Lawson's empire for £1,000.

Lanchester began designing a car from the ground up in 1895, and he started to produce an air-cooled petrol engined machine in 1900. Until the early 1930s, quiet, well-made cars were the Lanchester trademark.

Montague Napier of the London engineering firm of D. Napier and Son began making cars in 1899. He was soon joined by Francis Selwyn Edge, who was to play a major role in Napier's success. A dynamic salesman, publicist and businessman, Edge became the distributor for Napier and other major makes, keeping them in the public eye for many years.

The Locomotive Act had made Great Britain unusually dependent on imports. David Scott-Moncrieff, the British historian, has noted that in 1906 Parliament took notice of Great Britain's exporting of an average of two cars a month to France while importing 400 a month from France alone. On returning from an American trip, S. F. Edge, in an address to the Coventry Engineering Society in January 1910, warned that 'a very serious menace grows up in America.' Prophetically, Edge went on to say that as soon as American manufacturers filled their home needs, Great Britain would be flooded with cheap, well made motor cars. Apparently Edge, and eventually other English manufacturers, attempted to offset this 'menace'. By 1910 Napier had plants in Genoa and Boston but by 1912, when America exported 23,720 motor vehicles (while importing only 868) she had become the world's largest car maker.

American car makers had been slow to adopt the modern, front mounted engine layout. Not until after 1900, when European and British builders had almost universally accepted the French-inspired concept, did the United States stop making motorised wagons and carriages. Out of a US population of 76 million in 1900, only 4,100 owned an automobile. Within the next decade, the annual production of American cars soared to 181,000. By 1907 many American cars were a match for the Europeans in design and performance. And, in 1908, an American automobile earned world-wide fame when it captured the incredible New York to Paris race.

On February 12, 1908, six cars and 250,000 people lined New York's Times Square awaiting the start of the New York to Paris race. Jointly sponsored by the *New York Times* and the Paris newspaper, *Le Matin*, the original route called for driving across the United States (it had never been done in winter), shipping the cars to Alaska on coastal steamers, then crossing the Arctic via a largely imaginary network of frozen rivers and seas. Once in Asia, the cars were to drive across Siberia, through Russia and central Europe before reaching France.

When the Alaskan route proved impossible (only the Thomas Flyer was shipped to Valdez to attempt it), the crews shipped the cars to Japan and went on to complete the 170-day, 22,000-mile journey overland. It was an age when performance was the accepted way of promoting automobiles, and the public avidly followed every titbit of racing news. The New York-Paris race was reported, day by day, around the world. Winning it was the best

sort of advertising for the E. R. Thomas Motor Company and for American cars.

Although the Thomas Car Company of Buffalo was not to survive World War I, the round-the-world Thomas Flyer was rescued from a junkyard and restored to a place of honour in the Harrah Museum.

Until American automobile manufacturers grew large enough to operate their own mills and foundries, Indiana rivalled Michigan as a producer of American cars. Some historians believe it was the Great Lakes that made the difference. In addition to providing cheaper freight transportation than the railroads, many of the raw materials needed by the foundries were to be found near their shores. A more contemporary view, however, is that the good burghers of Michigan were a more adventurous lot and were eager to provide the expanding automobile industry with financial support. In 1915, when the total US production of automobiles reached 895,930, over 450,000 were made in Detroit.

Edward Joel Pennington's 1896 "autocar" was a three-wheeler that developed 2hp.

When the Indianapolis Speedway opened in 1909, it reflected favourably on the entire Indianapolis motoring community. Also, it provided a convenient test track for car builders long before each Detroit giant constructed his own testing facilities.

The small city of Auburn, Indiana, was home to 21 car manufacturers including such classics as Auburn, Cord and Duesenberg. Among the early Indianapolis builders were National, founded in 1900, Marmon which started in 1902, and early the following decade, Stutz.

The first Nationals, made between 1900 and 1903, were electrics. Petrol powered cars entered the National line in 1903, and the electrics were dropped in 1905. The next year National introduced one of the first American six-cylinder automobiles. Indianapolis continued as the home of the National until 1924, when the last model, the 6-71, rolled out of the plant.

One of the founders of the Indianapolis Motor Speedway, Arthur C. Newby, owned National, and as could be expected the company promoted its machines by racing. In 1911 Len Zengle's National captured the Elgin Trophy and the following year Joe Dawson won the second 500 mile race. The first Indianapolis victory went to another local firm, Marmon, builders of well-made, nicely styled cars from 1902 until 1933. Ray Harroun, a Marmon engineer who also captained their racing team, drove a special Marmon six, the Wasp, to defeat Ralph Mulford's Lozier. The only driver in the 500 without a riding mechanic, Harroun appeared to earn more fame for his use of a rear view mirror, an American racing first, than for winning.

One of America's best-liked cars, the dream of several generations of schoolboys, was the

The Thomas Flyer in Alaska during the 1908 New York-Paris race, which it won.

Stutz Bearcat. Harry C. Stutz began making cars in 1911, and Stutz remained in his control until 1919 when he left to build the H.C.S. Three-time national AAA champion, Earl Cooper, drove for Stutz, defeating Barney Oldfield and Ralph De Palma to win the 1913 Corona California road race. Steel magnate Charles Schwab bought Stutz and in 1926, hired the brilliant engineer-salesman-entrepreneur, Frederick Moskovics, as president. Moskovics began building handsome, straight-eight powered touring cars in the European tradition, and he successfully renewed the Stutz racing programme.

Two cruel blows made 1928 a difficult year for Stutz. Moskovics and Frank Lockhart, winner of the 1926 Indy, designed the Miller-powered Stutz Black Hawk Special in which young Lockhart lost his life. And Stutz suffered a widely-publicised defeat at the hands of C. T. Weymann, the French custom body builder, when Weymann's Hispano-Suiza beat a Stutz in a 24-hour, $25,000 match race at the Speedway. Impressed with the Stutz, Weymann bought a Black Hawk out of his winnings and entered it in the 24 Hours Le Mans of 1928 where it finished a close second to the winning Bentley. As with many thoroughbred cars, Stutz was unable to survive the depression.

The trend toward closed cars started slowly following World War I. In 1919, the Fisher Body Company made 103,000 open cars and 31,000 coupés. During the next five years, Fisher's sale of open cars more than doubled, reaching 239,000 in 1924. However, during the same period, the number of Fisher-made coupés increased ten-fold, from 31,000 in 1919 to 335,000 in 1924. When, also in 1924, Roy Chapin priced both his Hudson coupé and touring car at $1,500 and his Essex coupé sold for only 100 dollars more than the Essex roadster, it was the first time coupé prices competed with those of open cars. From that time on, the open car was doomed to complete decline.

At a time of bread lines, open cars, particularly luxury touring cars such as Stutz, were an anachronism. The society the automobile had transformed was beginning to change into a dependent society designed to serve the automobile itself. In 1935, a verse of Stephen Vincent Benet's poem *Nightmare Number Three* took a far from utopian view of man's relationship with the automobile:

. . . But the cars were in it, of course . . . and they hunted us
Like rabbits through the cramped streets on that bloody Monday.
The Madison Avenue buses leading the charge.
The buses were pretty bad—but I'll not forget
The smash of glass when the Duesenberg left the show-room
And pinned three brokers to the Racquet Club steps
Or the long howl of the horns when they saw men run,
When they saw them looking for holes in the solid ground . . .

As early as 1896, Milton O. Reeves was running his four wheel, three seater Motocycle around Columbus, Indiana. But Reeves will be best remembered for his strange Sexto and Octo, six and eight-wheeled cars built before he closed down in 1912. The automobile business was booming back home in Indiana. Haynes-Apperson began building cars in Kokomo in 1898. In South Bend, the established Studebaker wagon works first marketed electric cars in 1902 and petrol driven buggies in 1904.

Indiana and Michigan may have had a higher concentration of car manufacturers but automobiles were being made throughout the East and Midwest.

During the majority of its 59 years, Packard's 'Ask the Man Who Owns One' was more meaningful than most automobile slogans. Until 1935, when they produced the medium-priced 120, Packards had been large, graceful well-made cars. In August, 1898, James Ward Packard, a prosperous manufacturer of electrical products, bought the 13th car made by Alexander Winton. On the 50 mile trip from the Winton factory in Cleveland to Packard's home in Warren, Ohio, the Winton all but fell apart. When Packard complained, the testy Winton is reported to have said,

'If you're so smart, why don't you make a car for yourself.'

Packards were made in Warren until 1903 when the plant moved to Detroit. James Ward Packard stayed in Warren, day-to-day Packard management going to Henry Joy. Packard entered five cars in the 1902 New York to Buffalo endurance race, and all five finished. A Packard cut three days from Winton's coast-to-coast record, and, in 1904, the Packard Gray Wolf finished fourth overall and first of all American cars in the Vanderbilt Cup.

Packard became the Allies largest maker of aircraft engines in World War II. After the war the Soviet Union bought Packard's old body dies from which the Russians made the Zis. In 1954, Packard merged with Studebaker and in 1958 they ceased production.

During the first decade of the new century, Ohio could boast many makes. The Stoddard-Dayton, produced in Dayton from 1904 to 1913, captured the Speedway's inaugural race, a five mile event, in 1909 two years before the first 500. Overland began in Terre Haute, Indiana, in 1903 with a handsome, single cylinder roadster with an out-front, under the bonnet engine in the French manner. They moved to Indianapolis in 1905 and then joined Willys in Toledo, Ohio in 1908. In Cleveland, the White Sewing Machine Company began selling steam cars in 1900, but by 1910 had switched to petrol engines prior to converting their entire production to lorries. First made in Cleveland in 1899, the Stearns-Knight was considered one of America's more advanced automobiles, a reputation it retained until the mid 1920s when it was acquired by Willys-Overland.

Also made in Cleveland, from 1900 to 1931, was the Peerless which, with Pierce-Arrow and Packard, was one of America's famous 'Three P' quality cars. Peerless made a disappointing European debut at the Gordon Bennett races in 1903 and 1904, but they later raced there with considerable success as the Peerless Green Dragons driven by Barney Oldfield. Both the Peerless and Barney were featured in 'The Vanderbilt Cup', a Broadway musical starring Elsie Janis.

Few marques excite the collector as does the Mercer. Experts say that a good 1911 Type 35 Raceabout would very likely bring a quarter-million dollars. The first Mercers were made in Trenton, Mercer County, N.J. in 1909 by the bridge building Roebling family. From 1911 to 1915, they were among America's most successful racing cars. Ralph De Palma, captain of the Mercer team, and Barney Oldfield were among the early giants who piloted the bright yellow cars.

When Washington Roebling II went down with the Titanic, Mercer lost one of its staunchest supporters. The last Roebling brother died in 1918, and Mercer was bought by a Wall Street syndicate who interested Emlen Hare, a former Packard executive, in forming a new corporation which included Mercer, Locomobile and Simplex. But by 1925, the Hare group was out of business.

Philadelphia contributed the Chadwick, made from 1904 until 1916. The Great Chadwick Six touring car, introduced in 1907, became the first to employ supercharging when a blower was installed in one of the racing models.

In addition to the Thomas, upstate New York was the site of the Pierce-Arrow and Cunningham plants. Neither the stately Pierce-Arrow, first made in Buffalo in 1901, nor the well-engineered Cunningham, produced by a respected Rochester builder of fine carriages, survived the depression.

New England too had its share of prominent pioneer car makers. Locomobile started in 1899 as a steam car after John Brisbane Walker and A. Lorenzo Barber paid the Stanley brothers $250,000 for their steam car patents.

Following a disagreement with his partner, Barber began building Locomobile steamers in Westboro, Mass., moving to Bridgeport, Conn., the following year. Walker retained the Stanley plant at Tarrytown, N.Y. where he made the Mobile steam car from 1899 until 1903. The Stanleys repurchased their patent rights in 1901 and Locomobile switched to petrol-powered cars designed by A. L. Riker, a former builder of electric cars in Brooklyn.

Locomobile then produced an outstanding line of luxury touring cars. When George

Robertson won the 1908 Vanderbilt Cup on Long Island in a Locomobile, it was the first victory for an American car in international competition. Old number 16, the Vanderbilt winner, is now owned by Peter Helck, the distinguished painter and automobile historian. By 1920 Locomobile's fortunes had faded, and they joined other prestige makes, Crane-Simplex and Mercer in the Hare group. W. C. Durant took over the Hare group in 1922, but Locomobile ceased production in 1929.

Outstanding among New England's automotive pioneers was Hiram Percy Maxim, the nephew of Sir Hiram Maxim, the English inventor. Young Maxim was intrigued by the thought of using the Otto engine to propel a road vehicle, rather than provide power to drive machinery. Although a graduate of Massachusetts Institute of Technology, Maxim was unaware of similar work on internal combustion engines in the United States and Europe at the same time.

The explosion that followed Maxim's experiment (petrol dripped into a sealed six-pound shell casing) encouraged him to continue. Late in 1894, he joined Colonel Pope's Columbia Bicycle Company in Hartford, Conn., and in 1895, the Columbia Electric became the first of Colonel Pope's many makes. During the following year, Hiram Maxim built a petrol powered Columbia and the 500 electric and gasoline Columbias sold in 1900 made Colonel Pope's machine the sales leader of its time.

The Pope-Hartford, the product of another of Colonel Pope's several car building companies, was made in Hartford from 1903 to 1914. At $500, the Pope-Tribune, produced from 1904 to 1907, was cheapest of the Pope cars. Top of the line was the Pope-Toledo, made from 1903 until 1910. When Herb Lytle's Pope-Toledo finished 12th in the 1905 Gordon Bennett Cup race at Clermont-Ferrand, France, it marked the first time an American car had completed a European race.

Another New England made car, was manufactured by the American Locomotive Company of Providence, R.I. from 1905 until 1913. Originally built under licence from Berliet of Lyons, France, Alco began making their own six cylinder model in 1908. This large, well-engineered, rugged car captured the 1909 and 1910 Vanderbilt Cup races.

Of the car makers now in business, only the American Motors Corporation formed in 1954 by the merger of Hudson and Nash has remained independent of Detroit's Big Three. Nash and Hudson stayed in production until 1958 when AMC began marketing the Rambler. This name dates from 1902, when Thomas B. Jeffrey of Kenosha, Wisconsin, predecessor to Nash, sold the popular single cylinder, chain drive Rambler runabout for $750. This was among America's earliest mass-produced automobiles, 1,500 being sold in 1902 alone.

The Detroit department store owner, J. L. Hudson, and Roy Chapin, who had been with Olds, started the Hudson Motor Car Company in Detroit in 1909. In 1918, Hudson introduced the smaller, four cylinder Essex. Combined Hudson-Essex sales in 1929 reached 300,000, placing them third in US sales volume. A railway engineer's son, Walter Chrysler started working as an apprentice mechanic in the Union Pacific workshops in Kansas and became manager of American Locomotive's works in Pittsburgh. He was 37 when he joined the Buick Division of General Motors in 1911, and he was made its president early the following year. When Chrysler left Buick in June 1920, because of interference from W. C. Durant, president of General Motors, he was earning an astronomical $500,000 a year, although much of it came from shares.

Bankers retained Chrysler at a million dollars a year for two years to reorganise the ailing Willys-Overland company. Following Willys, Chrysler moved on to help Maxwell. Chrysler took charge of Maxwell shortly before they absorbed Chalmers, another popular American make. Maxwell had its beginnings in the United States Motor Co., with Stoddard-Dayton and Brush. After this firm collapsed, Jonathan Maxwell retained the marque. Chalmers started in 1907 as the Thomas-Detroit under the ownership of Thomas of Buffalo, makers of the Thomas Flyer, but was soon sold to Hugh Chalmer, vice-president of the National Cash Register Company, who gave it his name. Both cars sold well before World War I; sales of the Chalmers 6 exceeded 10,000 in 1915 and the lower priced Maxwell 4 sold 100,000 cars in 1917, the year that Henry Ford, the sales leader, produced 622,351 Model Ts. But the post-war era was another story and Chrysler discontinued the Chalmers in 1923 and the last Maxwell in 1925. Chrysler put his great engineering trio, Fred Zeder, Owen Skelton and Carl Breer (whom he had induced to leave Studebaker) to work and they soon came up with their high compression 1924 six cylinder model. It was the first real Chrysler engine, and was an advance over the engines used in other medium priced cars.

Four years later in July 1928, Walter Chrysler paid $175,000,000 to make Dodge part of the Chrysler Corporation. John and Horace Dodge, owners of a Detroit machine shop, had supplied Ford with engines and chassis for 11 years before 1914, when they began making cars bearing their own name. The Dodge brothers received a $25,000,000 share settlement from Henry Ford when he reorganised in 1916.

William Crapo 'Billy' Durant began to form General Motors in 1908. Buick, Cadillac, Olds and Oakland, which became Pontiac, were among his early acquisitions. Between 1908 and 1910 alone he acquired some 25 more firms. Durant was born in Boston in 1861 into a family of means. His grandfather had been a former governor of Michigan and Durant tried his grandfather's timber business, but he preferred selling. By the time he was 21 he was co-owner of a Flint insurance agency. He is said to have made a million dollars before he was 40 by selling the Durant-Dort, a small road cart, the patents of which his partner had purchased for two thousand borrowed dollars. In 1904 Billy Durant was in New York making money on Wall Street, when he was asked to assume the presidency of Buick, a job he accepted in November 1904.

David Dunbar Buick, a partner in the Detroit plumbing supply firm of Buick and Sherwood, invented the process that enabled porcelain to be fused to cast iron. But he was intrigued by the motor car and after making his contribution to modern bathroom decor, Buick left the plumbing business in 1901. After running out of funds, and partners, several times, Buick had his car, with the characteristic Buick overhead valve engine, ready early in 1903.

Buick's latest backers, the Briscoe brothers, were becoming impatient and soon moved their support to Jonathan Maxwell. David Buick no longer had much of a financial stake in the company when the Briscoes sold out to James Whiting of the Flint Wagon Works. Another year passed with very little to show for it before Durant was brought in.

Under Durant, Buick production began to rise. David Buick soon left the company with a generous settlement which he lost through poor investments. He tried the oil business, car spares manufacturing, land dealing and, in 1927, when he was 72, he returned to Detroit to teach in a trade school. He died in 1929.

Durant began forming General Motors in 1908. How he selected the word 'General' arose from a meeting Durant had with the House of Morgan's George Perkins. When they failed to agree, Perkins testily told Durant not to use 'International' as he, Perkins, had first thought of it. Durant is said to have scratched out 'International' on the spot and to have substituted 'General'.

By 1910 GM was so deeply in debt that the banks made Durant's retirement as GM president a condition for a large loan. Durant did not remain idle. Within a year he organised the Mason Company and the Little Motor Company, and he provided the backing for Louis Chevrolet to open a small factory in Detroit. Durant knew the Chevrolet brothers well. He had hired them to race for Buick in 1909, when he had a successful racing team.

Durant's new enterprises boomed. The low priced Little and medium priced Chevrolet both sold well, but after three years Louis Chevrolet became disenchanted. He sold his shares back to Durant in December 1913 and returned to Indianapolis to build Frontenac racing cars and make widely used racing car components. In his later years Louis Chevrolet's career took a downward turn. During the depression he is said to have worked as a mechanic in a Chevrolet factory. His health failed shortly afterwards and he died in poverty in Detroit in June 1941.

After Durant left, General Motors shares floundered as the banks, which had the last word, declined to pay GM dividends. Meanwhile Durant's Chevrolet shares were rapidly increasing in value, and he began trading Chevrolet shares for GM ones at five to one.

On September 16, 1915 Durant walked into a General Motors 'directors' meeting with a retinue, all loaded down with GM share certificates. 'Gentlemen' Durant announced quietly, 'Chevrolet has bought General Motors.' Following a hasty re-organisation, Durant became the new General Motors president. Pierre S. Du Pont, whose Delaware chemical company had been buying into General Motors at Durant's urging, was made chairman of the board.

Almost immediately Durant went on another buying spree. Many of his new purchases turned out to be astute ones—Delco, Hyatt Roller Bearings, Fisher Body—but he did not know when to stop. The post World War I slump slowed car sales, and a Du Pont-Morgan syndicate was needed to rescue General Motors. This time Billy Durant was out of GM for good. He formed Durant Motors in 1921 (the Durant Star of 1923 offered the first production station wagon) and did fairly well until the depression closed him down in 1932. In 1936, when he was 75, he opened a supermarket in Asbury Park, N.J. Shortly before he died in 1947, he had tried to find backing for a chain of ten pin bowling alleys. A visionary to the end, Durant felt that bowling would become an important family recreation.

It has been said that the automobile was invented by the Germans, developed by the French and popularised by Americans. All of them, and many more, had a hand in it.

Certainly, the still short history of the motor car has been a fascinating one and hopefully this historical summary will have been of help in understanding the early days of the 'horseless carriage'.

The first Chevrolet, a six-cylinder, was produced in 1912.

A.C.

John Weller built his first car, a 20hp four-cylinder, in 1903; he later developed a commercial three-wheeler, the Auto-Carrier —hence A.C.—and with backing from pork butcher, John Portwine, put it into production in 1905. A passenger version, the Sociable, appeared in 1908 and A.C. built their first four-wheeler five years later. It was a pretty little car, with a 1,100cc Fivet engine and a bull-nosed brass radiator, and the same basic design was put into production after the Armistice, but with a 1½-litre Anzani power unit. A.C.'s renowned 1991cc single overhead-camshaft six-cylinder engine, designed by Weller in 1919, was used in its cars from 1922 to 1963, during which time power output was trebled from 35 to 103bhp. During the 1920s, A.C. was controlled by S. F. Edge, formerly with Napier, but went into liquidation in 1929. In 1931, the Hurlock brothers acquired A.C., and under their control a series of sporting models using the Weller 2-litre ohc six was developed, with power outputs of 60, 70 and 80bhp—and 90bhp in supercharged form. A preselector gear change was optional.

The first postwar A.C. range was in production from 1947 to 1957. Their streamlined coachwork concealed mechanicals little changed from pre-war, apart from the adoption of hydraulic front brakes. Horsepower was in the mid-70s and maximum speed in the mid-80s. From late 1952, four admirably fashioned body types were available: two- and four-door saloons, a convertible coupé, and a four-seater sports tourer by the Buckland Body Works.

The 100mph-plus Ace two-seater sports, first shown at Earls Court in 1953, was popular for a decade among a discriminating and moderately affluent clientele. John Tojeiro's tubular chassis on a 7ft 6in wheelbase and alloy bodywork made for a dry weight of only 15cwt. The firm suspension was independent all round, using transverse leaf springs. Performance similar to the Ace's was available from the Aceca, a companion two-seater fixed-head coupé introduced late in 1954 at £1,215 plus purchase tax (42 per cent at the time!). For a premium of £210 an optional 1,971cc Bristol engine (enlarged to 2,216cc in 1958) was available from 1956, giving a top speed of 118mph.

Weller's 1919 masterpiece had now become a plucky anachronism and was finally

1951 2-litre Saloon six-cylinder; 1,991cc; four-speed gearbox; 80mph.

pensioned off in 1963. The modified Ford Zephyr 2,553cc six used in the 1961-2 Aceca was little more than a stopgap measure. An heroic if inelegant solution was provided by former American racing driver, Carroll Shelby, with an American Ford 4,260cc V8. From that potent source, mated with a suitably modified Ace chassis and suspension, sprang a Q-ship among sports cars, the 1962 A.C. Cobra, capable of over 150mph and standstill to 60mph in 4.2 seconds. Before another year was out, the Cobra became available with the Ford 4,727cc engine, with which it came seventh at Le Mans in 1963 and fourth in 1964. In 1965, the Cobra won the World GT Championship outright. The ultimate Cobra was the 427, with the 7-litre Ford V8, marketed through Shelby American Inc.

When the Cobra went out of production, the chassis was utilized for a more civilized GT car, the A.C. 428, available in both coupé and convertible forms.

1938 16/80 Sports six-cylinder; 1,991cc; 90mph; also available in supercharged form.

1954 Ace six-cylinder; 1,991cc of A.C. design but later available with Ford or Bristol engines also developed into Cobra.

Alfa Romeo

Founded in 1909 to take over the former Darracq Italiana assembly plant, A.L.F.A. (Lombardy Automobile Works Limited) of Portello on the outskirts of Milan, was acquired in 1915 by the industrialist Nicola Romeo, who added his name to the marque. Left unchanged was the trademark, combining the Visconti Cross of St. George and the Sforza snake swallowing an unfortunate infant. The chief designer, Giuseppe Merosi, formerly with Bianchi, remained until 1926, creating a number of successful sports and racing types. His successor, Vittorio Jano, was the genius behind the firm's years of greatest glory. His P2 Grand Prix 2 litre supercharged straight eight won its first race, at Cremona in 1924, and its first grand epreuve, the French Grand Prix, in the same year. Alfa became the world champion make in 1925, and as late as 1930 a P2 won the Targa Florio.

Between 1928 and 1930 Jano's six-cylinder 1,500 and 1,750cc twin-cam supercharged sixes triumphed in nearly every sports-car event. These cars, also available unblown, are renowned for their superb handling, and the exemplary refinement of their coachwork, such as in the Zagato example shown here. These observations also apply to the later 2.3 litre straight eights that won Le Mans from 1931-34, and the Mille Miglia of 1932-34.

Nicola Romeo retired in 1930, and in 1933 the company was taken over by the Italian Government. The same year, Enzo Ferrari began a five-year term in charge of the firm's racing programme. The Monoposto twin-supercharged P3 straight-eight won seven Grands Prix in 1932 and six in 1933. It was later enlarged to 2.9 litres, then to 3.2 litres in an attempt to match the potent, Nazi-backed Auto Unions and Mercedes. Ultimately, it couldn't match them, but Nuvolari *did* defeat the Germans on their home ground in the 1935 Grand Prix at the Nurburgring in a 3.8 litre P3. In the light-racing (voiturette) class,

1930 1750 Gran Sport six-cylinder; ohc; four-speed gearbox; one of the premier sports cars of the 1930s.

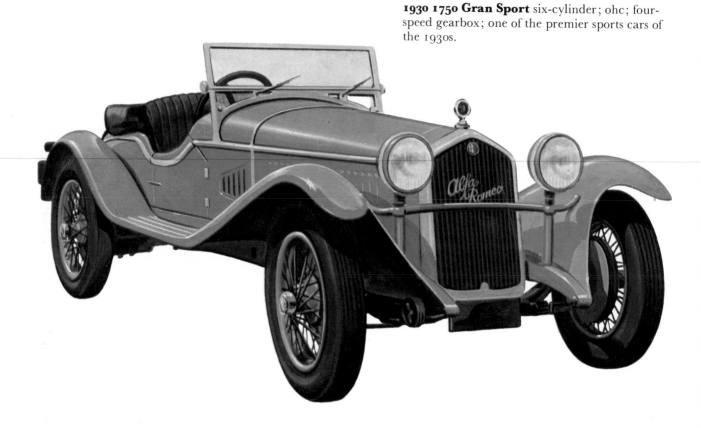

Gioacchino Colombo's supercharged 1.5 litre Type 158 Alfetta straight-eight of 1938 showed promise that was fulfilled after the war, when it won nearly every Grand Prix, making Giuseppe Farina World Champion in 1950 and Juan-Manuel Fangio in 1951. Sports cars in the last pre-war years included Jano's 2.3 litre unblown six of 1934-38, enlarged to 2.5 litres in 1939, and the 2.9 litre eights that won the 1937 and 1938 Mille Miglia.

Portello was badly damaged in the war, but by 1947 the reconstructed plant was producing an updated 6C 2500, the 'Freccia d'Oro' (Golden Arrow) with steering column gear change. The introduction of the 1900 sedan in 1950 was a radical change for Alfa, a four-cylinder with all-steel integral body/chassis in the standard version, though coachbuilders could still exercise their talents on a flat-platform variant. Nevertheless, the 1900 was capable of more than 100mph and eminently controllable, with the added attraction of low fuel consumption. During 1954, the 1900 was superseded by the somewhat larger 2000. More importantly, the 1,300cc Giulietta was introduced, bringing twin overhead camshaft performance and masterly styling to a popular market. In 65bhp form, the Spyder convertible shown here was especially popular; among the hardtop models, the costlier 90bhp sprint coupé was much in demand. The Giulietta was succeeded by the Giulia of 1962-68.

1956 Giuletta Spyder Sports two-seater version of the four-cylinder 1,300cc vehicle.

Allard

Gone but not forgotten, Sydney Allard's sports and racing cars enjoyed a phenomenal success during the early 1950s. A crashed 1934 Ford V8-40 saloon formed the basis of the first Allard car; Londoner Sydney Allard transformed it into an effective two-seater trials car, and the demand for replicas led to the start of production. From 1937 until the fateful autumn of 1939, he produced these stark two-seaters selling from £450 to £625, at his Adlards Motors Ford dealership in Putney. Some cars were fitted with the V12 Lincoln-Zephyr engine. Directly after the war, the firm was revived as the Allard Motor Co Ltd, and relocated in Clapham. Allard used the 3,622cc Ford Pilot V8 engine in three limited-production types: the short-chassis J (also available with a 3.9-litre Mercury engine), the two-seater or three-seater K1 roadster and the four-seater L1, from which the 1947 drophead coupé was derived. All had three-speed transmissions in unit with the engine, box

section frames, and aluminium bodies. Coil-spring independent front suspension and much needed hydraulic brakes were adopted in 1949.

Development culminated with the most successful open-bodied Allards, the J2 and K2 of 1949-52. In standard home-market form they used the 3.9-litre ohv Ardun-Mercury V8, but 5.4-litre Cadillac and Chrysler power plants were generally installed in examples exported to the United States, where their victories in such road races as the 1950 Bridgehampton compensated their owners for a degree of brutality. In international racing, running only on top gear for more than half of the 24 hours of the 1950 Le Mans, a J2 with Cadillac engine finished third. Then in 1952, starting from Glasgow, a well-prepared Allard P-type saloon with 4,375cc side-valve Mercury engine won the Monte Carlo rally over an icy course.

Allard followed his Monte Carlo triumph with the P2 Monte Carlo saloon, featuring a

1950 K2 3,622cc Ford V8 engine with three-speed gearbox; 90mph.

new tubular chassis that also served the Safari station wagon introduced later in 1952. Though these cars were available with engines to suit any requirements and came closer than their predecessors to being adapted to all-round use, they, and the later J3 and K3 open types, were overwhelmed by competition from Jaguar in price, performance, versatility and prestige. By the mid-1950s the large Allards, like the Bristol, were made only to special order as Grand Touring coupés (mainly with C-type Jaguar engines) and were discontinued altogether in 1961.

The Allard Palm Beach of 1952-5, powered by British Ford fours and sixes, marked the firm's entry into the light sports-car range. This attractive 100mph roadster (a saloon version was added in 1954) with a wheelbase of 8ft, three-abreast bench seat, and coil springing was obviously directed at the American market, but sales were disappointing.

The 1956 Palm Beach Mark II, a two-seater with attractive body, independent torsion-bar front suspension, and a choice of

1951 J2 4,375cc or 5,440cc V8 engines; three-speed gearbox; weight only 18¼cwts giving about 110mph with larger (Cadillac) engine.

British Ford Zephyr or Jaguar engine also failed to gain wide acceptance and was dropped in 1959.

1954 Palm Beach available with 1½-litre Ford Consul or 2½-litre Zephyr engines.

Alvis

Alvis of Coventry took their name from an aluminium piston manufactured by G. P. H. de Freville, who designed the company's first car, the 1920 10/30.

This was noted for its sporting performance —6omph from a 1½-litre side-valve car was quite unusual in those days—but it was the pushrod ohv 12/50 of 1923, the creation of the company's new chief engineer, Captain G. T. Smith-Clarke, which really made the Alvis Company's reputation. One of the great vintage sports cars, the 12/50 was produced until 1932; its performance was proved in 1923 when a tuned version won the 200-Miles Race at Brooklands at over 93mph. The 12/50 also formed the basis of the original front-wheel-drive Alvis of 1925, a sprint car with a duralumin chassis. And in 1928 came their—and the British car industry's—first catalogued front-wheel-drive model, a four-cylinder ohc 1½-litre, available with or without supercharger. Two unblown fwd 'Alvi' won their class in the 1928 Le Mans race, but the model had limited sales appeal, and proved an expensive aberration for Alvis.

For 1933, the 12/50 was replaced by the far less attractive Firebird, but it was sporting sixes which were the company's mainstay during the 1930s. The 2½- and 2.7-litre overhead-valve Speed 20, 90mph six, introduced in 1932, was supplanted in 1926 by

the Speed 25. Except for early Speed 20s, these models incorporated synchromesh transmission and independent front suspension.

Perhaps the ultimate Alvis was the 1937-9 4.3-litre (4,381cc) six. A truly thoroughbred sports machine, it was the fastest production saloon of its days, with a 100mph-plus top speed.

Best of the 1930s Alvis four-cylinders was the 1937 12/70 designed by George Lanchester.

After the war, a consistent single-series policy was initiated. The first offering, the dignified, sporty TA14 saloon with solid front axle, was rather heavy for its 1,892cc engine developed from the 12/70.

Starting with the TA21 of 1950-3, an ohv six of 2,993cc was used exclusively by Alvis. It was originally rated at 86bhp and gave a top speed of 85mph; these figures were soon improved on. Late in 1950 the four-door saloon was joined by a convertible and the faster TB21 tourer.

In 1955 Alvis introduced a handsome close-coupled two-door saloon body by Graber of Berne, Switzerland, on the TC21/100 six-cylinder chassis. A convertible coupé was added for 1958, when Graber coachwork was standardized. The last Alvis, the 130bhp TE21, made its debut in 1964. It featured four

1939 4.3 Tourer six-cylinder; 4,381cc; three SU carburettors; one of the four pre-war genuine 100mph cars.

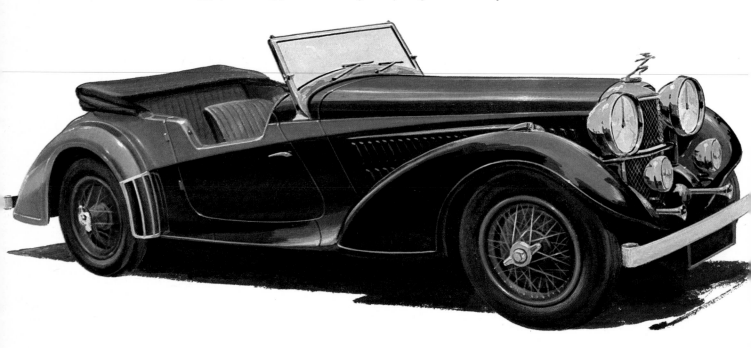

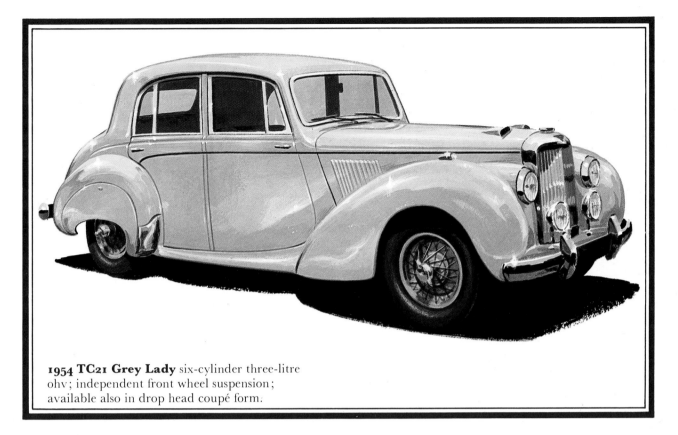

1954 TC21 Grey Lady six-cylinder three-litre ohv; independent front wheel suspension; available also in drop head coupé form.

headlamps and a five-speed ZF transmission, with options of power steering and an automatic transmission. In 1965 Alvis came under the control of Rover. Two years later it ceased production of all except military vehicles when Rover was absorbed by British Leyland.

1965 TE21 six-cylinder; 2,993cc; 130bhp @ 5000rpm.

Armstrong Siddeley

Armstrong Siddeley Motors of Coventry, established in 1919 with a merger of Armstrong-Whitworth of Newcastle and Siddeley-Deasy of Coventry, traced its roots back to the modified Peugeots marketed in 1902 by John Davenport Siddeley. During the inter-war decades the firm produced high-quality, rather stolid, cars at the rate of 1,000 or so a year. Except for the cheapest, smallest models, they were distinguished by bluff vee-radiators. The emphasis was on comfort and dignity, so the 1933 hiduminium-engined Siddeley Special 5-litre was quite uncharacteristic of the marque.

After the war came a range named after the parent Hawker Siddeley group's famous warplanes—Typhoon, Lancaster, Hurricane and, from 1949-50, Whitley. The engine for these stylish 'semi-knife-edged' vehicles, based on a prewar overhead-valve six, was of only 2.3 litres, a surprisingly small volume given their performance. In 1953 came the Sapphire, named after a Hawker Siddeley jet engine, with a new six-cylinder power unit of 3,435cc and incorporating hemispherical combustion chambers, which boasted 150bhp in twin-carburettor form from 1954. Late in 1958 came the 4-litre Star Sapphire saloon, publicized by the slogan 'The Managing Director's Car'. It was accurately described as being 'tailor-made for the man at the top: the man who demands absolute efficiency, sparkling performance and club chair comfort'. Inevitably, the saloon was soon supplemented by a limousine version. This was the marque's final offering: production ceased in mid 1960 following the merger of Hawker Siddeley with the Bristol Aeroplane Company.

1953 Sapphire six cylinder; 3,455cc; up to 150bhp with twin carburettors.

1951 Whitley six cylinder; 2,300cc; ohv

Aston Martin

Aston Martin had its modest beginnings just before World War I, when Lionel Martin and Robert Bamford put a 1.4-litre Coventry-Simplex engine into a 1908 Isotta-Fraschini chassis and won the Aston Clinton hillclimb. In 1922 the partners began production of Aston Martin cars in West London, and during three years produced about sixty 1½-litre side-valve sports cars plus a few 16-valve twin ohc racers. Racing successes such as a second at Brooklands in 1922 failed to keep the firm above water and in 1926 it was reorganized under Auguste Cesare Bertelli, who introduced a new 1,500cc ohc model derived from a design he had evolved while working with Enfield-Allday. Bodywork was by Bertelli's brother Enrico, while final drive was by a David Brown worm gear. Starting in 1930, dry-sump lubrication was standardized. Aston Martin won the 1932, 1935, and 1937 Rudge-Whitworth Le Mans biennial cup, finished fifth overall in 1933 and third in 1935, and were first in their class in the 1935 Mille Miglia.

1930 1½ litre four-cylinder; ohv; high-efficiency engine.

In 1932 a conventional Hotchkiss drive was introduced in the International Le Mans series. That year's competition version, the 1933-4 Mark II, and the 1935-6 Ulster models—similar but more powerful cars capable of up to 100mph—boasted chromed external exhaust pipes. Control of Aston Martin passed to R. G. Sutherland in 1933.

The 1,500cc engines were discontinued in 1936, being replaced by the standard ohc 2-litre Model 15-98 of 1937-9 which incorporated a synchromesh transmission and wet-sump lubrication, though the higher-priced Speed version retained the dry-sump system and crash gearbox. In a radical departure, the 1939 Speed had a streamlined body as did Claude Hill's experimental Atom prototype saloon of 1939, which was to influence the postwar enclosed models. The firm's first postwar car, also by Hill, was an open model with a short-stroke 1,970cc ohv engine and hydraulic brakes, of which few were made.

1947 marked a great watershed for Aston Martin: the floundering firm was acquired by the industrialist, David Brown, who wanted to build, regardless of cost, fast cars that lacked nothing in finish or amenities—grand tourers *par excellence*. The first cars built under Brown's control were designed by Hill and St. John Horsfall and were based on the Atom, with improved braking, tubular chassis, and suspension based on that used in a prototype that won the 1948 Grand Prix of Belgium. A Spa Replica saloon was introduced at the London Motor Show later that year, joined by the DB1 (for David Brown) open two-seater, soon followed by a DB1 coupé.

The DB2 sports saloon made its debut in 1950. Aston Martin's standard 3-litre engine was replaced by a masterful 2,580cc twin ohc six that W. O. Bentley had designed for Lagonda, another recent Brown acquisition. The Italianate stressed-skin alloy body set the theme for future Aston Martins; the DB2 was one of ten makes exhibited at the Museum of Modern Art in New York in 1953 for excellence of design.

In 1954, the DB2 became the DB2-4, with occasional rear seating; the following year, a

2,922cc power unit developing 140bhp was standardized.

Among Aston Martins designed primarily for competition and as mobile laboratories for potential improvements in the production sports cars, the DB3 (1952) and DB3S (1953) open two-seaters had a tubular ladder-type frame and advanced suspension designed by Eberan von Eberhorst. Between 1957 and 1959

the disc-braked, five-speed DBRs, of 2.9 and 3.7 litres, were more consistently victorious on both sides of the Channel; in 1959 they gained the World Sports-Car Championship by winning at the Nurburgring, in the Tourist Trophy, and at Le Mans.

In 1958 the firm moved into the former Tickford coachbuilding factory at Newport Pagnell. Development of the road cars continued with the DB4 saloon, introduced in 1958 at £2,650 and produced until 1963. Its 3,670cc aluminium engine gave 240bhp in standard form, 303bhp in the shorter, lighter, and more costly five-speed GT coupé version with Vantage engine. Top speed exceeded 140mph, and the saloon could go from 0 to 100mph and all the way back in 27 seconds, making full use of its disc brakes. The body, designed by Touring of Italy, was welded to

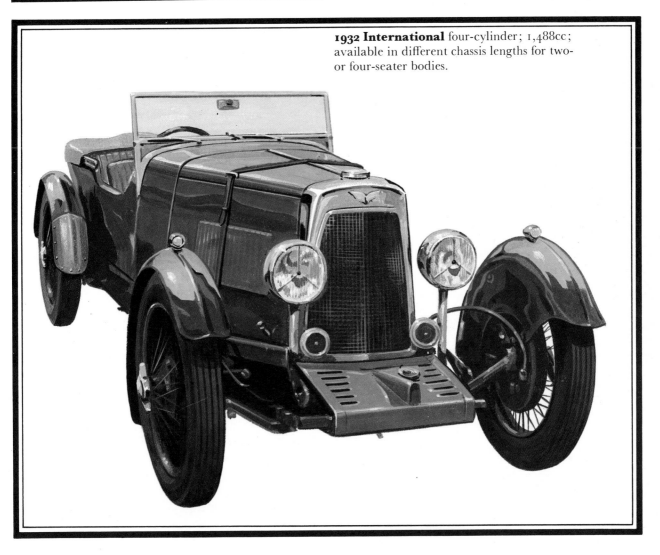

1932 International four-cylinder; 1,488cc; available in different chassis lengths for two- or four-seater bodies.

DB2-4 three-litre; six-cylinder; twin ohc; 140bhp @ 5000rpm.

the platform frame via small-diameter steel tubing, a method used in subsequent series.

The 3,995cc DB5 saloon and convertible of 1963-5 could top 150mph and introduced an optional automatic transmission. One of them, bristling with lethal gadgets, upstaged James Bond in the film of Ian Fleming's book *Goldfinger*. The 282bhp or 325bhp DB6 of 1965-8 had a five-speed transmission as standard. The last six-cylinder model, the

DB6 six-cylinder; 3,995cc; option of three SU carburettors or three Weber with raised compression ratio; also petrol injection.

stylish DBS coupé of 1968-70 (£4,473 basic), had four headlamps. The ultimate achievement to date is the DBS-V8, introduced in 1969 and known simply as the Aston Martin V8 since the Brown group sold the firm in 1972. The 5,340cc engine features four overhead camshafts and the V8 can attain 165mph.

Largely because of the costs entailed in achieving California's stringent emission standards, at the end of 1974 the company entered voluntary receivership. Two months later an Anglo/Canadian group acquired the firm and re-started production very successfully.

Auburn

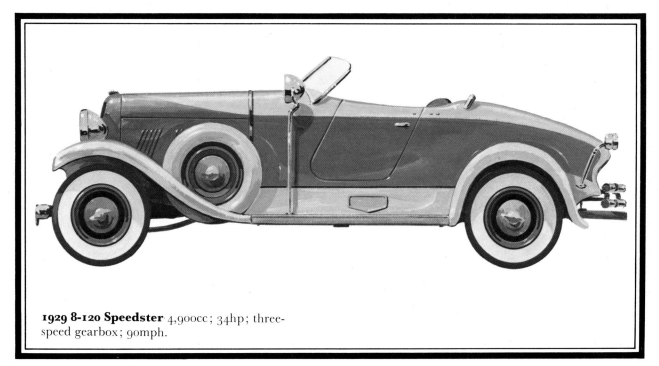

1929 8-120 Speedster 4,900cc; 34hp; three-speed gearbox; 90mph.

For almost a quarter century, Auburn was an obscure, low-production medium-priced car of no particular distinction. Its fortunes changed suddenly when Errett Lobban Cord took charge in 1924, when the company had to dispose of about seven hundred dated Beauty-Sixes (more than a hundred days' production at that low point) which were languishing outside its plant in Auburn, Indiana. By dint of inspired advertising and cosmetic surgery, super salesmen Cord cleared them out and for 1925 readied a radically different line of fours, sixes, and straight eights.

The first Cord-inspired cars, which continued with little external change during six model years, were instantly recognizable by a radiator shell like that of the Duesenberg Model A, and especially by a moulding line curving upwards from the bulkhead to the centre of the radiator top. The bodies were by Auburn itself, the Limousine Body Co of Kalamazoo, Michigan, and the McFarlan Motor Car Co of Connersville, Indiana, a firm dating from 1910 that was still producing its own splendid large Classics. Throughout Cord's period of control the Auburn-Cord-Duesenberg engines, of which the Auburn fours were dropped in 1927, were by Lycoming, who also supplied motive

power to Kissel, the last McFarlans, and other makes. During the second half of the 1920s Lycoming, Duesenberg, and the suppliers of bodies were absorbed into entrepreneur Cord's rapidly expanding empire.

Among the models produced between 1925 and 1930, designer James M. Crawford's open-model straight eights, phaetons, convertible saloons and rumble-seat roadsters, and the boat-tailed Speedsters styled by Count Alexis de Sakhonffsky are the most highly prized. The 8-88 of 1926-7 was surpassed by the 8-115 of 1928, which set many stock-car records and on one occasion bested the far costlier Stutz by climbing Pikes Peak, Colorado, in 21 minutes 45 seconds. The advertised figure of 115bhp for the 1928 Speedster, the highest in America at that time, was made possible by a new updraught twin choke carburettor. The similar 8-120 Speedster of 1929 shown here could attain 90mph and was listed at about $2,000. Its 4.9-litre engine, turned front to back, powered the L-29 Cord.

During 1931 the firm adopted the same mistaken strategy of most contemporary American luxury car manufacturers: it introduced a multi-cylinder monster, a 6.4-litre V12 designed by George Kublin and rated at 160bhp. The new car, with its big engine

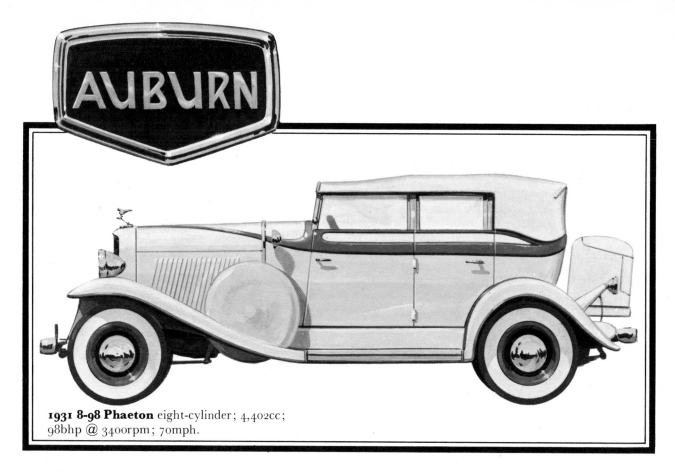

1931 8-98 Phaeton eight-cylinder; 4,402cc;
98bhp @ 3400rpm; 70mph.

and Columbia axle, had spectacular
performance, twice winning the American
stock-car speed championship and setting long-
standing mile and kilometre records for
unsupercharged standard cars in its two years
of production. In spite of these feats, sales
were disappointingly small, perhaps because
the basic price of $995 was too low to confer
snob status on its owners.

The year 1935 saw the début of the famous
851 Speedster (renumbered 852 in 1936), with
Gordon Buehrig's inspired restyling changes of
the 1933 Speedster body, with teardrop wings
and external exhaust pipes. The end product,
an insolently impractical vehicle carrying only
two passengers and affording minimal and all

1933 8-105 Speedster eight-cylinder Lycoming engine; 4,402cc; three-speed gearbox.

but inaccessible luggage space, succeeded in appearing completely new and was indisputably unique. Under the skin were a massive new frame, the old solid front axle, and the veteran eight, which, when August Duesenberg's centrifugal supercharger was specified, could develop 150bhp. Thus

equipped, this prime and potent classic–a dashboard plaque signed by record speed driver Ab Jenkins testified to a specific maximum in excess of 100mph for each unit—sold for about $3,500.

Including the less expensive unsupercharged examples, five hundred or so 851s and 852s were built before Auburn ceased all production in October 1936.

1935 851 Speedster eight-cylinder; 4,596cc; dual ratio near axles available as option; guaranteed 100mph in supercharge form.

Austin

1926 Chummy four-cylinder; 8hp; open four-seater version of one of the most popular British cars ever made.

Herbert Austin, formerly with Wolseley, founded the Austin Motor Car Company of Longbridge, Birmingham, in 1906. Before World War I it produced a great variety of fours and sixes ranging from 1,616 to 8,764cc, and from 1909 to 1911 it also marketed the first Seven, a one-cylinder Swift of 1,100cc with an Austin radiator shell and nameplate.

After the war, production centred on the 3,601cc Twenty, followed by the durable 1,661cc Twelve in 1921. Then came the immortal four-cylinder Seven for 1922, which remained in production for more than a decade. The engine had a capacity of only 747cc compared with the contemporary Morris-Cowley's 1,548cc, and the Model T Ford's 2,890cc, though the first cost of all three was roughly similar. By the same token, however, it travelled half as far again on a gallon of fuel ('Motoring at Tramfare') than either of the others, and paid far less horsepower tax.

'The Motor for the Millions', to cite another

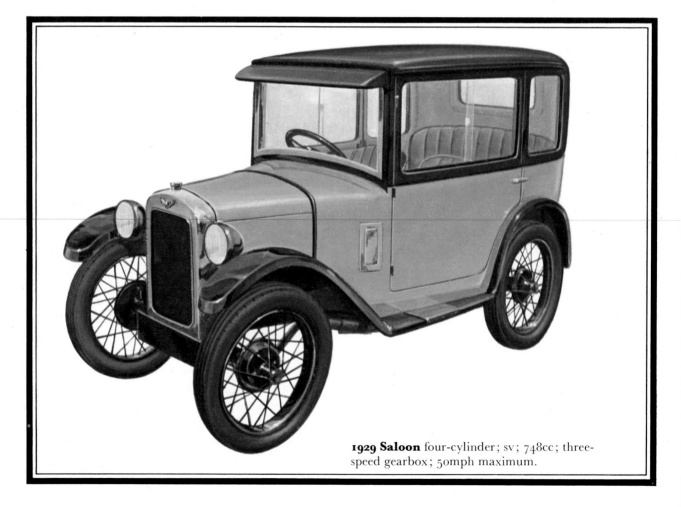

1929 Saloon four-cylinder; sv; 748cc; three-speed gearbox; 50mph maximum.

slogan, was aimed especially at young couples who otherwise would have had to make do with a motorcycle-cum-sidecar or with one of the flimsy cycle cars rife at the time. With a total length of 106 inches and a width of 46 inches, somehow it provided seating in the rear for two small children as well as for two reasonably trim adults in the front buckets. In fact it was a scaled-down companion of the other Austins, a real and respectable car.

Among the first Seven's unusual features was a manual pull starter in the driving compartment actuating a cable on a drum beside the flywheel. This arrangement was superseded by an electric starter at the end of 1923. The fuel tank, holding four gallons, was under the scuttle. Taking a leaf—leaves, rather—from Ford, the Seven had a transverse-spring front suspension until 1933. The four-wheel braking system was an advanced feature, though some of its advantages were nullified by the fact that the front brakes were operated by the handbrake lever, the rear brakes by the pedal.

The original open touring model was joined in 1926 by a two-door saloon that soon outsold the open cars. In the sporting field, from 1923 the factory had entered modified Sevens, some of them supercharged, in competition, with many victories which drew attention to the Seven's stamina. Specialist coachbuilders offered sports variants of the baby Austin, while in 1929 the production Ulster sports was available in supercharged form.

After 1933, the Seven was restyled, and lost much of its perky charm.

More than 290,000 Sevens were produced in Birmingham, and many more were built under licence abroad, notably by Datsun of Japan and by American Austin in Butler, Pennsylvania. The American Austin was essentially a restyled Seven with disc instead of wire wheels. Even with petrol at less than 20 cents a gallon its fuel economy failed to counterbalance its tame performance and tiny dimensions compared with the similarly-priced Model A Ford. As the Bantam, from 1935 to 1940, the car gained in weight and power

1931 Swallow special-bodied version, by the company that was later to become Jaguar, of the popular Seven.

but not in sales. The American Bantam people shelved the Seven to develop the original Jeep for the U.S. armed forces, of which it built more than 8,000 before losing out to Willys and Ford for lack of mass-production facilities.

After the Second World War, pre-war models were continued for a while, to be replaced in 1948 by the bulbous 40bhp, 70mph A40 Devon and Dorset saloons. Late in the next year came the even more bulbous 88bhp, 90mph A90 Atlantic convertible and sports saloon, designed primarily to broaden Austin's overseas market. It took America by storm initially, but perhaps it was just too American with its steering column gear change, and Pontiac-like chrome bonnet streak. Unlike the later Austin Healey 100/4 which used the same 2.7 litre engine it did not last long mainly because of premature rusting and unreliability.

Austins came in many shapes and sizes. Notable for dignity and prestige were the Sheerline and Princess saloons and limousines

1950 A90 Atlantic four-cylinder; 2,66occ; 88bhp; available as hard-top or soft-top coupés, the latter having optional power operation.

introduced in 1947, which were favoured by civic dignitaries. Not quite as good as 'The poor man's Rolls-Royce'—the Rover—they nevertheless looked far more expensive than they really were. Like most Rolls-Royces of the period they were powered by six cylinder engines of 4 litres or more. In 1960 they became a separate marque, known as Vanden Plas Princess.

Near the other end of the scale, among the various successors to the old Sevens and Eights, Pininfarina's A40 Countryman of 1959 stood out because of its utilitarian yet graceful body, which enabled it to serve both as an estate car as well as a saloon.

In 1952 Austin merged with Morris and Wolseley to form the British Motor Corporation.

1951 Princess Vanden Plas Saloon largest of the range of Austins; six-cylinder; 3,995cc; 130bhp @ 3700rpm; available as long chassis seven-seater and limousine.

Austin Healey

Following World War II, Donald Healey, formerly with Invicta and Triumph, made Riley-powered Healey sports cars which enjoyed many rally successes—the 105mph saloon version was the fastest British closed car of its day—and the export-only Nash-Healey in his factory at Warwick. Late in 1952 the British Motor Corporation took over his Austin A90-powered Healey 100, renamed it Austin Healey 100, and began to manufacture it in Birmingham the following May. This four-cylinder two-seater, with its smart full-width body (formed on the dies of an abortive MG TE), two-position windscreen, and rigid box-section chassis, gained instant popularity in the United States when it became available at $2,985 in mid-1953. It did well in the 1953 Le Mans and set international records for its class at Bonneville.

For 1957 the 100-4 was supplanted by the 100-6, whose additional cylinders gave greater smoothness with similar acceleration and top speed (105mph); this performance and exemplary reliability made it highly successful in international rallies. The length was increased to accommodate optional rear bucket seats for children of sporting parents.

In 1958 the 100-6 acquired a junior partner, the Sprite, priced at £669 (with purchase tax)

1958 Sprite Mk I cheap small sports car using four-cylinder, 948cc engine of Austin A35 origins; four-speed gearbox; 85mph.

and $1,799. The 948cc four of the Austin A35 was modified to give 45bhp and 80mph, while BMC's small chassis and suspension were hardly changed. The body, however, had an unusual front assembly that was hinged at the scuttle and carried 'frogeye' headlamps. An optional hardtop introduced in 1960 increased top speed to 85mph, thanks to lowered wind resistance.

1954 100/4 designed by Donald Healey using Austin A90 engine of 2,660cc; very successful in competition, having top speed of 115mph.

Bentley

Before Walter Owen Bentley founded Bentley Motors in London in 1919, he had pioneered the use of aluminium pistons in car engines and had designed the BR 1 (Bentley rotary) and BR 2 aircraft engines. His first production car, a 3-litre long-stroke four with overhead camshaft, won instant acclaim when it eventually reached the market in 1921 and was indeed the *beau ideal* of the Vintage sports car. The three chassis types—short, long, and the rare, ultra-short 100mph model—were available and 1,630 3-litres were produced up to 1929. A 3-litre won at Le Mans in 1924 and another, even though damaged, in 1927; such victories inaugurated the enduring Bentley mystique.

W.O.'s goals always exceeded his financial grasp. For 1926, instead of concentrating on the 3-litre, he perfected a 6,597cc six directed in the main at a sophisticated carriage trade that would value sprightly performance in stately saloons. But the anticipated sales failed to materialize. The 6½-litre engine was based on the 3-litre but had a camshaft driven by eccentrics rather than gears and a kingshaft; it was rubber-mounted to mask the engine's

1926 3-litre first of the 'W.O.' Bentleys; four-cylinder; 2,996cc; four-speed gearbox; available in a variety of chassis lengths with suitable bodies from limousine to stark open sports type.

harsh running. The open Speed Six of 1929, with higher compression and twin carburettors, was far more sporting; driven by the firm's financial angel, the diamond millionaire Woolf Barnato, it won the Le Mans 24 Hour race in 1929 and 1930.

The 6½-litre was hardly launched when Bentley started to develop a sporting successor to the by-no-means obsolete 3-litre. The new car was the renowned 4½-litre (4,398cc) four, essentially the 6½-litre minus two cylinders; the 100mm bore and 140mm stroke were identical. It was marketed from 1927 to 1931 with a five-year guarantee in normal use. In its 1927 Le Mans début it was eliminated in the same pile-up that damaged the victorious 3-litre, but in 1928 Barnato, with a broken frame and empty radiator, drove a 4½-litre to the first of his three successive triumphs on that course. Barnato's Speed Six led three 4½-litres over the finishing line at Le Mans to give Bentley a still unmatched 1-2-3-4 finish. Against Bentley's advice, racing driver Sir Henry Birkin had Amherst Villiers Superchargers fitted to a run of 50 4½-litres in 1930, in one of which he finished second in the *formule libre* 1930 French Grand Prix.

In 1930 W.O. presented his masterpiece, the 8-litre (7,983cc) 220bhp overhead-cam six; only 100 were completed, plus 50 of the less exciting F-head 4-litre, before the firm

went into a long-threatened receivership in July 1931. In all, 3,061 'real' Bentleys were built. As a result of the receivership, Rolls-Royce snatched control of Bentley from under the nose of Napier.

After a hiatus of two years, a totally new type of Bentley, the 'Silent Sports Car', emerged from the Rolls-Royce works at Derby. W.O. helped to develop it but left in 1935 to rejuvenate Lagonda.

The 3½-litre Derby Bentleys of 1933-6 were based mechanically on the Rolls-Royce 20/25; the chief points of difference were a lighter chassis of shorter wheelbase (10ft 6in against 11ft), two carburettors instead of one, and a top-gear ratio of 4.1 against 4.54 to 1. Despite a maximum speed of 90mph even in saloon form, the 3½-litre wasn't devised as a competition car, though Eddie Hall did take

second place in the 1934 and 1935 Ulster TTs with a works-backed two-seater.

The second Derby series, the 4¼-litre (4,257cc) based on the 25/30 Rolls-Royce, was made from 1936 to 1939. It had an edge in performance over the 3½-litre and could cope

1931 4½-litre four-cylinder; 4,398cc with two SU carburettors in standard form; also available in limited numbers as a supercharged car; very successful in competitions and still capable of high performance.

better with heavy saloon coachwork. The new
engine enabled Eddie Hall to take second
place in the TT yet again in 1936, at a
record 80.81mph.

After World War II, Rolls-Royce
and Bentley production moved to Crewe in
Cheshire. The Mark VI Bentley of 1946-51
was closely related to the Rolls-Royce Silver
Wraith, sharing the same engine, a 4½-litre
F-head six, again with two carburettors instead
of one. Being smaller and, at 4,000lb, about
10 per cent lighter than the Wraith, the
Mark VI had gratifying performance. Most
Mark VIs were equipped with standard steel
saloon bodies, making them competitive in the
prestige market at under £3,000 basic. In 1951
the engine was enlarged to 4,566cc to give a top
speed exceeding 100mph. From late 1952, the
Mark VI, boasting a more capacious boot,
became known as the R type. During the
model's last year, 1954-5, the engine grew
to 4,887cc and was soon adopted in the
Rolls-Royce Silver Cloud. Subsequent
Bentleys, starting with the S type of 1955-9,
are distinguished from Rolls-Royces mainly by
their radiator shell.

To supplement and outdo the Mark VI, in
1952 the R type Continental was introduced,
featuring a sweepingly curvaceous two-door
sports-saloon body by H. J. Mulliner. It was
longer, wider, smarter, lighter (by more than
a thousand pounds), faster (by 14mph), and
dearer (by £1,790 basic) than the standard
saloon and it gave its fortunate owners
(numbering 207 by the time the series was
discontinued in 1955) the ultimate in Grand
Touring.

1939 4½-litre six-cylinder; 4,257cc; four-speed
gearbox with overdrive; 90mph; by the time this
model appeared, Bentley had been taken over by
Rolls-Royce; this car was a development from
the Rolls 20/25 engine.

1959 S Type 4,887cc; automatic gearbox
standard; last of the six-cylinder series and the
first of the make sharing a common specification
—apart from radiators—with the comparable
Rolls-Royce model.

1955 R Type development of the first post-war Mk VI model; six-cylinder; 4,566cc; four-speed gearbox or optional automatic—the first Bentley to be so fitted; speeds of 100mph available.

BMW

BMW (Bayerische Motoren-Werke; Bavarian Motor Works), founded in 1916 to build aircraft and aero engines, produced the first of its famous flat-twin motorcycles in Munich in 1923; its first production car, the BMW-Dixi, was a licence-built Austin Seven, acquired when BMW took over the Dixi company in 1928, and built in the old Dixi works at Eisenach. It was succeeded in 1932 by the independently-sprung 3/20 PS. The first BMW six, the 303, appeared a year later. The first of a series of sporting sixes created by Fritz Fiedler, the 315 of 1934-5, developed 40bhp from its three-carburettor 1,490cc engine. The

1935 Type 55 Tourer six-cylinder; 1,911cc of high efficiency; four-speed gearbox; successful competition car with speeds of more than 80mph available.

similar 1,875cc model of 1936 developed 45bhp (twin carburettors) or 55bhp with three carburettors.

The most renowned pre-war BMWs were the 326, 327, and 328 sports sixes of 1936-9, with ingenious ohv gear operated by cross-over pushrods. Visually, these BMWs were distinguished by the narrow twin-oval grille that has remained a hallmark of all BMWs.

1937/38 328 Sports highly developed three-carburettor version of the 1,911cc, six-cylinder engine; one of the few genuine 100mph sports cars available before World War II.

For the 328 the power of the 1,971cc unit was raised from 55 to 80bhp by means of a free-breathing aluminium head and three carburettors. In this form it gained a class victory in the 1938 Mille Miglia, while a streamlined coupé finished fifth in the 1939 Le Mans 24 Hour race.

Following the division of Germany after World War II, the Eisenach factory in the Soviet Zone produced cars based on pre-war BMWs for a decade. The Munich factory, heavily damaged during the war, built only motorcycles until 1951, when the 72bhp 501 appeared. A near duplicate of the pre-war 326, it used the 1,971cc engine block and a saloon car body similar to the family version of 1936. In 1954 came the 95bhp 2.6-litre 502 eight-cylinder saloon, followed in 1955 by the 503 Gran Turismo cabriolet and coupé and the Type 507 sports, both of 3.2 litres and 140 and 150bhp respectively.

Also in 1955, to tap a less affluent market, BMW entered into a licensing agreement to manufacture the Italian-designed Isetta bubble car. This unique little vehicle's counterbalanced door at the front incorporated the instrument panel and steering column, so that one had unobstructed access to the two seats. The foldback roof top was weathertight when closed. The 293cc air-cooled engine, a single-cylinder BMW motorcycle type, was located forward and somewhat outboard of the right rear wheel, which, in turn, was separated by only 20in from its mate in order to obviate the need of a differential. A total length of 7ft 10in made city parking easy, and at 7cwt, the car could be squeezed into really tight spaces. Top speed was 53mph, fuel consumption 60mpg. The BMW Isetta 300 remained in production at home until 1963, and British licensees sold three- and four-wheeled versions from 1957 to 1964.

In 1957, Munich added the longer 9ft 6in, heavier 10cwt, faster (62mph), and more

1955 501B Saloon six-cylinder; 1,971cc with comfortable five-seater body; it became one of Germany's first post-war luxury cars.

expensive four-seater BMW 600 of its own design, with steel roof, a right-side door for rear passengers, a full-width rear track with differential, and a rear mounted two-cylinder 595cc motorcycle engine.

Despite these ingenious designs BMW fortunes reached a low ebb and the company was only rescued by the introduction of the 1500, an attractive sports saloon which led to the current range of fine cars.

1957 Isetta 300 bubble car with twin rear wheels set close together and capable of carrying three adults; single-cylinder; 298cc; top speed about 50mph.

Bristol

The Bristol dates from 1946, when the Bristol Aeroplane Company of that city began to produce the advanced 400 series close-coupled coupé and convertible based on BMW's 327 and 328 of the late 1930s. The use of aircraft metals meant that the Bristol's efficient ohv six-cylinder engine developed 85bhp from 1,971cc, aided by hemispherical combustion chambers and three carburettors. The frontal styling was pure BMW. Beneath the flowing aluminium bodies was a lightweight tubular steel frame, again reflecting Bristol's aircraft experience. Suspension was by independent transverse leaf springing at front, torsion bars at the rear. Steering was by rack and pinion. Initiating a Bristol tradition, the 400 was expensive for its time at a basic price of £1,750 in 1950.

Though available until the autumn of 1950, the 400 was supplanted by the longer and wider four-seater 401 saloon. It could attain 100mph, thanks to an aerodynamic body developed in the wind-tunnel. The running boards had disappeared, all lights were flush fitted, and the doors had push buttons instead of handles. The basic price in 1950 was £1,925, which included a sixteen-coat finish.

The 403 saloon, introduced at £2,100 in the spring of 1953, had a more robust engine developing 100bhp. That September came a short-chassis luxury coupé, the 405, employing aerodynamic lessons learned from the Bristol Brabazon aircraft. The spare wheel was located in a hinged compartment behind the left front wheel, with a similar arrangement at the right for the battery and other components, a feature adopted on subsequent Bristols. The range was supplemented the next year by the 405 convertible and four-door saloon, Bristol's only example of the latter body type and, by 1958, the only model offered.

The 406 saloon, announced in the summer of 1958, marked a number of departures for Bristol, now operating separately from the aircraft company. The body, by an independent coachmaker, was longer than that of any previous model and offered more interior space. Disc brakes were standard. The old

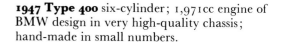

1947 Type 400 six-cylinder; 1,971cc engine of BMW design in very high-quality chassis; hand-made in small numbers.

1951 Type 401 further development of the 400 series but with luxurious four-seater streamlined bodywork worthy of aircraft manufacture, with which the company was associated.

1,971cc engine was increased to 2,216cc for smoother performance, though horsepower and top speed were hardly changed. Not so the price: £2,995 plus purchase tax.

From 1960, Bristols were assembled by a new firm, Bristol Cars Ltd. The six-cylinder engine, which had also been used by A.C., Frazer Nash, Cooper, and the export-only Arnolt-Bristol sports cars, was discontinued; a Bristol-modified Chrysler V8 power train was adopted, beginning with the 5,130cc 407 in 1961, graduating to the 6,277cc 411 in 1969. By then the basic price was about £5,000, falling between Aston Martin and Rolls-Royce.

1965 Type 409 V8 cylinder engine of Chrysler origin; 5,211cc; automatic transmission standard; more than 120mph.

Bugatti

One of the most gifted and individual car designers of all time, the Milan-born Ettore Bugatti, made engineering an art. Carlo, his father, was equally innovative in furniture and marquetry at the turn of the century, and his brother Rembrandt's animal sculptures in bronze won fame in the 1920s; both men's work is displayed in European and American museums.

At first designing cars for other makers, Ettore produced an advanced four-cylinder engine in 1900 when only 19. He then worked under contract with De Dietrich, Mathis, and Deutz before designing a light car which he planned to produce under his own name. Finally, in 1909, backing from the Darmstadt Bank enabled him to acquire his own factory, a former dyeworks, with numerous buildings and extensive land. It was located in Molsheim near Strasbourg in Alsace, a German province until 1918.

About 500 of the first production Bugatti, the Type 13, were built between 1910 and 1914. This stark two-seater 'bathtub', a 1.3-litre four with a single overhead camshaft, revolutionized light-car design. A standard model gained immediate prestige by winning its class and finishing second to a huge Fiat in the Grand Prix de France. At that time (1912), Bugatti also designed the 856cc Bébé for Peugeot.

When war broke out, the Francophile Bugatti left Alsace for Paris where he designed aircraft engines for the Allies. These were unsuccessful, but experimental examples worked on by the Duesenberg brothers at Elizabeth, New Jersey, led to the development of their post-war Model A power plant and thus indirectly to the wide adoption of straight eights in America. In fact, Bugatti had experimented with a straight-eight car as far back as 1913, but didn't go into production with a car of this configuration until 1920, when he built the 2-litre Type 30, which lasted until 1926. The first postwar models were substantially the pre-war Type 13, and that designation was retained for the short wheelbase racing version, though the long-wheelbase versions were now known as Type 22 (7ft 10½in wheelbase) and Type 23 (8ft 4½in wheelbase). A 16-valve version, originally designed for the 1914 Coupe de l'Auto won the 1920 Grand Prix des Voiturettes at Le Mans. This model became known as the Brescia after a spectacular 1-2-3-4 victory in the 1921 Voiturette race in that city.

Even more renowned is the Type 35 straight eight of 1924-30 with its many variants. The engine, derived from the Type 30 but with two intake valves and one exhaust valve per cylinder, had two more main bearings and improved lubrication, while the sky blue bodies were graceful as well as functional. Most Type 35s had Bugatti's alloy wheels in which the brake drums were cast integrally with the rim and flat spokes. Another enduring innovation, typical of Ettore's penchant for doing things the hard but

Cockpit of Type 35

Type 35B eight-cylinder, 2,261cc supercharged
engine; highly successful racing car capable of
over 120mph.

elegant way, was a hollow front axle with
cut outs through which the front leaf springs
passed. The marque enjoyed tremendous
sporting success; from 1924 to 1927 alone,
the marque as a whole was victorious on
1,851 occasions.

In effect ruler of a feudal fiefdom at
Molsheim, the imperious Ettore resolved to
build a conveyance that corresponded to what
he considered fit for monarchs. The result
was the legendary Type 41 Royale of 1927-32.
Remarkably, six survive. At about $40,000
for a complete car, only three were sold—
none to royalty—and three remained in the
Bugatti family for many years. Four are on
view in American museums: two at Harrah's,
one in the Briggs Cunningham collection, and
one in the Henry Ford Museum. The other
two were in the Schlumpf collection in France.

Graceful proportions tend to understate the
size of a Royale: 20 feet in length on a
14ft 2in wheelbase: a seven foot bonnet
conceals the long block of a 12-litre
straight-eight engine with its three valves per
cylinder, as in the comparatively diminutive
35. With 300bhp, performance ranged from 3
to 125mph in third, the highest gear, while
90mph could be attained in second. But

smoothness and silence rather than speed were
of prime importance.

The Type 46, introduced in 1929 as a
smaller Royale, had a 5.35-litre engine and
an 11ft 6in wheelbase, with the three-speed
transmission in unit with the rear axle.
With 120bhp, the top speed was in the 100mph
range. This model was marketed until 1936
and found several hundred buyers. A
development was the 4.9-litre Type 50 of the
early 1930s with twin overhead camshafts; its
racing derivative was the Type 54. Twin
overhead camshafts were also used in the
supercharged Type 51 2.3-litre racing car
introduced in 1931 which was ultimately
derived from the Type 35. The supercharged
Type 55 sports car of 1932-5 had a de-tuned
version of the 51 engine, the chassis of the
Grand Prix 4.9-litre Type 54, and it normally
wore handsome two-seater bodywork. It was
capable of 115mph. In a middle range was
the touring 3.3-litre Type 49 of 1930-4, usually
fitted with enclosed coachwork.

The last Ettore-designed cars in general
production were the supercharged Type 59
racing car and the Type 57 road car. The
3.3-litre Type 59 appeared in 1933; the last
Bugatti racing car produced in any numbers,

it had a claimed top speed of 130mph. The 57, also of 3.3 litres, was made until 1940. About 800 were sold—almost 10 per cent of the marque's total production over three decades. It had a comfortable 10ft 10½in wheelbase and attained a modest 95mph. Starting in 1935, more sporting variants began to appear; the short-wheelbase, high-compression 57S sports (125mph); the similar supercharged sports 57SC, with a top speed

of 135mph. In 1936, the 140mph 57G 'tank' appeared; a 'tank' won Le Mans in 1937 and again in 1939.

Meanwhile, all was not well at Molsheim. Ettore left the factory for good when his faithful retainers engaged in a sit-down strike in 1936, and Jean Bugatti, Ettore's promising heir who had conceived many of the most handsome 55 and 57 bodies died in 1939 while testing a 57G 'tank'. The Germans took over the factory complex in 1940; amphibious vehicles, torpedoes, flying bombs and snowploughs were some of the diverse items produced by them at Molsheim. Five years later, under Allied occupation, a fire caused by the Canadians damaged the plant; the Americans removed much of the machinery and plans. Ettore had to take the French government to court before his confiscated factory was returned; his designs for postwar

Royale Type 41 massive eight-cylinder of 12,760cc developing about 300bhp; even with very large limousine bodywork it was capable of high performance well over 100mph.

Type 55 supercharged eight-cylinder of 2,270cc and 135bhp; basically of Grand Prix model design; top speed 110mph.

types were never executed before his death in 1947. His successors' 57-based Type 101 coupé of 1951 did not go into serious production, and the new Formula 1 transverse rear-engined 251 of 1955 failed to finish a race. But the 1,200 or so *pur sang* Bugattis that survive will always be among the cars most coveted by collectors.

Type 57 eight-cylinder; 3,255cc; 130bhp giving about 95-100mph with conventional bodywork; also available as 57S with short chassis and 57SC with supercharger for higher performance versions.

Buick

1917 D44 six-cylinder; 3,650cc; ohv; very fully equipped and better-quality than most American cars of the period.

David Dunbar Buick, a Scots-born manufacturer of plumbing fixtures living in Detroit, built a prototype car in 1903, a two-cylinder with planetary transmission and overhead valves, the latter becoming an enduring feature of all Buicks. But by August 1904, when the first production model was sold, the fledgling firm had run out of funds and was soon taken over by the carriage-maker, William C. Durant of Flint, Michigan, in his first venture as a promotion wizard in the automotive industry. Buick was soon eased out and ended up two decades later as an instructor in a Detroit school for mechanics that traded on his name.

In 1908, Durant founded General Motors, with Buick as the keystone and sales of 8,800 put Buick in the front rank of American cars. Buick's 1908 four-cylinder was followed by the first six-cylinder which appeared in 1914. From then until 1921, these sturdy and dependable middle-priced cars, selling more than 100,000 annually under the management of Walter P. Chrysler, underwent little change in the rather bland appearance typified by the 1917 roadster. The 1922-3 series, advertised with the uninspiring slogan 'Power to Start, Power to

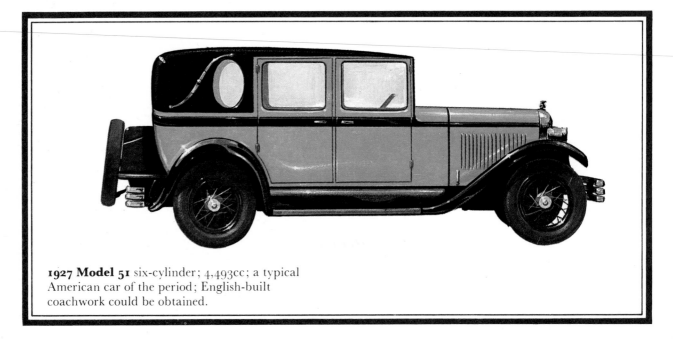

1927 Model 51 six-cylinder; 4,493cc; a typical American car of the period; English-built coachwork could be obtained.

1929 Model 55 Tourer

Stop', kept the rounded radiator and bonnet but the body sides were lowered to make them flush with the scuttle.

For 1924, the four's last year, four-wheel brakes and balloon tyres were adopted, along with body lines strikingly similar to those of the Packard. With only minor changes until 1928, Buick outsold all other American cars in their class. 'When better automobiles are built, Buick will build them', became the slogan. Smart variants of the enclosed bodies were offered in the senior series, while open models became more sporting, as saloon bodies superseded open-topped touring cars as standard family transportation.

A complete restyling in 1929 failed to woo the customer, and Buick sales lagged in what should have been a boom year. The trouble was that the bodywork was a little too rotund for contemporary taste, and the model became known as 'the pregnant Buick'. The 1930 models were less rounded. The following year, Buick announced that its range would consist of nothing but straight-eights, a policy maintained until 1953. To broaden Buick's appeal in the shrunken Depression market— 1933 sales were only just over 40,000—the newly appointed Buick Division President, Harlow Curtice, introduced the 1934 Special series. Independent coil-spring front suspension also came in 1934, followed by Harley Earl's basic restyling for 1936 (improved for 1937)

and a more efficient 'Dynaflash' engine and rear coil-springs for 1938. In 1941, the last full year before wartime cessation of car production, nearly 400,000 Buicks were sold. This figure was the result of talented engineering, conservative but attractive styling, and a broadened marketing range, from just above Chevrolet with the Special, through the middle-sized Super, the 165bhp Century, and the big Roadmaster and Limited, which vied with Cadillac for the luxury trade.

Some 1942 and most post-war Buicks had front wings which flowed back across the doors to merge with the rear wings—a radical styling step. The smooth but sluggish optional Dynaflow torque-converter transmission was introduced in 1948, followed by 'ventiport' holes in the bonnet and a toothy oval grille soon imitated by other makes and known abroad as 'the dollar grin'. In 1949, Buick also featured a two-door 'hardtop convertible' which was, in effect, a saloon without central door pillars.

For 1953, along with a switch to V8s for all models but the Special (which followed the next year), came the 188bhp Skylark convertible on the Roadmaster chassis, perhaps the most collectable Buick of the 1950s. Priced at more than $5,000, all it lacked was ventiports! Wire wheels, power steering, and Dynaflow were standard equipment.

In the latter half of the 1950s, Buicks

1953 Skylark V8; 5,278cc; 188bhp; equipped
with automatic gearbox and power steering.

suffered from controversial styling and a
decline in reliability. The marque came back
with tightened quality control and innovative
engineering, exemplified by the compact
Special of 1961, with a 3½-litre all-aluminium
V8 engine later modified for use in the Rover
V8 and the Range Rover; in 1962 it was
supplemented by a slightly smaller cast-iron
V6, a type of engine new to America.

More sought-after by collectors, however, is
the 1963 Riviera, a large four-seater hardtop
coupé that competed with the post-1957
Thunderbird as a luxurious 'personal' car. Its
styling was a successful blending of GM dream
cars and the American interpretation of razor-
edged British practice.

1963 Riviera V8; 6,653cc; 325bhp; 0-100mph
in just over 25 seconds.

Cadillac

1913 20/30 four-cylinder, six-litre engine with several unusual and advanced features, including an electric starter.

Henry M. Leland, 'master of precision', and now best known as the founder of Lincoln, was the guiding spirit of Cadillac from 1902 to 1917. His Leland and Faulconer foundry in Detroit built internal-combustion engines for Great Lakes 'Naptha launches' from about 1896, and entered the automotive field in 1900 by making transmissions for the Curved Dash Oldsmobile. In August 1902, after Olds had refused to adopt an improved Leland & Faulconer engine, Leland entered an agreement to supply the single-cylinder unit—designed by Alanson P. Brush—plus steering mechanisms and planetary transmissions for a new car, the Cadillac. It was named after the French explorer who had founded Detroit two centuries before.

The backers of the firm that was to build the Cadillac had previously been associated with Henry Ford in two ephemeral companies, the Detroit Automobile Company of 1899-1900 and the Henry Ford Company of November 1901-March 1902. Ford had resigned, 'determined never again to put himself under orders!' He had left behind him the unfinished drawings for a passenger car: Leland redesigned it to take his single-cylinder engine,

though the overall appearance was identical to the Model A Ford which appeared in 1903.

Cadillac built, in association with Leland & Faulconer, two prototypes which generated 2,200 orders at the New York Show. This instant success continued as the Cadillac's reliability became a byword. Built to exacting specifications under Leland's supervision—in 1904 he merged his firm with the Cadillac Automobile Co and became its general manager—this well-finished little car with the big cylinder (125mm bore and stroke) and two-speed planetary transmission sold in the range of $750 to $1,000 during its seven years of production, ending with a rating of 10bhp compared with the 7bhp of 1903.

In 1908 it won the Dewar Trophy, for a spectacular feat: under the auspices of the Royal Automobile Club, three Cadillacs were completely disassembled then all the parts were jumbled indiscriminately, and reassembled without a single stroke of a file and run 500 miles on the Brooklands track in Surrey with no untoward incident, thus demonstrating the precision and interchangeability of all components. Thanks to their durability and

1925 V63 V8; 5,228cc; three-speed gearbox; coil ignition.

to the esteem of their owners, a fair number of the approximately 18,000 one-cylinder Cadillacs have survived.

Starting in 1905 and continuing for a decade, four-cylinder Cadillacs appeared, the later ones equipped with conventional sliding-gear instead of planetary transmissions. They ranged from 20 to 50bhp and were priced from $1,400 to $3,750 for the then predominant open models. In the immediate period after Cadillac became a unit of General Motors in 1908, the basic price range was fairly narrow, from $1,400 in 1909 to $1,975 in 1913-4. Factory-built closed bodies, as distinguished from coachbuilt units, became available in 1910. For pioneering electric lighting and starting via Charles F. Kettering's system, Cadillac was awarded the unique accolade of

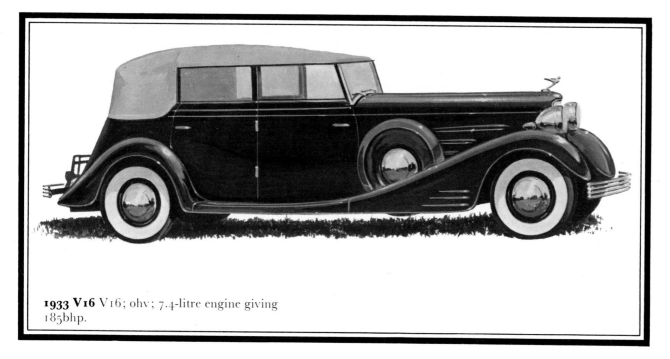

1933 V16 V16; ohv; 7.4-litre engine giving 185bhp.

a second Dewar Trophy in 1913. This emancipation of the driver from manual cranking and from fussing with acetylene lighting ensured the triumph of petrol-driven cars; from then on, the limited-range electric car and the complicated steam car were anachronisms. During the decade 1905-14, 67,167 Cadillac fours were produced.

For 1915, Cadillac dropped the four and, without the expected transition to a six, made automotive history with the Model 51 V8, the first V8 to go into mass production in America. Compared with the 1913-4 fours, the 1915 V8 touring car weighed 3,795lbs against 4,095lbs, had an engine of 5.1 against 6 litres but was rated at 60bhp compared with 40 or 50, had left-hand instead of right-hand steering, and sold for the same price—$1,975.

The factory coachwork remained unimaginative; even a 1924 V63, introduced with the slogan 'Expect Great Things', could be recognized as a descendant of the V57 used

by General Pershing in France and even of the 1913 fours. This continuity of design was paralleled in the use of the 5.1-litre V8 engine which remained essentially the same until 1927, except for such advances as detachable cylinder heads in 1917 and a dynamically balanced and counterweighted crankshaft in 1924. Four-wheel brakes were also adopted in 1923. Engine output increased modestly to 72bhp in 1924 and 87bhp in 1926.

Quality continued after Henry Leland and his son Wilfred left Cadillac in 1917 to found the Lincoln Motor Co. The 1925 V63 touring car, a favourite among police and gangland chiefs, wore the last of the Leland-type bodies, modified by somewhat smartened lines and a Duco pyroxylin finish. The 1925s pioneered crankcase ventilation and thermostatic control of the coolant temperature.

In 1926 and 1927 the bodies were transitional, with a lower look. Starting in 1928, the advanced styling of Harley Earl, the creator of the 1927 La Salle, took over, with little change until 1932. The 1929 convertible coupé exemplifies early Earl designs. Under the 1928's skin was a new 5.6-litre V8 developing 90bhp, every one of which was needed to propel the nearly 5,000lb car. In this period, Cadillac was the first car

1929 Convertible Coupé eight-cylinder; 5,573cc; three-speed gearbox with synchromesh introduced as new feature; one of America's quality cars.

1938 60S V8; 5,573cc; 90bhp @ 3000rpm;
various wheelbase lengths available for custom
coachwork.

in the world to have a synchromesh
transmission.

For 1930, Cadillac introduced chief engineer
Ernest Seaholm's overhead-valve V16 of
7.4 litres and 185bhp, another first that was
emulated in America only by Marmon and
an experimental car, the Peerless. All through
the 1930s and into 1940, V16s remained in
limited production as GM's style leader and
ultimate prestige car. Examples powered by the
45-degree-V engine of 1930-7 hovered around
6,000lb and ranged from 11ft 6in to 12ft 10in
in wheelbase. With bodywork by Fleetwood,
exclusive body builders to Cadillac since 1926,
prices ranged from $5,350 to $9,500.

Of the 3,863 ohv V16s built in 1930-7,
about two-thirds were sold in the introductory
year. From 1932, annual production was
advertised as being limited to 400 cars, a figure
that was never attained. The modernized 11ft
9in wheelbase V16 of 1938-40, with a much
lighter 135-degree 7-litre Seaholm engine of
equal horsepower, underlined Cadillac's hold
on the luxury-car market but sold a total of
only 511 units. The basic price was $5,140
during all three years. From 1931 until 1937,
Cadillac also offered a 6-litre V12, rated at
135 to 150bhp, that would be more noteworthy
were it not overshadowed by the V16.

The V8, Cadillac's mainstay throughout,
continued with the development of the 1928
5.6-litre flathead engine until 1948, first
to 5.7-litres in 1930, then to 5.8 in 1936,
by which time, just as now, Cadillac was
outselling all other American luxury makes
combined. From 1936 until 1942, basic models
cost only about $1,500 to $1,800—about the
average annual wage of those Americans
fortunate enough to be employed full time.
Dignified Series 75s and other long-wheelbase
examples with Fleetwood bodies were far
dearer.

Along with other GM lines, Cadillac V8s
adopted front ventilating panes in 1933, along
with more rounded bodies. Independent coil-
spring front suspension followed in 1934, while
the external boot disappeared. The 60 Special
saloon of 1938-40, still an eye-catcher,
anticipated subsequent styling trends. Hydramatic drive became optional in 1941, when all
Cadillacs underwent restyling.

For 1948, Harley Earl and his associates
introduced new body lines that featured modest
tailfins inspired by the P-38 fighter plane. The
styling continued with the 1949 fastback coupé,
but the 5.4-litre engine was all new. It marked
the Cadillac V8's adoption of overhead valves;
compared with the old 5.7-litre L-head, it

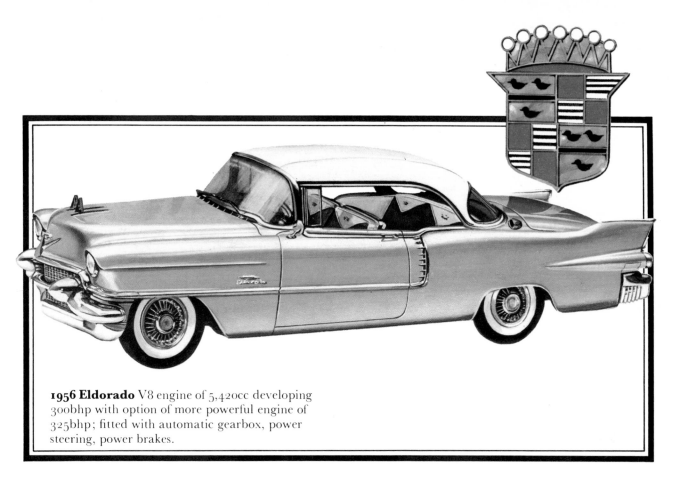

1956 Eldorado V8 engine of 5,420cc developing 300bhp with option of more powerful engine of 325bhp; fitted with automatic gearbox, power steering, power brakes.

weighed 771 against 992lbs, had a larger bore and shorter stroke, delivered 160 against 150bhp and was more efficient, giving gratifying fuel economy as well as top performance. In the 1950 Le Mans race, Briggs Cunningham's Cadillacs finished tenth and eleventh, and a Cadillac-powered Allard J2 was third. The mechanical dimensions remained unchanged through 1955, though the horsepower race with Chrysler extracted

1959 Fleetwood 60 Special V8 engine; 6,393cc; 325bhp @ 4800rpm; all automatic or power equipment standardised; over 110mph.

250bhp by that year through modifications in compression ratio and carburation.

For 1956-7, the engine was increased to 6 litres, with power in the 300bhp range. At the top of the line and by far the most expensive American car of its day was the Eldorado, listed at $13,704 for the 1957 Brougham style. Besides prestige, the buyer got fuel injection, air suspension, special fabric or hide upholstery, and a rather cramped rear compartment. The 6.4-litre 325bhp 1959 Fleetwood Special marks the ultimate in Cadillac's contribution to 'Eisenhower Baroque'.

Chevrolet

W. C. Durant's Chevrolet Motor Company's first offering was the 4.9-litre Classic T-head six of 1912, designed by Louis Chevrolet and Etienne Planche and built in Detroit. Although it was fairly expensive at $2,150, 2,999 were produced in that year. Chevrolet's almost doubled in output in 1913, when they introduced the L-head four and six (phased out in 1915), which were made in Flint, Michigan.

The Classic was succeeded in 1914 by two smaller Chevrolets, the 2.8-litre Model H four at $750 and the 4.4-litre Model L six at $1,425. The Hs of 1914-16, the Royal Mail roadster and the Baby Grand touring car, were deservedly popular, bringing total Chevrolet production to more than 13,000 in 1915.

Chevrolet was so successful that Durant used it to regain control of General Motors, of which Chevrolet formally became a unit in 1918. The 1916 model year marked the introduction of the 490 series, so called from its initial dollar price (soon increased) to compete with the Model T Ford. The 490

used an overhead-valve four much like the Baby Grand's, but was smaller and lighter. Its advent raised Chevrolet production to nearly 63,000, an impressive showing but hardly a threat to Ford's 735,000. Actually, the 490 did not equal Ford in quality, but it offered a sliding-gear transmission and conventional appearance. In its final year, 1922, it ranked second to Ford with 209,000 against 1,174,000 units.

All along, more expensive cars bore the Chevrolet emblem: a 4.7-litre V8 of 1917-18 and a 4-litre four of 1918-22 both far rarer than the 490. Acting on the advice of Alfred P. Sloan, general manager of Chevrolet after Durant's second and final ousting from GM late in 1920, the corporation instituted a single-model policy for the marque at the low end of the model range. The Superior fours of 1923-28 retained the 490 engine but underwent continuous improvements to chassis and running gear. The 1925 models with smarter lines, Duco finish in colour, and an aluminium radiator shell, were a departure from previous stodgy design. In that year,

1915 Royal Mail four-cylinder; 2,818cc; 24bhp; three-speed gearbox; magneto ignition.

1920 490 four-cylinder; 2,818cc; three-speed gearbox; fitted with electric self-starter.

the two-millionth Chevrolet appeared, and saloon cars began to outsell the touring car and roadster. The 1927 models with disc wheels and a body belt moulding, outsold Ford for the first time.

For 1929, using two-upmanship against Ford's Model A four, Chevrolet presented a six, the neat styling of which bore a family resemblance to the Cadillac. The new ohv engine, soon nicknamed 'Cast Iron Wonder' from its piston material, was so good that it remained basically unchanged until 1953. Over the years, it gained a fourth main bearing, doubled its horsepower from 46 to 92, and

1925 Superior engine as for the 490.

1955 Nomad six-cylinder; 3,860cc or V8 4,343cc engine; 12-volt electrics; overdrive with synchromesh gearbox available optionally.

went from 3.2 to 3.5 litres.

Chevrolet's first V8, introduced in 1955 under the aegis of Chief Engineer, Edward N.

1960 Corvair four-door six cylinder; 2.3 litre; air-cooled rear engine.

1968 Corvair Monza open version of the small Chevrolet air-cooled six-cylinder rear engine of 95, 110 or 140bhp.

Cole, was revolutionary. This 4.3-litre engine was lighter than the companion 3.9-litre six and gave 162bhp against the 123 (or 135 with Powerglide transmission) of the six. The bore was bigger than the stroke, and the pistons were of aluminium. With optional tuning equipment, the V8 could accelerate to 60mph in less than 10 seconds. The body styling was an added attraction, especially in the Nomad station wagon which drew an immediate response from buyers who wanted utility with performance. The 1956 and 1957 Nomads were also sought after.

The El Camino pickup stands out among the 1959 Chevrolets. All of them were overstyled and bulky, 17ft 7in long, 6ft 8in wide, and 5ft 6in across the front seat. Such features were almost justifiable in this luxury-utility model. Engine options ranged from the 135bhp six to a 348bhp V8.

Starting as a four-door compact saloon in 1960, the rear-engined, air-cooled Corvair 2.3-litre six had moderate appeal in the family market. Later Monza versions, however, became increasingly popular among enthusiasts until Ralph Nader's book *Unsafe at Any Speed* (1965) documented the car's handling deficiencies.

Corvette

Designer Zora Arkus-Duntov's Chevrolet Corvette first appeared as a sporty 1954 convertible and soon developed into a true sports car. Then, as today, the body was of moulded glass fibre reinforced plastics. The engine was the 3.8 litre six, modified to produce 150bhp. Underneath were a box-section chassis, Hotchkiss drive, and dual exhausts. Top speed with Powerglide transmission (no options available) exceeded 100mph, with a zero to 60mph time of 11 seconds. More desirable in many respects is the 1956 model with 4.3 litre V8, hardtop and three-speed manual gearbox.

For 1957-61 the engine had a 4,637cc V8 with optional fuel injection. Other options starting in 1958 included a four-speed all synchromesh manual transmission and competition modifications, giving a 0-60 time of 6 seconds. A year after adoption of a 5,358cc engine in 1962, the Corvette chassis, running gear, and body underwent radical changes resulting in the Sting Ray of 1963-67, more potent than ever but gimmicky on the outside, with false vents, multiple insignia, retractable headlamps, and for 1963 a split rear window. By this time the Corvette could hold its own against the Jaguar E type, with a 130mph top speed.

1954 Corvette six-cylinder; 3,860cc; 150bhp; automatic transmission; 100mph; reinforced plastic body.

1965 Stingray V8; 5,363cc; 250/300/340 or 360bhp versions; the 360bhp will attain 140mph.

Chrysler

1924 six-cylinder; 3,293cc; 68bhp @ 3200rpm; speeds of about 70mph made this a popular car with both gangsters and the police.

Following a notable career in car production for other firms, Walter P. Chrysler organized his own company in 1922, taking over Maxwell and Chalmers in Detroit. There, with the talented engineering team of Fred M. Zeder, Owen R. Skelton, and Carl Breer, he designed a car that made most other American makes obsolete overnight. Mechanically, this L-head, 3.2-litre six-cylinder Chrysler 70 featured light alloy pistons, four-wheel hydraulic brakes, a comparatively high compression ratio of 4.7 to 1, using a cylinder head based on the principles of Harry Ricardo, and a counterbalanced seven-bearing crankshaft.

Introduced in January 1924 at $1,695, it sold 32,000 units during its first year. A companion four-cylinder superseded the Maxwell in mid-1925 (Chalmers had been dropped in 1923), and in 1926-8, Chrysler ranked seventh among American makes.

A luxury six, the 4.7-litre Imperial E80 of 1926-7, featured fluting on the bonnet and cost from $2,595 to $3,595, selling with the slogan 'As Fine as Money Can Build'. It was succeeded by the longer L80 of 1928, developing 112bhp with the high compression for the day of 6 to 1. The regular line, starting at $2,795, was supplemented by superb coachbuilt creations by Le Baron, Locke, and Dietrich.

For 1931-3, 6.3-litre straight-eight Chrysler Imperials successfully copied the appearance of the Cord L-29 but not its front-wheel drive. Among early Chrysler successes in competition was a 1927 Imperial's transcontinental run of 79 hours 55 minutes, followed in 1928 with third and fourth places at Le Mans (after Bentley and Stutz) with the 4-litre six-cylinder 72s, successors of the 70. In 1931, an Imperial set six stock-car records at Daytona Beach, Florida.

During 1928, Chrysler acquired Dodge and launched the low-priced Plymouth and De

1929 Imperial six-cylinder; 4,074cc; top of the range and usually sold with large seven-seater coachwork.

1934 Airflow available as six-cylinder, 3,957cc or eight-cylinder, 4,893cc; one of the earliest mass-produced streamline designs.

Soto. Styling for all four lines consistently bore a strong family resemblance. In its combined production, from 1933 to 1950, the Chrysler Corporation held second place among American car makers, behind GM and ahead of Ford-Lincoln-Mercury.

Contributing little to the production race were the Chrysler, Imperial, and Custom Imperial Airflow series of 1934 to 1937, of which fewer than 30,000 were sold during these four years. The first Chrysler succeeded because it was years ahead of its time; the Airflow design failed because it was premature. The car itself was tough and fast; a standard coupé set 72 records in Utah; the concept and mechanical execution —largely Carl Breer's—were brilliant; seating amidships and the engine located well forward

1950 Town and Country straight-8; 5,394cc; 135bhp @ 3200rpm; almost unique American styling used for short period in the 1950s.

1958 300D V8; 6,423cc; 380bhp @ 5200rpm; available with injection giving 390bhp; limited production model.

resulted in a lowered centre of gravity for the unitary frame-cum-body.

But it was the body that killed the Airflow. Although its contours, derived from wind-tunnel tests, followed streamlining dictated by nature, it lacked appeal for the public. Such compromises as a dummy 'V' radiator shell to replace the waterfall grille were unavailing, and Walter Chrysler's pride and joy expired.

The Chrysler marque exceeded sales of 100,000 cars only once during the 1930s and fell to 25,000 in 1932. The 1940-1 models were more popular, and production rose to 163,000 in 1952, the highest figure until 1965. Such acceptance was ascribed more to engineering than to sensible but humdrum

styling. An exception was the rare Town and Country sedan-wagon of 1942 and its successors of 1946 to 1950, also trimmed in wood but essentially saloons and convertibles.

The advanced Fire-Power overhead-valve V8 engine, featuring hemispherical combustion chambers, double rocker arms, and deeply buried spark plugs, was introduced in the 1951 New Yorker and Imperial models and retained until 1958, by which time it had gone from 180 to 345bhp. It also powered the 300 series introduced in 1955, tuned to even higher output. The 300 series continued with other engines and less flamboyance until the 300L of 1965. Fire-Power engines were also used by Allard, Cunningham, the French Facel Vega, and the Italian Dual-Ghia.

Cisitalia

Under Piero Dusio, this small Turin firm won fame shortly after World War II in racing and in body design. Its first cars were single-seaters powered by the Fiat 1100 (1,089cc) engine modified to yield 50 or 60bhp. Like subsequent Cisitalias, they had a tubular space frame and suspension of advanced design. For a brief period, these cars formed a special competition class, and one driven by Tazio Nuvolari finished second overall in the 1947 Mille Miglia while Piero Taruffi won the 1947 Italian Championship with a Cisitalia. In the late 1940s, Carlo Abarth, Ferdinand Porsche, Robert Eberan von Eberhorst, and others designed for Cisitalia a complex front-wheel-drive racing machine, the supercharged flat twelve-cylinder engine which was said to achieve 300bhp from 1½ litres. But Dusio ran out of money and the car never had a chance to prove itself.

Of more lasting significance, two-seater Cisitalia road cars pioneered the subtly styled and functional 'Farina line', soon emulated by larger firms. Pinin Farina's bodies had straight or nearly straight sides and high integrated quarter panels that superseded wings; a nearly flat bonnet lay in a valley between the two front panels. The 202 GT, designed in 1946 and put into

production in 1948, has been exhibited since that year at the Museum of Modern Art in New York, the only car so honoured. Similar convertibles and coupés, some by Frua, appeared during the late 1940s. Their modified Fiat 1100 engines gave a top speed of 90 to 100mph. After a hiatus of more than a year for refinancing—and an abortive attempt to shift production to Argentina—in 1952 the 1100s were joined by a Farina-bodied three-seater coupé and a two-seater convertible powered by a 2.8-litre aluminium-alloy B.P.M. marine engine giving about 145mph. Few of these expensive models (about $8,500 in the United States) were sold. Production of all types ceased in 1958. The last Cisitalias, of 1961-5, were modified Fiat 600s that could not compete against Abarth and other specialist firms.

Coupé four-cylinder; 2,772cc; 160bhp @ 5300rpm; De Dion rear suspension; developed originally from Fiat parts.

Citroën

The chevron emblem of the Citroën is derived from the double helical gears that André Citroën manufactured before presenting his first car, the Type A, a 1.3-litre four, in 1919. Constantly expanding his efficient operations to reach an output of 100,000 ten years later, Citroën was dubbed the Henry Ford of France. Unlike the American, he offered a comprehensive range during the 1920s, incorporating many innovations, such as all-steel bodies and power brakes. The little two-seater, the 856cc 5 CV of 1922, was extremely popular. Because of its yellow body, it was dubbed *Citron pressé*— 'lemonade'—which could also be interpreted 'Citroën in a hurry'. A fleet of Citroëns equipped with Kégresse half-tracks at the rear made the first motorized crossing of the Sahara in 1922-3; equally impressive were later expeditions from Algeria to Madagascar and from Beirut to Peking.

In 1932, Citroën launched a new range with 'Floating Power' engines; then, to ensure the future of his company, by now one of France's 'Big Three', André Citroën not only demolished and rebuilt his Quai de Javel factory within three months during 1933, but also brought out the following year the revolutionary *traction avant* 7 CV, with its low-slung monocoque body, all round torsion-bar independent suspension, and a wet-liner ohv power unit. That year of technical triumph ended in

1922 5CV four-cylinder; 856cc; three-speed gearbox; France's family car of the 1920s, the equivalent of Britain's Austin Seven.

financial failure: the firm was acquired by the Michelin tyre company and André Citroën died in July 1935. Under the new regime, more than 700,000 of the 7 CV and more powerful variants such as the *Onze Legère*, *Onze Normal*, and the 15 CV were sold before the type was discontinued in 1957.

In sharp contrast to the agile, fast-cornering *traction avant* was their little brother, the 2 CV (Deux Chevaux), designed and built in prototype form but not put into production until 1948. Truly the French People's Car, this ugly duckling was *très pratique* for anyone indifferent to status and content with a cruising speed in the forties. Though the 2 CV was utilitarian in appearance and equipment, it had front-wheel drive and the engine was an air-cooled ohv two-cylinder midget of 375cc

1938 (Light 15) four-cylinder; 1,911cc; front-wheel-drive; the larger-engined version of two similar models; more than 65mph.

1956 DS19 four-cylinder; 1,911cc; 75bhp @ 4500rpm; widely acclaimed as the vehicle of the future with very advanced detail specification; more than 85mph.

(later enlarged) that could wring over 50 miles from a gallon of fuel. Thanks to the push-back cloth roof in the 'convertible' and the removable rear seat in that model and the station wagon, sizeable loads could be carried. Comfort was ensured by very soft suspension and seats with rubber bands stretched on the tubular seat frame.

The DS19 Citroën, in production without fundamental change from 1955 to 1975, was as far ahead of its time when introduced as the old *traction avant* had been. A unique hydro-pneumatic system flattened rough roads and enabled the ground clearance to be varied from $6\frac{1}{2}$ to $11\frac{1}{2}$ inches. It also controlled the DS's brakes and transmission; these components, however, lacked power assistance on the less expensive ID models that broadened the range from 1956. Both types shared traditional Citroën front-wheel drive and an aerodynamic four-door body with plastic roof. Comfort and handling were superb, but the 1934 long-stroke engine design, retained in most models until 1967, restricted both performance and refinement to a standard not quite in keeping with a great nation's top car after the demise of such famous luxury marques as Delage and Delahaye.

1957 2CV two-cylinder, air-cooled engine of 425cc developing 12bhp; front-wheel-drive 'people's' car.

Cord

1930 L29 eight-cylinder; 4,934cc; 125bhp; front-wheel-drive; one of the first commercial applications of fwd.

After taking over Auburn and Duesenberg in 1929 the expansive Erret Lobban Cord launched a luxury car honoured with his name and priced between them at about $3,000 when fitted with standard coachwork. As might be expected, the L-29 Cord was handsome and was notable for its front-wheel drive, used for the first time on an American car with a respectable production run. (Granted, the short-lived Ruxton by Moon appeared earlier in the same year, and Harry Miller's front-wheel-drive racing cars had been famous since 1924.) Mated with a 4.9-litre 125bhp straight eight side-valve engine by Lycoming, another Cord subsidiary, were the transmission, differential and front axle. Thanks to the front-wheel drive, the chassis was set so low as to permit the roof line to stand only 5ft high compared with the more usual 6ft or so that was customary at the time, while still providing adequate

Supercharged Beverly Sedan

Standard Beverly Sedan

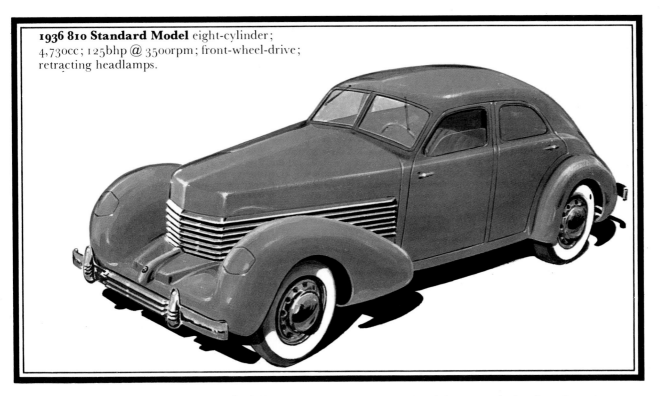

1936 810 Standard Model eight-cylinder;
4,730cc; 125bhp @ 3500rpm; front-wheel-drive;
retracting headlamps.

headroom. The striking but dignified lines were enhanced with custom bodies by Hayes, Murphy and other coachbuilders, and they received the compliment of imitation in the conventional drive Chrysler Imperial of 1931. About 4,400 of the L-29 appeared before production had to be discontinued after only two years. The mechanically complex drive, badly-chosen gear ratios, low-geared steering, traction troubles on steep hills, and comparative costliness in the great Depression that soon followed its debut, all contributed to the early demise of the first Cord.

Two years later, Auburn and Duesenberg sales were declining so, to prevent his automotive interests from foundering, Cord decided to produce a sporting luxury car. Its gifted designer was to be Gordon Buehrig, a veteran of such firms as Stutz and General Motors, whose first project with Cord was a smaller Duesenberg on the Auburn chassis.

In mid-1934 that project was abandoned in favour of an all-new Cord with no relation to either Auburn or Duesenberg; this would feature front-wheel drive coupled to a reversed V8 Lycoming engine of 4,730cc and 125bhp. Development work on the project continued for about six months. The new car was so

close to its final form early in October that Buehrig patented the body design. Among the advanced features that enabled him to take this unusual step were the rear-hinged, grille-less 'coffin-nose' bonnet with Venetian blind louvres continued on three sides, headlamps—adopted from aircraft landing lights—that could be wound down into the wings, and minor touches like flush tail lights and a flush door over the fuel filler cap; the convertibles had wind-up windows all round and a top that could disappear into a metal-covered well. Unlike many highly styled cars, Buehrig's Cord provided ample space for its passengers. Except for its restricted glass area, the body remains a masterpiece of inspired originality.

Despite obvious reasons for optimism, in January 1935 Mr Cord blew cold on his project and suspended it; no doubt he was deterred by cost considerations, and he may have hoped that the attractive 1935 Auburn, restyled by Buehrig, would salvage the company. By the time he changed his mind again and ordered a resumption of work in July, the firm's financial resources were shrinking and the New York Automobile Show, a compulsory showcase for 1936 models, was only five months away. Worse still, the car could not be exhibited there unless a hundred examples had been produced by opening day. That meant fabricating a hundred bodies largely by hand, since the Auburn plant lacked facilities for stamping from large dies and there was no time to sub-contract the work. The roof of the saloon, for example, was assembled from seven panels. Also, the front-wheel-drive system posed problems that should have been solved methodically over a period of time, rather than in a near frenzy. The upshot was that the striking new Cord was exhibited at the show without its four-speed transmission, in what might have been a fiasco comparable with that of the Tucker a decade later. Orders flooded in on the basis of the car's appearance and novelty. Potential buyers couldn't know that the protrusion in front concealed a void, and then the orders dried up as Christmas passed without promised deliveries of functioning vehicles.

Deliveries finally began in March, after public confidence had been shaken. The situation was not helped by a tendency of some early examples to overheat and to jump out of gear. These teething troubles were soon surmounted but they were not forgotten and the complex front drive was often too noisy and it always bore down too hard on the outer universal joints. Then there was the competition from the luxury car field, at a time when some models of the well-seasoned Cadillac sold for less than the 1936 Cord Series 810's modest basic price of $1,995. Not surprisingly, production ceased in 1937, after a two-year total run of 2,320.

The 1936-7 Cords were notable for performance as well as aesthetics. In standard 125bhp form they had a top speed just short of 90mph, although the slow-responding preselector transmission made for sluggish acceleration. With the supercharger available

1936 810 Winchester Sedan

1937 812 Phaeton Sedan as in the 810, but supercharged to give 175 bhp and over 100mph.

on the Series 812 of 1937, gross horsepower was 195 and top speed surpassed 100mph. This, coupled with roadholding and cornering qualities unequalled in America, was enough to justify a Cord advertisement's boast: 'Any driver that passes the Supercharged Cord *knows* he does so only with the Cord driver's permission.'

All 1936-7 body types are highly prized, whether they be four-door saloons, two-door and four-door convertibles, or the long-wheelbase 1937 *berline* with chauffeur division, oddly out of character in a car meant more than most others to be owner-driven.

The financial failure of this brave venture compelled E. L. Cord to abandon the manufacture of cars. Still a millionaire, he moved to Nevada, where he died in 1974. Gordon Buehrig went on to Ford and contributed to another great quality car, the Lincoln Continental Mark II of 1956-7.

1936 Runabout and Supercharged Convertible

Daimler

Britain's oldest surviving marque, Daimler, originated from a meeting between Gottlieb Daimler and a young British engineer, Frederick R. Simms, in the late 1880s. Simms acquired the British rights to the Daimler engine and, in 1893, founded the Daimler Motor Syndicate under the arches of Putney Bridge, where Daimler engines were fitted into river launches. The first Daimler-engined car arrived in England in 1895, and Simms sold his rights to the British Motor Syndicate, which launched the Daimler Motor Company in January 1896. The first Daimler cars to be built in Coventry appeared in 1897, and were closely based on the contemporary Panhard and Levassor; the marque gained prestige in 1900 when the Prince of Wales purchased a 6hp phaeton. Some four years later the now traditional Daimler fluted radiator shell was introduced on the chain-drive L-head fours, most of them large and powerful, that made up the firm's range until 1909.

In that year, Daimler was the first to adopt the 'Silent Knight' double sleeve-valve engine. The sleeve-valve soon became standard, and its silent, sedate running gave the Daimler a great following in society. Continued Royal patronage helped too, though George V's lofty cars of 1910, 1925 and 1931 showed scant progress in styling. By the late 1930s, however, non-royal saloons with bodies by Hooper or Barker had a fairly modern appearance.

In the late 1920s, some of the 7.1-litre Double-Six V12s designed by Chief Engineer Lawrence Pomeroy, Sr, of Vauxhall fame were strikingly handsome. Pomeroy also designed the first fluid-flywheel transmission soon used in conjunction with the Wilson Preselector gearbox to give the easiest gearchanging until the advent of automatics, and the 4.6-litre straight eight of 1935-40; as with other Daimlers introduced since 1933, it had overhead rather than sleeve valves.

From 1946 to 1959, Daimler production centred on six-cylinder cars of comparatively modest size. The sole exception was the heavy 5.5-litre DE36 straight eight of 1946-53. It is best remembered for the extravagant bodies built for Managing Director Sir Bernard Docker and his wife. Among the most pleasing sixes of the 1950s are the 75bhp 4-litre Conquest saloon (originally priced at £1,066 plus tax) of 1953-6 and the livelier Conquest Century (100bhp and 100mph) in open and convertible form.

The last true Daimlers before Jaguar took over in 1960 were two widely differing cars, the dignified but fast (119mph) Majestic Major 4.6-litre V8 saloon, and the SP250. This glass-fibre bodied two-seater 2½-litre V8 sports car could reach 123mph, but the ugly body was poorly made and the car soon succumbed. Its engine also powered the Jaguar-bodied Daimler 250 saloon of 1962 to 1968.

1953 D-N six-cylinder; 2,433cc; 75bhp @ 4200rpm; fluid flywheel and pre-selector gearbox; automatic chassis lubrication.

Delage

Though Louis Delage built some of the finest French cars of all time, his company started modestly enough in 1905, building single-cylinder runabouts with De Dion power units. Sporting successes brought the marque to public notice, and by 1910 the company had prospered enough to move into a new factory at Courbevoie, near Paris. In 1909 the first four-cylinder Delages had appeared, initially with Ballot or De Dion engines, but soon with power units of Delage's own construction; a 30hp six appeared in 1911.

Delage's racing cars were as unorthodox as the touring models were conventional: among their notable victories were the 1911 Coupé de l'Auto, the 1913 Grand Prix de France at Le Mans (not to be confused with that year's French Grand Prix, won by Peugeot) and the 1914 Indianapolis 500, in which Delages were first and second.

After four years of wartime armaments production, Delage introduced a 4½-litre six, the CO, and a 3-litre four, the DO in 1919. Among notable successors were the four-cylinder, 2.1-litre DI of 1923-8 with overhead valves and the impressive 6-litre GL of 1923-7, with overhead camshaft and power brakes. Meanwhile competition-model sixes, eights, and twelves, developed regardless of cost and complexity, enhanced the Delage name by setting a land speed record of 143.24mph in 1924 and winning the French and Spanish Grands Prix in 1925.

Among road cars of the late 1920s, the 3.2-litre DM series, a six-cylinder based on the DI four, was especially fast and competent in sporting DMS versions. Delage ended its most glorious decade with the straight-eight 4,050cc ohv D8 of 1929.

It was continued in various desirable forms until World War II, by which time the engine had grown to 4,743cc. Many D8s could top 100mph even when pulling heavy coachbuilt bodies. Beginning in 1932, they had smaller companions of equal distinction in various D6-series sixes; competition examples of these cars finished second at Le Mans in 1939 and 1949.

From 1935 Delages were built by Delahaye but retained their identity. The only new postwar Delage was the 3-litre Olympic D6. Owing to French taxation policy it found few buyers, and no Delages were made after 1954.

1938 D8 Cabriolet straight-8; 4,300cc giving 100bhp; four-speed Cotal electric gearbox; maximum speed around 100mph.

Dodge

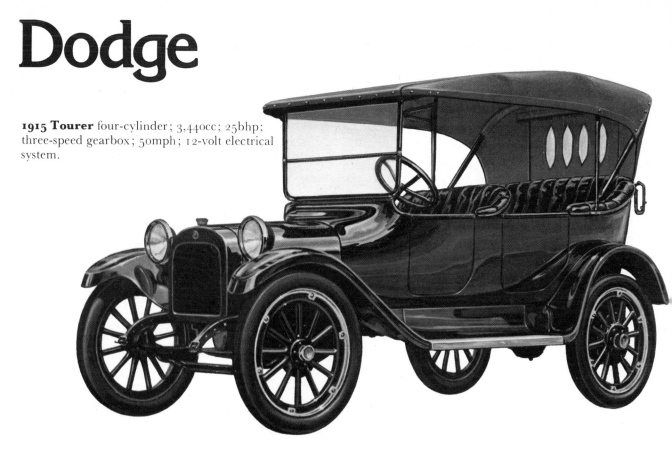

1915 Tourer four-cylinder; 3,440cc; 25bhp; three-speed gearbox; 50mph; 12-volt electrical system.

In their Detroit machine shop, John F. and Horace E. Dodge made transmissions for the Curved Dash Oldsmobile, starting in 1900. In 1903 they contracted to supply engines, transmissions, and chassis for Henry Ford's first production car, the Model A, and continued to furnish engines to Ford for eleven years. They held 100 shares of stock, costing $10,000 and representing a one-tenth interest in the Ford company, and used the dividends from Model T sales to launch the Dodge Brothers' car in 1914. Five years later, they won a lawsuit for $19 million in back dividends from Ford, who then bought back their shares for another $25 million.

The 1915 model Dodge, a 25hp L-head four introduced at $785, remained basically the same for more than a decade. It was a sensible vehicle of a quality not apparent from its appearance. The word 'dependability' entered the language via Dodge advertising. Among its pioneering features were an all-steel body and a 12-volt electrical system with a dynastart which automatically restarted the engine if it stalled with the ignition on. The car was an immediate success, ranking third among American makes in 1915 with 45,000 sales; five years later it was third with 141,000. In 1916, US Army forces led by General John

J. Pershing used it in pursuit of the Mexican rebel leader Pancho Villa.

John and Horace Dodge both died in 1920, but their enterprise continued to prosper as the product underwent detail refinements. In 1928, two higher-priced lines were added; the low-slung Victory Six saloon with welded, monopiece bodywork and the Senior Six saloon and rumble-seat roadster.

Meanwhile, in 1925, the Dodge heirs had sold the firm to a New York banking syndicate for $146 million, but the new owners had no experience of the motor industry, and Dodge was soon on the edge of financial disaster. Three years later, Walter P. Chrysler acquired Dodge and its prized dealer network for $70 million in stock plus $56 million payments on Dodge bonds, a move that enabled his corporation to become one of the Big Three among US car makers. As early as 1929 the four-cylinder cars and the six-pointed-star emblem were dropped and most Dodges had a Chrysler appearance. The 1930 Senior Six, however, was still in the pre-Chrysler tradition.

From 1930 to 1933, straight eights as well as sixes were offered.

A silent synchromesh transmission was adopted in 1933, followed the next year by independent front suspension. During the 1930s,

1933 Sedan six-cylinder; 2,795 or 3,310cc, the latter giving 75bhp @ 3600rpm; free-wheel and automatic clutch optional; hydraulic brakes.

Dodge, now fourth biggest American manufacturer, lost most of its individuality and took on a close resemblance to the other marques in the Chrysler Corporation—Chrysler, De Soto and Plymouth. Unlike Chrysler and De Soto, however, Dodge never adopted the controversial Airflow styling, though their 1935 models were similar to the Chrysler Airstream line. Except for the lack of a 1934-7 Airflow series as made by its sister marques Chrysler and De Soto, Dodge continued its resemblance to those marques and to Plymouth. Underneath, starting in 1953, 3.8-litre overhead-valve V8 Red Ram engines, then developing 140 against 103bhp, supplemented

the flathead six. High, stodgy bodies were succeeded by Virgil Exner's Forward Look of 1955-6, available in three colours.

Exner's Flight Sweep bodies of the late 1950s had futuristic lines and massive tail fins. By 1959, three eights ranging from 255 to 305bhp were offered. The old six was succeeded in 1960 by a slanted ohv engine of 3.7-litres, still used in 1976 in some Dodge Darts, which became compacts in 1963. The larger Dart exemplifies the sculptured styling of 1960-2. Dodges in various sizes and engine displacements continue as near twins of Plymouth.

1955 Sedan six-cylinder; 3,773cc; 110bhp @ 3600rpm; or V8 version of 3,955cc giving 150bhp @ 4000rpm.

Duesenberg

The self-taught brothers Fred and August Duesenberg, German-born and Iowa-bred, built the two-cylinder Mason car in Des Moines, Iowa, in 1906. Their Mason four-cylinder racing-car engines of 1910 were successful from the start, and in 1913 they founded the Duesenberg Motor Company in St Paul, Minnesota. There they built high-performance marine engines as well as racing cars that won many events in the hands of Eddie Rickenbacker, Ralph Mulford, and other star drivers. Upon America's entry into World War I in 1917, the Duesenbergs were awarded contracts to construct twelve- and sixteen-cylinder aviation engines (the latter an unsuccessful Bugatti design) along with marine and tractor power plants.

After the Armistice, they sold their wartime Elizabeth, New Jersey, factories to Willys-Overland, and the rights to their four-cylinder race-bred engine to the Rochester Motor Company, which in turn supplied it to such high-quality marques as Biddle, ReVere, and Roamer. At a new factory in Indianapolis, the Duesenbergs developed overhead-cam straight-eight engines that did well in the 1920 Indianapolis 500 and set an unofficial land speed record of 156.04mph later that year.

Before that, the Duesenbergs had built prototypes of their 4.2-litre Model A passenger car, which had pioneered the straight eight engine and hydraulic four-wheel brakes in the United States. Less visible advances were the overhead camshaft, hemispherical combustion chambers, optional aluminium pistons, tubular axles, and a molybdenum-steel frame. Despite Duesenberg's racing triumphs, climaxed by victories in the French Grand Prix at Le Mans in 1921 and at Indianapolis in 1924 and

1925, only 500 or so Model A's were sold before they were discontinued in 1926; about 50 survive.

E. L. Cord of Auburn bought the Duesenberg plant in 1926 and assigned Fred to create a supercar regardless of cost. With August's aid, he did just that in the renowned Model J Duesenberg of 1929. At 265bhp, its 6.9-litre Lycoming straight-eight engine with double overhead camshafts and four valves per cylinder

1929 Model J eight-cylinder; 7,495cc; four valves per cylinder; 110mph giving 12mpg.

far outclassed other American luxury cars and vied with Europe's finest in performance—having a 116mph maximum speed and zero to 100mph in 20 seconds. Though massive, with a total weight of about 3 tons and wheelbases of 11ft 10½in and 12ft 9½in, it was eminently drivable if not easy to park. Power brakes were adopted for 1930. The $8,500 chassis plus a coachbuilt body brought the total price to a minimum of $13,500—more than three times the price of a complete standard Cadillac.

For 1932, near the nadir of the Depression, Fred and August outdid themselves with the even costlier SJ, a J with the engine beefed up to accommodate a centrifugal supercharger. This 320bhp marvel with its exposed exhaust pipes needed only 17 seconds to accelerate to 100mph on its way to 130mph. Soon the car's market among the very wealthy became saturated; the last engines were delivered in 1935 and the last bodies fitted in 1937, when Cord's empire was liquidated. Fewer than 500 of the prized Js and SJs were built, of which more than half are still cherished in good homes.

DuPont

It was a good thing that Éleuthère Paul DuPont was a member of the fabulously rich Delaware munitions family, considering the cost of building the mere 537 cars made by his DuPont Motors Corporation during its life-span, 1919-32, at factories in Moore, Pennsylvania, and (from mid-1930) Springfield, Massachusetts. Of these, nearly 200 were Model Gs of 1928-32, a handful of which survive, expensively restored, in speedster, phaeton, and saloon body styles in addition to the most renowned of all, the 1930 town car now in the Harrah collection.

DuPont bodies were custom built, most of them by the firm's own G. Briggs Weaver. Actual construction of the town car's sybaritic coachwork was carried out by Merrimac of Merrimac, Massachusetts. The engine, a modified Continental L-head straight eight of 5.3 litres and 114bhp could haul the 11ft 9in wheelbase three-ton vehicle up to the mid-seventies in top gear.

Performance was better with the far lighter speedsters, built on a 10ft 5in wheelbase and profiting from engine modifications that produced 140bhp and nearly 100mph. Besides two-seater types, there were four-seater Le Mans Replicas, so called from DuPont's unsuccessful entry in the 24 Hours of 1929. One DuPont speedster was a present from Mary Pickford to her husband, Douglas Fairbanks, Sr, and another was damaged during the twenty-second lap of the 1930 Indianapolis 500. DuPont's claim to fame lies in its early use of a grille in front of the radiator and by 1931, American cars that lacked a grille looked undressed. Today, DuPonts are prized for their rarity and workmanship.

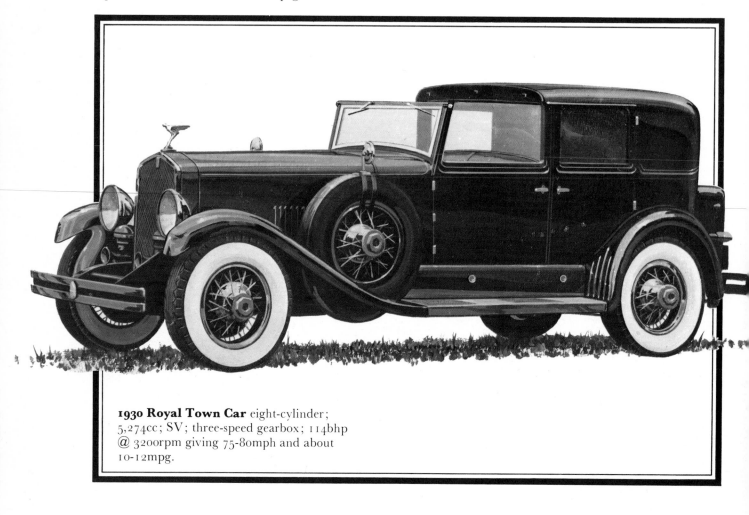

1930 Royal Town Car eight-cylinder; 5,274cc; SV; three-speed gearbox; 114bhp @ 3200rpm giving 75-80mph and about 10-12mpg.

Essex

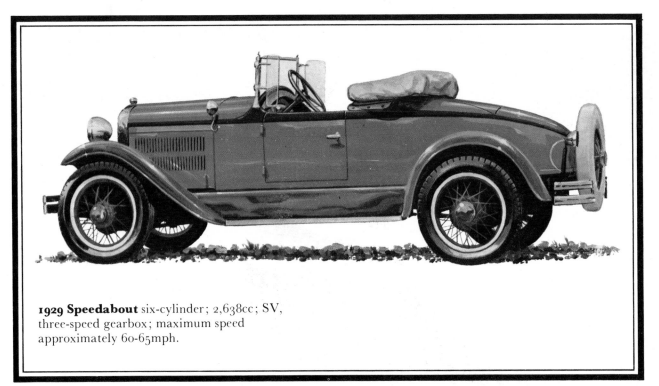

1929 Speedabout six-cylinder; 2,638cc; SV, three-speed gearbox; maximum speed approximately 60-65mph.

At the end of World War I, Hudson introduced a smaller line, the Essex four. All Essexes from 1919 until 1923 had a sturdy F-head (inlet valves over exhaust valves) engine of 55bhp and 2.9 litres capable of 60mph, enough to set a transcontinental speed record in 1920. The instantly recognizable angular bodies boasted radiator shutters for winter motoring. The two-door saloon of 1922, called a coach, pioneered the popularizing of enclosed cars in the low-priced field at only $200 more than the $1,095 open models.

Essex reached its zenith of popularity in the mid-1920s, when a high-revving, long-stroke L-head six succeeded the four. To minimize construction costs, the 1924-6 bodies were devoid of curved panels. Displacement increased from the 2.1 litres of the 1924 model to 2.35 litres for 1925-7, when the car matched the 55bhp of the original fours but was somewhat faster, thanks to the engine design and lighter weight. These little square cut sixes owed their popularity to a low price (never more than $900) and the humming engine, reminiscent of a sewing machine when it ran well. Unfortunately, it tended to throw connecting rods, and detractors referred to the Essex as the '10,000 mile car'.

From 1928 onwards, a gradual approach to grace, improved reliability, still lower list prices, and increased engine size—ultimately to 3.2 litres—failed to stop American sales from lagging, though the British assembly plant on the Great West Road near London continued to serve an appreciative public. During 1932 the Essex was superseded in the Hudson range by the Terraplane six and eight.

1929 Coach six-cylinder; 2,638cc; SV, three-speed gearbox; maximum speed approximately 60-65mph.

Ferrari

Ferrari has symbolized the ultimate in racing and Grand Touring cars since the late 1940s. Enzo Ferrari, the firm's founder and guiding spirit, first won fame as a tester and racing driver for Alfa Romeo in the 1920s and then as manager of Alfa's Scuderia Ferrari racing stable in the 1930s. From 1933, the team's cars sported the prancing horse still used by Ferrari, taken from the mascot of the World War I Italian ace Francesco Baracca. Ferrari built his first car, Type 815, for the 1940 Brescia Sports Car Grand Prix. During the Second World War, Ferrari was reduced to making grinding machines, first at Modena and then at the village of Maranello, 12 miles south, where his newly founded factory was relocated in accordance with the Fascist government's decentralization programme. The move proved unavailing as the plant was bombed in 1944 and 1945.

The indomitable Enzo soon rebuilt it and took up the production of racing cars, his lifelong passion. The first example of the 125 series was completed late in 1946. This 1½-litre V12 was largely the creation of Giaocchino Colombo, who had designed the memorable straight eight Alfa Romeo 158 of 1938. The 125 engine defined the configuration for most later Ferraris. Its banks of six cylinders, each with a single overhead camshaft, formed an angle of 60 degrees. The block and crankcase were a single light alloy casting with cylinder liners of cast iron; the heads were also of alloy. The Tipo 125 appeared in three basic configurations: 'Sport', 'Competizione' and 'Gran Premio'. The first two were unsupercharged, and developed 118bhp, being equipped with a twin-choke Weber carburettor; they differed externally in the style of body fitted—all-enveloping

coachwork on the 'Sport', two-seater GP type body with cycle wings on the 'Competizione'. The supercharged 125 'Gran Premio' first appeared in 1948 with a single-stage blower, and developed 225bhp in this form. The following year a twin-stage supercharger raised power output to 300bhp. Ultimately, the 125 GP could develop 315bhp. For 1948, the V12 was developed to produce the new Tipo 166 2 litre, current until 1953. Among their victories were the Mille Miglia, Targa Florio and Tour of Sicily of 1948 and 1949, and the Le Mans and Monza races of 1949. In the form in which it won the Mille Miglia, the Tipo 166 had three Weber carburettors and an output of 140bhp, giving a 136mph top speed.

For Formula One, Ferrari's new designer, Lampredi, created a new unsupercharged V12. Originally of 3.3 litres, it grew to 4.5 litres in 1950. This engine, and Lampredi's 2-litre twin overhead camshaft fours of 1951 enabled Ferrari to eclipse Alfa Romeo and Maserati in nearly every Grand Prix event of 1951-3, with Alberto Ascari being the firm's star driver.

The fast touring models, being eminently usable on the road and not generally subjected to the punishment inflicted on outright racers, are the Ferraris most prized by collectors; these models include the 2.6-litre Inter, 195 Sport, and 212 Export models of 1948-53, all V12s. Bodied by Vignale, Ghia, and Touring in coupé and convertible styles, they were eagerly sought by a wealthy and discriminating clientele. The first of the smooth egg crate-grille Pininfarina bodies was a cabriolet (convertible) on the 212 Inter chassis of 1952. Other coachbuilders continued their work, but Pininfarina soon became predominant.

Ferrari himself has said: '. . . I am mainly interested in promoting new developments . . . Were my wishes in this respect to be indulged, there would be no production of standard

4.1 America V12; 4,102cc; 220bhp @ 6500rpm; three Weber carburettors; five-speed gearbox; 150mph.

models at all but only a succession of prototypes.' From the welter of type designations created by a firm whose total output seldom exceeded 500 cars a year, it is just possible to single out a few road-going models of the 1950s and 1960s that were produced in appreciable numbers over several years.

The 4.1-litre 342 America of 1951-2 was the first of the large displacement machines. Aimed at Americans who wanted superb performance and unquestioned snob appeal, it succeeded admirably. Lampredi's V12, originally yielding 230bhp at 6,000rpm was reduced to 200bhp at 5,000rpm, while the weight was increased from 2,000 to 2,640lb. In this form it still achieved 115mph. It was succeeded late in 1953-5, by the 4½-litre four-speed 375 America capable of 155mph; the special 4.9-litre 375 Plus won Le Mans and the Carrera Panamerica in 1954. For 1955-9 it was onward and upward with the 5-litre SuperAmerica, capable of 161mph.

The 400 SuperAmerica of 1960-3 equalled or excelled the 410's performance—up to 185mph—with 4 instead of 5 litres. The four-speed transmission was equipped with overdrive. These cars were great favourites among the jet set.

Ferrari introduced the 3-litre V12 250 Sport in 1952: it was a smaller-engined version of the original 3.3-litre Grand Prix engine. A 250 Sport won the 1952 Mille Miglia against stiff opposition from Mercedes-Benz. In 1953 came the first of the famous 250 GT Series, the 250 Export, followed a year later by the 250 Europa, which was succeeded in 1956 by the production 250 GT, with a greatly refined specification which included the substitution of independent coil springs for transverse springs in the front suspension. The maximum speed was 126 to 167mph, depending on the final drive ratio. Starting in 1960, overdrive was standardized on some body types. In 1960 the 250 GT pioneered the 2+2 coupé, with tiny seats in the rear. The classic Testa Rossa sports/racing car won the Buenos Aires 1,000 Km, Sebring 12 Hours, Targa Florio and the Le Mans 24 hours, as well as the World's Sports Car Championship in 1958, 1960 and 1961.

For 1964-6 came the 4-litre 330 GT and the 500 5-litre Superfast which replaced the 400 SuperAmerica. These were still front-engined V12s with solid rear axles. The 1964-7 3.3-litre 275 GT which replaced the 250 GT 2+2, retained the front mounted engine but introduced independent rear suspension in the touring line up. Rear-engined sports/racing cars with independent rear suspension, V6 engines as well as V12s, won the four Le Mans from 1962 to 1965. By 1968, all Ferraris had independent rear suspension and the rear engined Dino V6 of 1.6 and 2 litres (2.4 litres from 1969) doubled the firm's market potential.

1969 Dino 246 V6; 2,418cc; 195bhp @ 7600rpm; four oh camshafts; five-speed gearbox.

Fiat

During the first two decades of their existence, Fiat built everything from voiturettes to expensive road machines and formidable racers, always in limited numbers, before entering the mass production market with the 1½-litre Type 501 four of 1919-26; some 76,000 of this and the similar Type 502 of 1924 (a long-wheelbase version usually seen as a taxi) found buyers among families of moderate means. Their output was surpassed by the advanced 1-litre Type 509 of 1924-9, a four with overhead valves, semi-servo wheel brakes, and the then adequate top speed of 50mph; 92,000 were sold, thanks to Fiat's newly introduced hire-purchase organization and a brisk export demand.

Even more popular was the Type 508 Balilla of 1932-7, a side-valve, 1-litre short-stroke four with hydraulic brakes, capable of 75mph. The faster two-seater overhead valve sports variant of the middle 1930s is the most desirable style—only a thousand were produced against 112,000 of other 508s in many body types. Of the latter, the choicest are the spiders (roadsters), torpedoes (sport tourers), coupés by Castagna, and the 508S Mille Miglia coupé.

During the 1920s there was no lack of prestigious Fiats. These were led by the Type 520 6.8-litre V12 Superfiat of 1921-2 of which

no more than 30 were made, and its derivative, the 4.8-litre Type 519 six of 1922, and the 3,740cc Type 525 six; one of these was presented to the Pope in 1929 by Giovanni Angelli, head of Fiat. The racing programme was resumed from 1921 to 1927, with notable success, while in 1924 old 'Mephistopheles'—it was mostly raced in England and re-engined by Ernest Eldridge—was fitted with a 21.7-litre six-cylinder airship engine. In its original, 1908 incarnation, this racer had a four-cylinder engine of 18.2 litres—and broke the world land speed record at 146mph.

The 1930s were not a propitious time for luxury models. For the owner who wanted more car than Balilla, Fiat made the Ardita four of 1.7 and 1.9 litres on a family-sized 8ft 10in wheelbase and equipped it with hydraulic brakes. The 1933 Castagna-bodied Ardita coupés were outstanding in both styling and performance. Variants of the Balilla and Ardita were the first production types for Simca in France.

In 1936 came a landmark car for Fiat, engineer Dante Giacosa's short-stroke, ohv 1500 six-cylinder with backbone frame, independent front suspension and hydraulic brakes. It was so satisfactory that it underwent little change until 1949. Abandoning the boxy tradition, it featured a streamlined body with

1933 Ardita four-cylinder; 1,758 or 1,944cc giving 40 and 45bhp respectively @ 3600rpm; 60-65mph.

1935 Balilla four-cylinder; 995cc; 36bhp @ 4000rpm; three-speed gearbox; 73mph giving about 30mpg.

sharply slanting grille. It was followed later in 1936 by the tiny, yet almost as aerodynamic, L-head 500A four, nicknamed 'Topolino' (Mickey Mouse). The engine, mounted ahead of the radiator, developed 13bhp at a brisk 4,000rpm—enough to attain an evental 53mph through the four gears. It carried two adults on centrally positioned bucket seats, behind which was space for luggage or an uncomplaining child or two. The 500A put four wheels within reach of impecunious Italians. With a total length of 10ft 8in, it was the smallest and most popular mass-produced car in the West. It was succeeded by the 500C of 1948-57 with overhead valves, 16.5bhp, and 60mph. In between the 500s and the 1500s, the 1,089cc ohv Millecento of 1937-50 was capable of 70mph as a four-door saloon and 90mph as a sports coupé.

1936 Topolino four-cylinder; 570cc; 13bhp @ 4000rpm; 50mph claiming 50mpg.

1958 Multiplas four-cylinder; 633cc; 22bhp rear engine; estate car offered with alternative seating giving 4/5 or 6 seats.

Ford

'I will build a car for the great multitude.'
That was Henry Ford's declared aim when,
75 years ago, on June 16, 1903, he founded
the Ford Motor Company after years of
experiment and two previous abortive attempts
to establish motor manufacturing companies.
Ford, born in 1863, was the son of a farmer
who had emigrated from County Cork, Ireland,
in 1847, at the height of the potato famine;
as young Henry grew up on his father's farm
in Dearborn, Michigan, he came to loathe the
unnecessary drudgery of farm life. 'My earliest
recollection,' he was to recall, 'was that,
considering the results, there was too much
work on the place.' A fall from a horse in
1872 convinced him that, as soon as he was
old enough, he should try to develop some
more reliable form of prime mover than animal
power. And when, four years later, he saw a
traction engine for the first time, he realized
that he was 'by instinct an engineer'.

Ford built his first internal combustion
engine in 1893, his first car in 1896; his
mechanical talents inspired a group of Detroit
businessmen to found the Detroit Automobile
Company (Mechanical Superintendent, Henry
Ford) in 1899. It collapsed after a year with
a loss of $86,000, having built maybe a dozen
cars. The Henry Ford Company, formed under
similar circumstances in 1901, lasted for three
months before Ford resigned after disagreeing
with his backers; bereft of its figurehead, the
company was renamed 'Cadillac'.

The infant Ford Motor Company began
operation in a former carriage works on Mack
Avenue, Detroit, and initially 'had to strain
every nerve to make ends meet': most of the
$28,000 originally invested had gone before
the first order for a Ford car, from a Chicago
doctor named Pfennig, arrived on July 15. It
was the decisive turning point in the company's
fortunes: from then on, the orders kept flowing
in, and some $20,000-worth of cars was sold
in a month.

Ford's first car was known as Model A: it
was an 8hp gas-buggy with a horizontally-
opposed twin-cylinder engine beneath the
driver's seat. Total production of this model
was 1,708 cars. Having tasted instant success
in a notoriously uncertain industry—Ford was

one of the few of the 57 new car manufacturing
companies founded in 1903 to see 1904—
Henry Ford developed his products fast,
seeking his ultimate motorcar. He moved
quickly and spasmodically through the
alphabet of models; Model A was joined in
1904 by Model B, a big, not-very-successful
vertical four, then succeeded later the same
year by the 10hp Model C. Model F was a
de luxe development of Model C; Model K
was a powerful 40hp six which proved to have
too many horsepower for its two-speed
epicyclic transmission; Model N was a light
15hp four-cylinder which created a sensation
with its $500 price tag and was subsequently
made in two de luxe forms, Model R and
Model S.

But it was on October 1, 1908, that Henry
Ford unveiled his 'universal car', the Model
T, a car 'so completely simple that no one
could fail to understand it'.

Light and strong, because of the extensive
use of vanadium steel in its construction, Model
T had a four-cylinder, 2,953cc engine with
three main bearings. It showed Ford's early
mastery of foundry techniques with a
monobloc cylinder casting and a detachable
cylinder head; in unit with the engine was a
two-speed, pedal-operated epicyclic
transmission.

Model T soon proved itself as a 'go-anywhere'
car; in June 1909 a Model T won the
4,100-mile New York-Seattle race for the
Guggenheim Trophy, crossing from coast to
coast in 22 days under appalling weather
conditions across terrain where roads hardly
existed. And in October 1911, the Edinburgh
Ford agent made the first ascent by car of
Britain's highest mountain, Ben Nevis, at the
wheel of a Model T. It was said that you
could go anywhere in the homely Model T
except in society.

As demand for the Model T increased, so Ford
sought ways of increasing production. And in
1913, apparently inspired by the methods of
the Chicago meat packers, Ford introduced
the motor industry's first moving production
line, which enabled him dramatically
to cut the time taken to produce a motor
car. By 1914 Ford, with one-sixth of America's

automotive labour force, was making almost half the nation's cars—all Model Ts, by that time 'any colour the customer wants so long as it was black', for black paint dried the quickest.

At peak, Model T output exceeded two million cars a year, and by the time that Model T finally went out of production, an estimated 16.5 million had been built in Ford plants all over the world.

For Ford had early on become an international company. Almost as soon as the company was founded, Model As were being shipped to Europe, Africa and Australasia, and by 1911 sales in Britain had grown to such an extent that it was deemed worthwhile to establish Ford's first overseas factory in a converted tram factory at Trafford Park, Manchester, on Britain's first industrial estate. By the outbreak of the First World War, Ford was far and away Britain's biggest manufacturer, with annual sales approaching 10,000. Nevertheless, Model T was still

basically an American car, and sold principally because of its robust, durable construction and its low cost. When the 1920 Motor Car Act, based on the rated horsepower of engines, increased the Model T's annual road tax to £23, sales began to decline. Over 300,000 Model Ts were built at Manchester before production ceased there in August 1927.

Though its styling had altered dramatically over the years, the 1927 Model T was at heart little different from its 1908 forebear. It still had brakes on the rear wheels only, and its foot-operated gearchange, commonplace enough in Edwardian days, had become mere eccentricity. Something different was needed: but when Ford closed down production of Model T in the summer of 1927, he had little idea as to what shape its successor should take.

The new car was the most eagerly awaited model of the year, and when it was finally unveiled on December 2, 1927, some 10 million Americans queued to see the New Ford in the first two days. To become known as Model

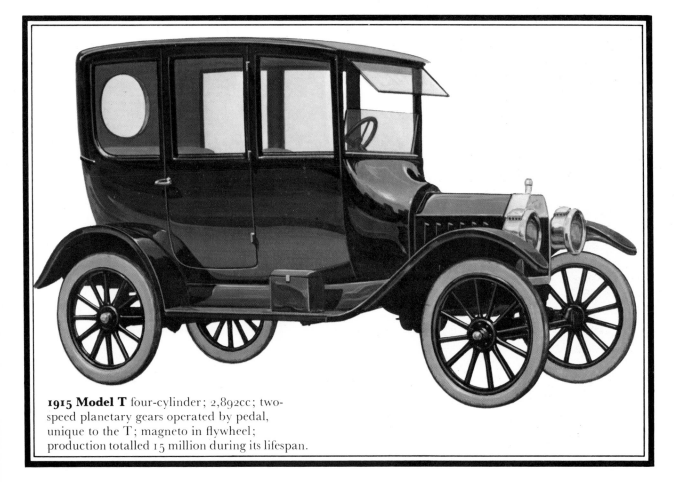

1915 Model T four-cylinder; 2,892cc; two-speed planetary gears operated by pedal, unique to the T; magneto in flywheel; production totalled 15 million during its lifespan.

A, the New Ford had a conventional three-speed gear box (which 'changed as easily as slicing butter') and was the first production car ever to feature safety glass in the windscreen as standard: but it was the Model A's snappy styling—created by a team led by Henry Ford's son Edsel—that really caused a sensation, for it was based on Ford's luxury car line, the Lincoln, and a wide choice of colours and trim fabrics was available, in heady contrast to the monochromatic Model T.

The first official purchase of the Model A was for 'America's Sweetheart', Mary Pickford, who was given a Sport Coupe by her husband, Douglas Fairbanks, as a Christmas present, the sale being made by Edsel Ford himself.

Though over 4 million Model As would be made between 1927 and 1932, it could only be a stopgap. Ford had waited too long before changing over from the Model T, and had lost momentum and industry leadership as a result. In Europe, especially, where most countries taxed vehicles on the size of their power units, the 24hp Model A sold poorly compared with smaller-engined cars designed to meet local conditions. True, a small-bore 14.9hp Model A was offered, its power unit built in Ford's Cork, Ireland, factory; but it cost £5 *more* than the 24hp model, and was lacking in power, so it proved to be a both-ways loser.

Sales of Model A plunged in the Depression, and, by the time that Ford's huge new factory built on reclaimed Thames marshland at Dagenham, Essex, was ready to go into production in 1931, there was virtually no demand at all for Model A cars, nearly all the sales being made consisting of commercial vehicles. The financial position of Ford of Britain, incorporated three years before to spearhead Ford's European operations, was desperate. The Dagenham factory had cost £5 million to build, and there was insufficient money to repay the firm's commitments.

The company could no longer rely on Model A to sustain it: a new policy and new models

1928 Model A four-cylinder; 2,877cc; available in a wide variety of body styles, the sedans becoming more popular.

were needed to carry Ford through the 1930s. As early as 1928, Henry Ford had shown the head of Ford of Britain, Sir Percival Perry, designs for a light car, and, when he visited Europe in 1930, had declared that he planned to build such a car. Perry was less enthusiastic, predicting that the development costs of an all-new model would add a disproportionate amount to the financial burdens of the newly-formed British company. Ford was insistent, and requested that Perry should select 15 British and French light cars for shipment to the Ford headquarters at Dearborn, Michigan, for examination and evaluation.

'Fifteen cars seem an awful lot,' complained Perry, 'but if Ford wishes to make comparisons, I think he should see everything . . .'

Worsening financial conditions forced Perry to change his mind over the viability of the small car project. The Dagenham factory began operation in October 1931 with scarcely a car on the order books; of the vehicles produced there during the latter months of 1931, only five were cars, the rest trucks. In mid-October, Perry appealed to Dearborn to design a small car to save Dagenham from financial disaster.

The response was immediate and dramatic: Henry Ford initiated a development programme which would rival the changeover from Model T to Model A for speed. Design parameters were laid down: the new baby Ford for Europe had to have a smallbore engine of around eight taxable horsepower, light weight, a 90-inch wheelbase, narrow track.

Recalled Chief Engineer Laurence Sheldrick: 'The job was done pretty darn quick! It was a characteristic Ford in all respects, with torque tube drive, transverse springs and certain valve and tappet features on which Henry Ford insisted.'

Work on the new model continued round the clock; by mid-December, Dagenham's General Manager Rowland Smith was summoned to Dearborn to help with the development of the new 8hp Model 19. One January morning, he was underneath the car adjusting the brakes when the 67-year-old Henry Ford appeared, ordered him to move over, and also lay under the car wielding a

1934 Model Y four-cylinder; 933cc; 22bhp; one of the first true £100 production cars; more than 55mph; 35mpg.

spanner. Disguised by a radiator badge bearing the name 'Mercury' (which was rejected by Perry but later adopted for Ford's mid-price US range), the Model 19 was soon making trial runs in the Dearborn area.

By mid-February 1932, just four months after the first designs were being made on the drawing board, the Model 19 made its public debut, at Ford's own motor exhibition at the Albert Hall in London. Britain's oldest dealer principal, the septuagenarian A. E. Rumsey of Bristol, dapper in gold pince-nez and goatee beard, stepped forward to pull the dust-sheet from the new car and the crowd surged forward to inspect what would become known as the Model Y.

'Nothing like it has ever occurred in the motor industry in this country,' reported a delighted Perry to Edsel Ford, while Rowland Smith telegraphed Dearborn: 'Have never seen Ford dealers so enthusiastic . . . Public opinion and Press everywhere proclaim 8hp car just what is wanted here . . . Anticipate that many months will elapse before we can overtake the demand.'

The new model was received with equal enthusiasm in Ford's other European markets: 14 prototypes had been completed and were shown at special exhibitions from Norway to Portugal to gauge public and trade reactions. These resulted in the car being substantially remodelled, with a sleeker, more capacious body and redesigned power unit before it went into production in August 1932.

Model Y was the ancestor of all Ford light cars for the next quarter-century, and quickly achieved its purpose by giving Ford a big share of the small car market—54 per cent in 1934. Morris countered by introducing the Eight, a 'Chinese copy' of the Model Y, with almost identical styling but improved mechanical specification, including hydraulic brakes, so Ford slashed profit margins to the bone to produce the first—and only—fully-equipped saloon car ever marketed at £100.

For many people, the £100 Ford Popular represented, as had the Model T to a previous generation, the key to the open road. Sales of this lively and durable little car boomed, giving Ford overall sales comparable to those of Morris and Austin, representing almost a quarter of 'Big Six' production.

'Model Y was our only salvation . . .' said a grateful Perry.

Ford's European factories at Cologne, Barcelona and Asnières, near Paris, built the Model Y in the early days, too, though it never reached the popularity it had in Britain, because high local production costs kept the selling price high. In Germany, Ford sought to turn this into a positive aspect by offering, on a series production basis, a well-equipped, if over-bodied, cabriolet version of their Model Y 'Köln'.

In 1932, Model A had been succeeded by what was to become known as Model B (though Edsel Ford had insisted that it should be called the 'Improved Model A'). Basically the same mechanically as its predecessor, with the same choice of 14.9hp or 24hp power units, the Model B sold even less well than had the A in Europe. Dagenham production was only 8,784—possibly the fact that the smallbore version of the B was unfortunately codenamed the 'BF' didn't help—and when the Model B was phased out in 1934, it was replaced by another Dearborn-designed light car, the 10hp Model C, which had an 1,172cc engine.

Cologne produced its own version of this small Ford, too, under the name 'Eifel', replacing it just before the war with the curvaceous 'Taunus', still with the same power unit.

Model Y and Model C were developed, via the short-lived 'Eight' and 'Ten' announced in 1937 (and significant as the first Dagenham-designed cars), into the Prefect ('The Ten ahead of its Class') and the Anglia 8hp, the latter appearing shortly after the outbreak of war in 1939.

If these two cars formed the backbone of European Ford production in the 1930s, no less significant was 'Henry Ford's last mechanical triumph', the V8, which had gone into production in the early part of 1932. Using the same chassis as the Model B, the Model 18 V8 incorporated Ford's revolutionary mass-produced V8 power unit, which had cylinders and crankcase cast in one, proof that Ford foundry techniques were well ahead of the rest of the industry.

Model 18's 3,622cc power unit gave it the sort of performance normally associated with the sports cars of the day—80mph maximum speed, 0-50mph in only 12 seconds— though its brakes were only just up to coping with such velocities. Ford called it 'the greatest thrill in motoring', and press reports spoke glowingly of 'leaping forward at an astonishing speed . . . seeming to be swept along before a giant hand and not pulled along by machinery . . .'

The Model 18 caused a sensation in America, where it sold well; but because of this demand, which far outstripped supply, the new V8 only reached Europe in small numbers. In England, for instance, only 911 Model 18s, imported from Ford-Canada because of the more favourable tariffs on Empire goods, were sold.

A radically restyled, improved V8, Model 40, appeared for 1934. This was the first Ford V8 to be built in Europe as well as America; it was produced at Cologne and at Cork in Ireland, though not, surprisingly, at Dagenham, where Sir Percival Perry felt that tooling-up for the production of the V8 could prove detrimental to his small-car production. A four-cylinder version, Model B-40, was marketed in mainland Europe, where horsepower tax made the big, 30hp V8 expensive to run. Cologne's interpretation of Model 40, known as the Rheinland, was often fitted with series production cabriolet coachwork, and in this form was perhaps the most handsome V8 variant produced anywhere in the world.

France, too, was responsible for some covetable V8s, built under the name Matford in the Strasbourg factory of Emile Mathis, who had entered into an agreement with Ford in 1934 whereby he acquired some much needed capital and Ford some vital extra production capacity. It was to be a stormy relationship, for Mathis had felt that he would retain rather more independence under the agreement than Ford had intended, and it would last only four years before a parting of the ways was agreed upon, with Mathis being paid over $1 million and his factory reverting to him after 1940; Ford acquired a new plant at Poissy, near Paris.

Series-production coupes and cabriolets were a feature of Matford production, too, the most common being bodied by Janer. Matford also introduced a small-bore 22hp V8, the Alsace (which had been designed in Dearborn); a similar low-tax V8 engine was used in Dagenham's 1936 Model 60 and its successor, Model 62. The 22hp V8 was not as successful as the larger power unit, and went through four fairly major design revisions in its short lifespan. When Dagenham introduced the postwar Pilot V8, using a modified version of Model 62's bodyshell, it had the 30hp engine in all but the pre-production prototypes (and this at a time of strict petrol rationing).

Dagenham's first production V8 was the Model 48, which had more modern coachwork and a lower, more rigidly-braced chassis, with the engine moved forward 18 inches to give better weight distribution; top speed was now 87mph.

With the 1929 Model A, Ford had been the first manufacturer to offer a factory-produced station wagon body; this style, known as the 'Utility Car' in Europe, was to reach its greatest

1954 Skyliner new type V8 engine with six-cylinder option giving 130 or 115bhp respectively; special feature was the tinted transparent panel in roof.

elegance on the V8s of the 1930s, and owed its success to the fact that Henry Ford owned large expanses of hardwood forest near Iron Mountain, Michigan, where a body plant had been established to provide wood framing for Model Ts. Here the station wagon bodies were produced on an assembly line from maple, birch and basswood for shipment to Ford plants all over the world.

The V8 continued to develop throughout the 1930s: the year 1936 saw the Model 68, with a more streamlined radiator grille, improvements in the seating and road-holding, while the 1937 Model 71, with cable instead of rod brakes, had more than a hint of the styling of the revolutionary new Lincoln-Zephyr about it. Models 81A and 91A were the last V8s seen in Europe before the war halted production, but in America development continued until the last civilian V8 left the production line on February 10, 1942.

Ford was quickly back into production after the war; Dagenham's first postwar Anglia appeared on May 26, 1945, followed by the Prefect a month later, while in America the first civilian model, a 1946 Super Deluxe Tudor Sedan, came off the line on July 3, 1945, and was personally delivered to President Truman at the White House. The driver was 28-year-old Henry Ford II, who was to take over control of Ford Motor Company the following September, when his 82-year-old

grandfather at last relinquished the presidency of the manufacturing giant, retiring to his estate at Fair Lane, where he died at the age of 83 on April 7, 1947.

Aided by the famous 'Whiz Kids', Henry Ford II immediately began the huge task of turning Ford Motor Company into a modern enterprise; in September 1946 an international Division was set up to coordinate Ford activities outside the US. Nevertheless, the postwar products from Ford's European factories had very little in common: after experimenting with ohv engines in the late 1940s, Dagenham introduced the integral-construction Consul and Zephyr in 1950, which broke new ground with independent front suspension and overhead valves. For some years, Cologne remained faithful to the Taunus 'Bückel', which, despite its streamlined styling, reminiscent of the 1938 V8-81A, had the sidevalve 1,172cc engine which Dagenham was still using on the resolutely old-fashioned Prefect. The French plant at Poissy built the Vedette, an American-inspired V8 which was just too costly to buy and run in postwar France, and whose poor

1956 Thunderbird V8; 4,457cc; 200bhp; 120mph; one of the modern American sports cars but with 'civilised' aids such as power seats and electric windows.

1965 Mustang V8; 4,727cc; 271bhp @ 6000rpm; four-speed manual gearbox; more than 125mph; lower-powered options were available including a 2.8-litre six.

sales were a major factor in the decision to cease building Ford cars in France in 1954 (though the design was to be continued by Simca, who took over the Poissy plant).

In America, the first all-new model from the new regime was a complete departure from previous Ford practice. Work started in late 1947 on a design with full-width styling created by George Walker, an independent Detroit styling consultant, with Ford engineers carrying out a crash programme to develop a new chassis and tools to make and test the car.

The new look was previewed in April 1948 when basically similar Lincoln and Mercury models appeared in the showrooms, then, on June 8, the 1949 Ford line was unveiled at the Waldorf Astoria Hotel in New York. The first-ever Ford to have independent front suspension, the new model had cost an estimated $118 million to develop, and caused almost as great a stir as its classic predecessors.

Another step forward came in 1954, when the old flathead V8 was replaced by an ohv unit. That year saw some wild colour schemes, and an unusual model called the Skyliner, a pillarless coupe with a tinted glass half-roof and a bonnet ornament in the shape of a delta-winged jet.

Though hardly a sports car as Europe understood it, the 'stunning' Thunderbird of 1955 was described as 'America's first luxury sports car'. Produced as the result of extensive market research, the T-Bird, initially powered by a 4.2 litre Mercury V8, could be had with automatic transmission, power steering and brakes and automatic windows, but its styling was a lot 'cleaner' than most of its contemporaries, and it sold well.

By the time it went out of production in 1964, the Thunderbird had completely changed character, and a new concept of sporty car was needed to attract the car-conscious 'youth market'. The result was the Mustang, which was to become the most successful new car of all time—until Ford broke its own record in 1976 with the introduction in Europe of the Fiesta baby car.

Mustang was introduced as a convertible with hard-top and two-plus-two models, with the choice of a 3.3 litre straight-six or a 200bhp 4.7 litre V8 (later on, a 'muscle car' variant, the GT350, appeared, with a 305bhp Cobra V8). It was yet another example of Ford's ability to produce the right car at the right time which has recurred—with that notable exception, the Edsel—throughout the company's 75-year history. Ford today is the world's biggest 'family firm', with sales of 150 million vehicles since 1903. A recurring advertising theme for many years has been 'there's a Ford in your future': it is equally true to say that nearly every motorist has a Ford in his past!

Franklin

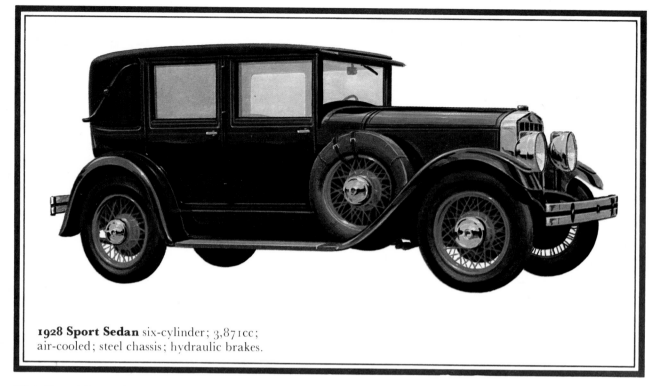

1928 Sport Sedan six-cylinder; 3,871cc;
air-cooled; steel chassis; hydraulic brakes.

The Franklin of Syracuse, New York, was America's most successful mass-produced air-cooled car, before the Chevrolet Corvair appeared as a four in 1902. Innovative from the beginning, it was a pioneer with its mechanically operated overhead valves, float-feed carburettor, and low unsprung weight. By 1912, the first model year for the sloping Renault-type nose, retained for more than a decade, it had introduced automatic spark advance, Hotchkiss drive, and pressure-fed engine lubrication. These were soon followed by a central gear change, all electric lighting and starting, and aluminium pistons. In contrast, two seemingly archaic but effective features, laminated ash frames and buggy-type full elliptic springs, remained on all models until 1927 and 1932 respectively. Sixes supplemented the fours in 1905 and replaced them entirely in 1914.

Until 1928, top speed was never much higher than 50mph, but conservative owners found compensation in a smooth, quiet ride, long engine life, high tyre mileage thanks to the car's light weight, and phenomenal economy—40 mpg was claimed for the 1918 open models. In 1922, the appearance was made conventional but not enhanced by the adoption of a raked-back dummy radiator shell.

For the Series II in 1925, smart European-inspired bodies designed by Frank De Causse gave a radically different image without much change under the skin. For 1928, four-wheel hydraulic brakes were adopted and the stroke was lengthened by 18mm in an effort to participate in the then leisurely horsepower race. That year's Airman series, honouring Charles Lindbergh as well as the engine type, was still an elegant laggard. For 1929 the bore was increased by 6.25mm, yielding an unimpressive 67bhp from a 4,500cc engine. Restricted by an old cylinder design and downdraught blower system, Franklin was being literally left behind.

With the 1930 Series 14, performance became competitive, thanks to finned aluminium heads for each cylinder (which themselves were finned horizontally) and an ingenious side-draught arrangement of cooling-air flow regulated by thermostatically-controlled shutters in the 'radiator', an enlarged valve area, increased compression ratio (5.3 to 1) and a bigger carburettor. This talented engineering by Carl Doman and E. S. Marks was complemented by pleasing new body

1925 Tourer six-cylinder; 3,871cc; ohv; air-cooled engine; chassis frame of laminated wood.

lines. Prices ranged from $2,485 for the factory saloon to $7,500 for coachbuilt bodies by Dietrich, Locke, and other coachbuilders. As a concession to modernity, the chassis was steel, but full elliptic springs were retained. With this car and the next year's similar Series 15, Franklin reached its zenith in design but not in sales, which plummeted to under 3,000 in 1931.

In a foredoomed effort to stem the tide, Doman and Marks devised and introduced a V12 in 1932. The engine was a 150bhp masterpiece capable of 95mph, and the bodywork was styled by Ray Dietrich. For 1933 the price was cut from $4,000 to an uneconomic $2,885. Under pressure from bank creditors in 1934 the firm offered the medium-priced Olympic with Franklin engine and 'radiator', and Reo body and chassis. Car production ceased during that year. Under new auspices, the factory turned to light-aircraft engines, one of which, converted to water-cooling, powered the Tucker.

1934 Club Sedan six-cylinder 4,495cc; air-cooled; the last model produced and sold before the company went bankrupt.

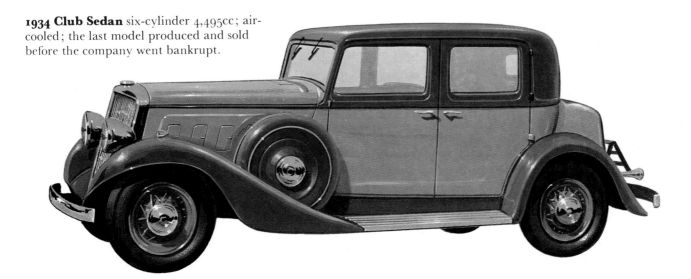

Frazer Nash

Frazer Nash's ancestor was the GN, a sporting cyclecar made from 1910 to 1925 and named after its designers, H. R. Godfrey (the 'G' of HRG) and Archie Frazer-Nash. Post-World War I GNs were chain-driven, and Frazer-Nash followed this tradition in the stark sports cars he built at Kingston-on-Thames from 1924-6, and at Isleworth thereafter. In contrast to the GN, which in its heyday of the early 1920s was turned out at the rate of fifty or so a week, the highly individual Frazer Nashes (the cars lacked a hyphen, along with most other amenities) seldom totalled such a figure in any given year.

The 'Chain Gang' types underwent little essential change for a decade and half; they had light construction, multiple chain-and-cog final drive to a solid rear axle and quarter-elliptic springs all round. Under Frazer-Nash and from 1929 under H. J. Aldington, various engines were tried and modified for performance: first Anzani and Meadows, both 1½-litre fours, Blackburne twin overhead-camshaft sixes (used in some Invictas as well) of 1½ or 1.7 litres, and the firm's own ohc 1½-litre Gough four. Capable of 80 to 90mph in their most potent versions, Frazer Nashes shone in Alpine Trials and rallies. The narrow, bathtub tailed TT Replicas of 1932-8, of which fewer than a hundred were built, remain the Frazer Nash *par excellence*.

During 1924-39, the firm marketed slightly modified 2-litre German BMWs under a Frazer Nash nameplate. Beginning in 1947, a BMW 328-based engine developed for Bristol and modified by Frazer-Nash powered a new model with tubular chassis, transverse-spring independent front suspension, torsion bar rear suspension and conventional sliding-gear transmission. Capable of more than 100mph, the new Frazer Nash was named the Le Mans Replica after finishing third in that race in 1949. Two years later it also won the Targa Florio, the first British victory in this event, after which the streamlined models were named Targa Florio. From 1953, fixed-head coupés complemented the open sports versions. The last Frazer Nashes, smooth Continental coupés of the late 1950s, had 2.6 and 3.2 litre BMW engines and cost £2,500 before purchase tax.

1925 Sports sold in a wide variety in the 1930s using four- and six-cylinder engines of several different proprietary makes but using, in all cases, chain drive; some models were supercharged giving speeds of up to 100mph.

Graham

1932 Convertible available as six-cylinder of 3,679cc or with choice of eight-cylinder engines of 3,960cc or 4,905cc.

The brothers Joseph, Robert and Ray Graham, who had prospered by building Dodge-powered Graham trucks, bought the Paige plant in Detroit and introduced a line of Graham-Paige L-head sixes and eights in 1928, the new firm's only really profitable year. All but the cheapest of these stylish but conventional cars featured four-speed transmissions, then unusual in America. Open models of the 1928-31 period and coachbuilt saloon bodies and limousines by Le Baron are especially desirable.

The 'Paige' suffix was dropped in 1930. Amos Northrup's expensive-looking Blue Streak styling of 1932-4, featuring pontoon wings and vee-shaped radiator grille, was soon imitated by other car makers. A striking appearance, reasonable price (as low as $995 for the eights), and outstanding performance failed to sell many cars, as did the centrifugal supercharger option first offered in 1934.

The regressively styled Grahams of 1935-7 had few selling points except the supercharger and surprisingly good economy. The eights were discontinued in 1935 and production was soon transferred to Dearborn. In an attempt to gain extra sales, Graham launched a cheap 2.8-litre six in 1935. Even though it could reach 75mph

and do better than 20mpg and was priced at a mere $595, it sold poorly and in fact only 23,000 Grahams were sold in 1935. The 3.6-litre Cavalier fared no better in 1936, despite its handsome styling and optional supercharger. When the low-priced Crusader six was dropped in 1937, Nissan of Japan bought the dies, tools and engine blocks and built a car based on it.

Gambling on a radical change, Graham management launched the 'sharknose' style in 1938. The gamble didn't pay off, but the car is undeniably eye catching.

1938 Sedan six-cylinder; 3,560cc; 106bhp @ 4000rpm; with supercharger and aluminium cylinder head; overdrive and vacuum gearchange optional.

Hispaño-Suiza

This marque was the creation of the Swiss engineer Marc Birkigt and from 1904 to 1911 was produced only in Spain; hence the name Hispaño-Suiza. With the exception of the Alfonso XIII, a fast, minimal-bodied four-cylinder voiturette of 1912-20 with the odd but effective bore-stroke ratio of 80mm to 180mm in its early years, the most famous Hispaños originated in France where an assembly plant was opened in 1912—and produced 'H' sixes of 1919-34 and the V12 of 1931-8.

The H6B 6.6-litre was revolutionary when it appeared in 1919. Its aircraft engine inspiration was symbolized by the flying stork mascot of Georges Guynemer's Stork

Squadron, whose Spad fighters were powered by Hispaño. The car's engine had a single overhead camshaft, dual ignition, and nitrided steel liners for the aluminium block. It delivered—somewhat noisily—135bhp and a top speed of about 90mph, coupled with sufficient torque to crawl at 3 or 4mph in top gear. The four-wheel servo-assisted brakes were adopted by Rolls-Royce. The steering, as in all European quality cars of the era, irrespective of the rule of the road, was always right-hand. In chassis form, ready for the coachbuilder, the H6B weighed about 2,500lb and cost about the same as a Rolls-Royce Silver Ghost, though its design was 14 years more modern. In 1924

1928 Convertible six-cylinder; 6,597cc; single ohc; three-speed gearbox; over 90mph; one of the world's most expensive cars.

the H6B was joined by the longer-stroke 8-litre H6C Boulogne capable of more than 100mph. For the less affluent Spanish market, there was a 3.7-litre version of the H6B, the Barcelona, a somewhat disappointing machine.

Like other makers of luxury cars on both sides of the Atlantic during the Depression, Birkigt felt compelled to produce a twelve, and his Type 68 appeared late in 1931. The 9.4-litre engine was of identical bore and stroke, while the later Type 68bis, of longer stroke, boasted 11.3 litres compared with the Cadillac V16's 7.4 litres. With no loss in efficiency and a welcome gain in silence, push-rod overhead valves were employed.

Regrettably, the three-speed transmission was retained, in which a first-gear ratio as low as 5.44 to 1 made restarts on hills difficult. But these cars were impressive in nearly every other particular: a wheelbase of 11ft 3in to 13ft 2in, a minimum top speed of 100mph despite a weight of up to three tons, acceleration from rest to 60mph in less than 12 seconds, and a phenomenal thirst.

Coincidentally with the V12s, Hispaño-Suiza introduced a comparatively small (4.6-litre) Junior six built in the newly acquired Ballot factory. This and the veteran 'H' sixes were superseded in 1934 by the 4.9-litre K6, powered by one bank of the T68bis V12. From the time of the Munich crisis in 1938, the firm ceased all car production in France to concentrate on aircraft engines and other war material. In neutral Spain, sixes of less than 4 litres, unimportant in the Hispaño canon, appeared for a few more years.

1932 Convertible six-cylinder; 6,597cc or 7,982cc; or V12 version with 9,424cc, this giving over 200bhp and 100mph.

Holden

Backed by a loan from the Australian government, eager for industry, General Motors launched 'Australia's Own Car' in 1948. This Holden was a compact four door saloon similar in specification to the Vauxhall Velox. It had a six cylinder, overhead valve 2.2 litre engine, unit construction, column gear change and 70mph cruising speed. In short, the quintessence of mediocrity, but the car was simple, tough, reliable, and dustproof. Although its dowdy styling changed little for eight years, in that time Holden had captured nearly half of the Australian market and annual production was approaching 100,000 units.

To keep on top 'Down Under', the 1957 model Holden represented a thorough but not radical revision, with nearly every dimension somewhat larger. During the five year run of this series, styling gradually decreed two-tone paint, 1955 Chevrolet or Pontiac type side mouldings, and a wrap-round windscreen. Station wagons supplemented the saloon.

From 1962, all Holdens had unexceptionable if not exceptional styling. To meet Japanese and Western competition, GM both shrank and expanded the low-medium size concept, from small sixes to 5.7 litre eights, and offered many options and body styles. Even so, by 1974 Holden's share of an enlarged market had declined to one third.

1957 six-cylinder; 2,171cc; 70bhp @ 4000rpm; three-speed gearbox; more than 80mph.

Hotchkiss

Hotchkiss et Cie, an armaments firm founded in the 1870s at Saint-Denis near Paris by the American inventor and manufacturer Benjamin B. Hotchkiss, exhibited its first car at the 1903 Paris show. This large four-cylinder car, advanced for its time, had mechanical inlet valves, a steel frame and the Hotchkiss drive, which came to be employed in a vast number of marques the world over. Hotchkiss drive imparts the driving and braking forces to rear leaf springs; the axle is saddled to the springs, which pivot at the front in a pin attached to the frame or underbody and are shackled to it at the rear.

Hotchkiss cars, whether large or medium sized, always gave an impression of luxury without ostentation and reliability without dullness. Though the firm continued to produce fours along with occasional light sixes, these qualities were best embodied in the larger overhead-valve sixes of 1928-54, all of them similar in concept whatever the model designation. The 3-litre AM80 of 1928 (with torque-tube instead of Hotchkiss drive!) won the 1932 Monte Carlo rally, as did the $3\frac{1}{2}$-litre Hotchkiss-driven version in 1933 and 1934; a similar model tied with a Delahaye in 1939. Then in 1949 and 1950 Hotchkiss won the gruelling winter event again, with 20cv 686 $3\frac{1}{2}$-litre saloons.

Fame and acclaim were not enough to cope with the post-war French tax structure, which penalized heavily owners of both new and old large cars, nor were sales helped by conservative styling and other features— independent front suspension was not adopted until 1949, and right-hand steering was retained to the end. Only 400 sixes and 2,276 Anjou 2.3-litre fours were produced in 1951, plus 29 of the advanced front wheel drive Hotchkiss-Gregoire 2-litre flat-four saloons which were introduced too late. Before the war, Hotchkiss had built another Gregoire design, the Amilcar Compound. In 1954, shortly after it had acquired Delahaye, Hotchkiss ceased production of private cars, though it still makes Jeep-like vehicles.

1952 Paris-Nice six-cylinder; 3,485cc; 100bhp @ 4000rpm; Cotal electric gearbox.

HRG

In 1935, in a workshop in Norbiton, Surrey, three competition motorists, Halford, Robins and Godfrey, combined to build a sports car which harked back to vintage standards of performance and appearance. Seeing that it was good, they soon started production in their own factory at Tolworth, Surrey. Through two decades, the car remained true to the original concept of a fast, light, stark, and above all traditional sports/racing machine. Ron Godfrey had originally worked with Archie Frazer-Nash, making the GN cyclecar and, like the GN and the Frazer Nash, the HRG had quarter-elliptic front suspension, though rear springs were semi-elliptic. In 1939 the original 1,500cc Meadows engine was superseded by highly modified Singer fours of 1,100 and 1,500cc with overhead cams and twin carburettors. Magneto ignition remained optional to the end. No mere anachronistic toys, HRGs won the 1½-litre class at Le Mans in 1939 and 1949, in the Alpine Rally of 1948 and 1951, and in the 24-hour race at Spa-Francorchamps, Belgium in 1948 and 1949. On the British scene they were successful in sprints, hill climbs and trials and in the Production Touring Car Race at Silverstone in 1949 and 1950.

Despite such triumphs and a modest price (£895 basic for the 1,500cc in the early 1950s and £820 for the 1,100cc, which was discontinued in 1953), hardly more than 200 of the classic two-seaters were produced. The last of the classic 1500s, introduced in 1955 and listed for sale until early in 1957, had hydraulic brakes, a new Singer engine, and a price of £1,280 basic for the home market, though actually all were sold abroad.

HRG also offered an unsuccessful aerodynamic version in the late 1940s. In 1955 the British motoring press generously publicized an advanced 1,500cc two-seater incorporating a modified twin-cam Singer engine, all-enveloping body, tubular chassis, cast-magnesium wheels, aircraft-type disc brakes and all round independent suspension, using transverse leaf springs and special shock absorbers. The admirable new car was still-born, a victim of economics; only two were completed.

1948 1500 four-cylinder; 1,496cc; ohv; 61bhp @ 4800rpm; four-speed gearbox; more than 80mph; 30mpg.

Hudson

1918 Runabout Landau six-cylinder
4,719cc; SV; three-speed gearbox; over 70mph.

Backed by the Detroit department store magnate J. L. Hudson, the Hudson Motor Car Co was started in 1909 to produce a car designed by Roy D. Chapin and Howard E. Coffin, both of whom had held important posts with Oldsmobile, Thomas-Detroit, and Chalmers. More than 4,500 of the first Hudson, a 20hp four with three speed sliding gear transmission and priced at $1,150, were sold in 1910. The more powerful Model 33 of 1911 was even more popular. Larger and more expensive fours followed in 1912 and 1913. A big (6.9-litre) six, the Model 54, also appeared in 1912, the year in which J. L. Hudson died; no more fours were built after 1916.

The memorable Super Six introduced in 1916 had a 4.6-litre engine which, thanks to a balanced crankshaft and the then high compression ratio of 5 to 1, developed 76bhp. The same side valve engine was used until 1926 when an F-head layout was adopted, to raise power output to 95bhp. Except for the traditional rounded Hudson bonnet, the body styling came to resemble the boxiness of Hudson's junior partner, the Essex, introduced in 1919. As with the Essex, the 1922 two-door saloon, called a coach, was priced at only $100 above the open models, thus pioneering the trend toward enclosed bodies.

Combined Hudson and Essex sales peaked in 1925-9 at an annual total between 227,000 and 300,000; in 1925, 1927 and 1929, the firm ranked third behind Ford and Chevrolet.

In 1930 Hudson introduced a 3½-litre side valve straight eight which became the company's sole offering in 1931 and 1932, in which year its capacity was increased to 4.2 litres. The 4.2-litre was available until 1952, by which time it was rated at 128bhp. During its long life, this flexible, smooth running and comparatively thrifty power plant established many speed and endurance records.

Despite the Hudson's merits and the Essex's improvements, their combined sales dropped badly from the very beginning of the Depression—to 114,000 in 1930 and 58,000 in 1931 and 1932. In mid-1932 the Essex name was dropped in favour of Terraplane. With an engine essentially the same as the last Essex's 3.2-litre unit, this new junior line for 1933 represented a significant upgrading in performance because of a 600lb saving in weight, down to 2,345lbs. The basic price was also lowered, from $775 to $565. Later in 1933 the even more brilliant Terraplane 4-litre eight was added. In 1933 the engine was bored out to 4.2 litres. Terraplanes established many hill climbing records and won twice at Pike's Peak. In England, their engines and chassis were modified for use in the Railton and Brough Superior sports cars. Later Terraplane 3½-litre sixes were rated from 80bhp to an eventual 101bhp. The Terraplane name

1938 Terraplane six-cylinder; 2,723cc; 76bhp @ 3800rpm; three-speed gearbox; 75mph; 20mpg.

was dropped in favour of Hudson 112 in 1939 and Hudson Six in 1940-2 and 1946-7; they had a 2.9-litre engine. Larger sixes, called Country Club, Super, and Commander, were offered along with the eight.

After 1932, Hudson sales fluctuated widely, from a low of 41,000 in 1933 to 144,000 in 1948. The latter figure, a leap from 100,000 in 1947, was almost equalled in 1949 and 1950. Hudson's partial comeback was inspired by a revolutionary body and chassis design that superseded the warmed-over pre-war models. All full sized Hudsons of 1948-54 had a rigid 'Step-Down' unitized body and frame construction, with frame members running along the side edges of the body and outside the rear wheels.

In 1951-4 the most powerful Hudsons were the 5-litre Hornets, thirsty side valve sixes developing 145bhp in their initial standard form and up to 170bhp for the 'Twin H-Power' version of 1954. Almost from the beginning, Hornets dominated stock-car racing in the United States. These were literally standard cars; for little more than $3,000 anyone could buy similarly equipped types.

Glory in competition impressed only a limited if traditionally loyal public: Hudson

sales fell from 93,000 in 1951 to 76,000 in 1952. As far back as 1950, management was preparing to broaden its market with a narrow four-door compact saloon that would have been the first in the States. Snags arose, and the Hudson Jet was not ready until

1952 Hornet six-cylinder; 5,048cc; 145bhp @ 3800rpm; three-speed synchromesh gearbox.

1953 Super Jet six-cylinder; 3,310cc; 114bhp @ 4000rpm; over 90mph.

March 1953, more than a year after Willys's Aero series. The Jet's engine was similar to the Hornet's, scaled down to 3.3 litres and developing 104bhp in standard form and up to 114bhp with optional equipment. The body, whether four-door or two-door, could seat six at a pinch and had plenty of headroom. Priced somewhat below $2,000, the Jet competed directly against Chevrolet, Ford and Plymouth without offering an impressive package.

All 'real' Hudsons, including the Jet, disappeared with the 1954 models after the firm merged with Nash to form American Motors. The name continued for 1955-6 with Packard or left-over Hudson engines in minimally modified Nash bodies, and for 1957 with Nash's V8. For the next decade, all A.M. cars were called Rambler.

Humber

Thomas Humber founded his bicycle works at Nottingham in 1868. The first Humber motor vehicles, made at Coventry and at Beeston near Nottingham, appeared in 1898 following some singularly bad motorcycles and tricars, including the notorious Pennington machines. Among the wide variety of early models, the first fours appeared in 1902 along with a two-cylinder type. Better known is the one-cylinder Humberette of 1903-4, a popular light car; the name was revived for an air cooled 1-litre vee twin of 1912-5. The only six made before 1927 was the 30/40 of about 1908, boasting 5,155cc. At that time, all production became concentrated at Coventry.

Oddly, for a make which had concentrated on fairly mundane transport, Humber built a team of three racing cars for the 1914 Tourist Trophy race. These twin overhead camshaft machines were very fast but none finished the race. Thereafter the firm reverted to building well-made but conservative touring cars. Their best known small car is the 8/18, powered by a 985cc engine giving 20bhp at 3,000rpm. It was usually clothed in a pretty, 'chummy' body which became quite popular. Later on, heavier coachwork reduced the performance and the model's popularity waned. The 8/18 used an F-head layout (overhead inlet, side

exhaust valves) and this feature was retained until the early 1930s. However, Humber were backward in other respects, eschewing front wheel brakes and retaining a transmission brake until 1928. A succession of well engineered and durable cars followed the 8/18 but few of the 30,000 cars made before 1930 still exist.

Perhaps the most pleasant of vintage Humbers was the 3-litre 20/55 six, which was to develop into the Snipe. This car appeared in 1927 along with the 14/40, a neat small car which could top 60mph. This was followed in 1929 by a light six, the 16/50, but despite a steady sale to the professional classes, Humber ran into financial difficulties that year and was taken over by the Rootes Group, run by the brothers William and Reginald Rootes, who had already acquired Hillman. Although the existing designs were carried on for a short while, the Rootes brothers soon began a rationalization programme and the Humber range became in effect de luxe Hillmans, catering to an upper-middle-class market at comparatively low prices.

In appearance, most Humbers of the 1930s were family saloons like the 1933 3½-litre Snipe 80 six. A four-cylinder 1,669cc Model 12 of 1933-7 was shorter, while the Pullman,

1934 Vogue four-cylinder; 1,669cc; SV; 42bhp @ 3800rpm; four-speed gearbox.

featuring occasional seats amidships, was longer. Only sixes were made in the last years of the decade. The last pre-war Snipe, of 3,180cc, became a renowned staff car during the war, in an open-bodied version.

An interesting 1934 variant of the 12 saloon was the Vogue, styled by Captain Molyneaux. At £355, it cost £70 more than its conventional counterpart. Also available in 1934 was a traditionally British sports tourer 12 with two cutaway doors and pneumatic upholstery, priced at £285.

After World War II, Humbers were assembled at Ryton-on-Dunsmore, near Coventry. The first postwar cars, near duplicates of pre-war types, appeared before the end of 1945. They included the new 1,944cc Hawk four saloon, enlarged to 2,267cc in 1950 and continuing until 1967. These engines were used in Sunbeams which had become part of the Rootes Group in 1935. Higher in the Humber range, the postwar six engines went from 2,731cc in the 1945-8 Snipe to 4,086cc in the 1948-52 Super Snipe. The 4,086cc engine also powered the 1945-53 Pullman limousine, which was widely used in car hire, government service and by undertakers.

For 1953, the Super Snipe and the Pullman (called Imperial when without the glass partition) went over to a 4,139cc overhead valve engine that made for better performance. The Super Snipe leaf spring front suspension was replaced by the independent coil type standard on Hawks from 1948.

The long chassis sixes were discontinued in 1954, followed by the identically powered Super Snipe two years later. The name of the latter was revived for a narrower and lighter car of 2,651cc and soon of 2,965cc. As station wagons, with such appointments as folding picnic tables behind the front seat, they were popular among well-to-do American suburbanites. From 1967, under Chrysler control, the Humber badge appeared only on the Humber Sceptre, which was a mildly modified Hillman Hunter saloon and in 1975 even this was dropped for the sake of rationalization.

1953 Super Snipe six-cylinder; 4,139cc; 113bhp @ 3400rpm; four-speed gearbox; 93mph; 16mpg.

Hupmobile

1923 **Tourer** four-cylinder; 2,998cc; SV; 55mph giving 17mpg.

The Hupmobile two-seater runabout made its bow in Detroit in 1908, just before the Model T Ford. Both were light four-cylinder vehicles of similar engine capacity, 2.8 litres for Hupmobile, 2.9 for Ford, each developing 20bhp. The Hupmobile however, had a two-speed sliding-gear transmission instead of Ford's planetary type, and at $750 was $100 cheaper. Ford's wheelbase was 8ft 4in against Hupmobile's 7ft 2in and it weighed 1200lbs against Hupmobile's 1100. At first, Robert C. and Louis Hupp marketed the runabout as a second car or as an inexpensive sporting conveyance. In 1911, however, Hupmobile began a long family tradition, with a touring car on a 9ft wheelbase, priced at $900 and equipped with three forward speeds.

Later fours, in the usual range of body types, attracted a large and loyal following among a clientele similar to Dodge's—one which valued

1931 **Century 8** eight-cylinder in a variety of sizes developing up to 100bhp; freewheel incorporated in transmission.

reliability above show. (Incidentally, Hupmobile adopted steel bodies in 1913, two years before Dodge.) The last Hupmobile fours, of 1925, were recognizable as descendants of models dating back a decade, and they still had two-wheel brakes.

In 1925, a straight eight of more modern appearance was introduced, followed by a six in 1926. For 1928, Hupmobile's last notably successful year, both were restyled as the Century Six and Eight. The New Century series of 1929 and later, of which the 1931 saloon is typical, included strikingly smart open and convertible types; these are rare, representing only a small percentage of the firm's rapidly declining output. It proved not to need the Cleveland, Ohio, plant acquired in 1929 when the Chandler car ceased production.

The Aerodynamic series unveiled in 1934, which the public perceived as freakish rather than advanced, failed to lift Hupmobile out of its mid-Depression slough of fewer than 10,000 units annually. No cars were made for several months from mid-1936, and the overweight and even more bulbous 1938s and 1939s were hardly come-back material. No more real Hupmobiles were built after May 1939.

Then, just when things seemed darkest, they became darker still when Hupmobile entered into an odd arrangement with the similarly floundering Graham organization. Both firms were to build, in the Graham factory at Dearborn, Michigan, rear-drive sixes using body dies of the defunct Cord, though Hupmobile would supply its own chassis and 101bhp engine. The Hupmobile Skylark and the Graham Hollywood were almost identical with the Cord 812 from the scuttle rearward. In front they were stubbier, with conventional teardrop headlamps. Both the Graham and Hupmobile offerings, at $1,250 and $895 respectively for saloons, lacked the Cord's finesse. Most of the flood of orders based on advance publicity were never filled; capital ran out, and the Cord dies were unsuitable for mass production. Hupmobile gave up in July 1940 after making only 354 Skylarks. Two months later, the last of 1,859 Graham Hollywoods staggered off the line.

1935 Sedan eight-cylinder; 4,968cc; 121bhp @ 3500rpm; over 75mph.

Invicta

Invictas are best known for the superb S series $4\frac{1}{2}$-litre cars, though they account for only 77 of a total production of approximately 1,000. In 1925, shortly after Noel Campbell Macklin and the sugar magnate, Oliver Lyle, introduced the marque, the Invicta had a 2.6-litre overhead valve Meadows engine and a top speed of only 6omph, thanks to Macklin's belief in gearing a car so that it could run from a standstill to maximum speed on top gear. The 2.6-litre was replaced soon after by a bored out 3 litre version of 1926-30, which twice won the coveted Dewar Trophy on the basis of reliability.

The first of the $4\frac{1}{2}$-litre Invictas, all series of which used an ohv six-cylinder Meadows engine conservatively rated at 115bhp, was exhibited late in 1928. The N.L.C. car of 1929 was built to the highest standards and was priced accordingly at £1,050 bare and almost twice that figure with a saloon body. Soon it was joined by the less luxurious Type A.

Both the N.L.C. and the A were overshadowed by the S series that had its debut at an inauspicious time, late in 1929. Its massive sports chassis with underslung rear springs had main components of nickel chrome steel and supporting units of gunmetal. The engine, the bulkhead behind it, the sump and the transmission housing were aluminium castings. External exhaust pipes emerged from the left side of the bonnet. Beneath it, synchronized twin ignition by magneto and coil led to two rows of six spark plugs each. The four-speed Meadows transmisssion was controlled from the right of the driver with a gate change.

The performance was in keeping with such delights: zero to 6omph in 14 or 15 seconds, with a top speed in the mid-90s. The S is often referred to as the '100mph' series, a pardonable exaggeration. Its forté was not sheer speed but fast and reliable touring, so that in competition it fared better in long distance rallies than in races. In it, Donald Healey won the 1931 Monte Carlo Rally despite badly bending the car against a Norwegian telegraph pole, and finished second in 1932. Two traits detracted from the S: at high speed the engine was rough and the car

had a reputation for becoming tail-happy at speed.

Much sought after when it was in production, the S type has become a collectors' item, capable of commanding huge prices, although it sold for a modest £875 when new. The company were developing an even more desirable car to follow the S, when they ran out of cash. This would have had a 4.9 litre twin cam engine and five speed pre-selector gearbox.

Hoping to broaden the market, in 1932 Invicta introduced a model with the same 9ft 10in wheelbase and 4ft 8in track but powered by the $1\frac{1}{2}$-litre overhead camshaft Blackburne six of 45bhp—to haul 2,800lb—only 450lb less than the $4\frac{1}{2}$-litre's weight. Few were sold, and fewer still of the 1933-5 supercharged versions that developed 90 and 100bhp at the expense of reliability. Between

1933 and 1935, half a dozen Invictas were assembled in London, the Cobham plant having been taken over by Railton. Advanced series of Darracq-based 2½ and 3 litres which were announced in 1937 never went into production.

The Invicta name was revived in 1947 with the Invicta Black Prince produced at Virginia Water, Surrey and powered by a 120bhp 3-litre Meadows six with twin overhead camshaft and dual ignition. The car had little connection with the old firm, except that its designer, W. G. Watson, had worked there with Macklin. Overweight at nearly 4,000lb, expensive at £2,300 basic (£3,580 including purchase tax for a saloon and even more for a convertible coupé) and unduly complex with its hydrokinetic automatic torque converter, only about twenty were sold until they were withdrawn from the market early in 1950, when AFN Limited, makers of the Frazer Nash, took over the moribund company.

1931 4½ litre S-Type Tourer six-cylinder; 4,467cc; ohv twin ignition; four-speed gearbox; 100mph.

Isotta-Fraschini

At the turn of the century, Cesare Isotta and Vincezo Fraschini of Milan formed a partnership to import Renaults. The Isotta-Fraschini name soon made its appearance on modified Renaults with one and two cylinder engines built largely from Italian-made components. In 1902 the partners graduated to their own four-cylinder chain-driven car, a 24hp model on Mercedes lines. By 1904, there were 12hp and 16hp fours in the range too. Isottas won a number of racing events over the next few years, notably the Coppa Florio in 1907, though their first racer, a 17.2-litre behemoth built for the 1905 Coppa Florio, was notably unsuccessful. In 1909, Oreste Fraschini and Giustino Cattaneo developed one of the first successful four-wheel braking systems, optional on 1911 model cars and standard equipment in 1914. Chain drive was retained on both large and small fours

until 1913 and survived in a redoubtable 90mph overhead camshaft 10.6-litre sports car of 1914.

During World War I, the firm built advanced aircraft engines designed by Cattaneo. He applied this experience to the Tipo 8, introduced in 1919 and initiating Isotta-Fraschini's single model policy. The 5.9-litre 80bhp overhead valve engine was the first straight eight to go into series production and had an aluminium block, nine main bearings and twin carburettors. These were cars for the rich—big and elegant but not outstandingly manoeuvrable or fast. All bodies were coachbuilt and about 370 examples of this exclusive conveyance were produced between 1919 and 1925. Among the coachbuilders and designers associated with the Tipo 8 and later Isottas were Castagna, Sala, Touring of Milan, Fleetwood of Fleetwood, Pennsylvania, and Detroit, and Le Baron of New York.

The best known Isottas are the even more impressive Tipo 8A of 1925-31 of which 950 were produced. The engine, bored out to 7.4 litres, developed 120bhp at only 2,400rpm. Top speed was about 90mph in standard form and more than 100mph with the 135bhp 8ASS Spinto unit, though even this made do with a three-speed transmission. Except for the 11ft 4in Spinto chassis, the wheelbase was 12ft 1in.

Cattaneo's last Isotta, the similar 8B of 1932-5 had a redesigned engine capable of 146bhp at 3,000rpm and a stiffer frame. The Depression market for cars of such ostentatious luxury was almost non-existent, and not more than 30 8Bs had found buyers when Isotta-Fraschini merged with the Caproni aircraft firm in 1936. The streamlined V8 rear-engined Type 8C

Monterosa of 1947 failed to attain production status.

Film idol Rudolph Valentino was often photographed driving Isottas and since his death in August 1926, nearly every example of the marque in America has been identified as an ex-Valentino. Actually, he owned only two Isottas, one posthumously. The first was a formal 1925 Tipo 8 town car with body by Fleetwood. Inspired by his role in the film *Cobra*, he mounted a sculptured cobra on his Isotta and Voisin radiator caps. Soon the emblem was adopted on other Isottas in preference to the firm's winged man holding a wheel aloft. Naturally a cobra also graced the 8A Fleetwood convertible which Valentino had commissioned and helped to design but which was not delivered until after his death.

Tipo 8A straight-eight engine of 7,372cc; ohv; three-speed gearbox; vacuum servo assisted brakes; fitted with bodies by all the major international coachbuilders.

Jaguar

1934 SSI six-cylinder; 2,134cc or 2,662cc engine with side valves of Standard design; four-speed gearbox; over 75mph.

In 1922, 21-year-old William Lyons and his friend William Walmsley formed the modest but impressive-sounding Swallow Sidecar and Coach Building Co. in Blackpool, to produce comfortable motorcycle sidecars. The product, prophetically, was competitive in price as well as comfortable. Britain beat a path to the Swallow workshop door, and in 1928 the company moved to larger quarters in Coventry.

The Swallow line had already been expanded to include smart bodies for Austin Seven, Morris, Standard and other popular makes. Then in 1931 Lyons arranged for Standard to supply underslung chassis on which he mounted sleek sports bodies. 'Rakish' was the inevitable adjective, but with Standard six-cylinder engines the top speed was hardly more than 70mph.

This was the original SSI, the 'SS' standing for either Swallow Sports or Standard Special.

The 1935 successor was capable of 90mph in the open sports SS90 version, but its 2½-litre Standard engine had reached the limits of modification short of supercharging, to which Lyons never resorted, and the body the limits

of lightening. Lyons was not satisfied until Heynes and Harry Weslake had devised a 2.7-litre overhead valve six, supplemented in the late 1930s by one of 3½ litres and developing 120bhp. With this larger capacity, the sports version attained the 100mph that had long been Lyons's target. Hence the number SS100 for the car, which shared the appropriate appellation of Jaguar, first used by Lyons for the saloon of 1936. The SS100 stayed in production until World War II, during which the firm manufactured aircraft parts, despite the massive German air raids of 1940 and 1941. At the end of the war the firm sold its sidecar interests and became Jaguar Cars Limited, dropping 'SS' from its cars as well. Rapid and efficient reconversion enabled the Jaguar works to introduce the Mark IV in 1946. This post-war series of sports saloons and drophead coupés were essentially like the pre-war models, but incorporated a hypoid rear axle. Three pushrod overhead valve engines were used: a 1.8-litre four supplied by Standard and sixes of 2.7 and 3½ litres from Jaguar.

The Mark V Jaguar saloon and convertible,

1937 SS100 six-cylinder; 2,664cc; 104bhp @ 4500rpm; four-speed gearbox; 95mph and 20mpg; available later with 3½-litre engine which gave speeds of over 100mph.

introduced in 1948 with the choice of the six cylinder engines, were fitted with hydraulic brakes and independent torsion bar front suspension. But the most striking changes from the Mark IV were in the newly rounded coachwork, featuring small faired headlamps, a raked windscreen, spatted rear wheel arches, disc wheels, and a deceptive air of massiveness allied with grace.

At the London Motor Show in October 1948, Jaguar unveiled the prototype of its

1948 MkV six-cylinder push rod ohv engines; 2,664cc or 3,485cc; 102bhp or 125bhp respectively; 90mph with larger engine.

1951 XK120 six-cylinder; 3,442cc; twin ohc; 160bhp @ 5200rpm; 120mph.

XK120 sports car that revolutionized post-war motoring. Lyons himself created the dateless flowing body, which set new standards of grace and function. Early examples were open, supplemented later by drophead and fixed head coupés; all were two-seaters, as befitted the type.

The twin overhead camshaft engine was even more noteworthy. Also of $3\frac{1}{2}$ litres (3,442cc to be exact), or smaller than the contemporary Chevrolet six, it developed 160bhp and enabled the car to exceed the 120mph promised in the car's name. Heynes and Weslake were the chief designers, with the collaboration of Walter Hassan and Claude Bailey.

Even this superlative machine had shortcomings: the twelve-inch hydraulic brakes looked capable of stopping an avalanche but proved inadequate at anything

1954 XK140 six-cylinder; 3,442cc; twin ohc; 190bhp @ 5500rpm; 120mph; available as two-seater roadster, fixed or drop head coupés.

near top speed; cooling was often inadequate; gear changing was comparatively slow; seating space was cramped for tall drivers. Still, the XK120 sold as fast as it could be produced. The great majority were exported, mainly to the United States, where affluent enthusiasts were ready to graduate from the MG or to try a more impressive and 'civilized' conveyance for their initiation into the sports fraternity. Bill Lyons was well on his road to knighthood.

Even in its earliest days, in 1949, the XK120 won priceless acclaim by achieving a world record of 132.6mph for a standard production car on the Jabbeke highway in Belgium. In 1953 a modified version did 172mph at Jabbeke.

The XK120 won many a road race and rally before production ceased late in 1954, but it was the C type that lent invaluable racing prestige to the marque. The C type was specifically designed for the demanding Le Mans 24 Hours where it won in 1951 and 1953. The chassis was mainly of welded steel tubing, with all components designed for lightness consistent with strength. The front suspension was of course modified for racing, while the heart of the ingenious rear suspension was a transverse torsion bar. The winning Jaguar in the 1953 Le Mans race owed its victory to disc brakes made by Dunlop. The engine did not require radical changes and was offered in C form as an extra cost option, along with wire wheels and fog lamps, on otherwise standard cars. Only 54 C types were built.

Late in 1954 the C type was superseded by the even more potent D type with an ultra-aerodynamic body framing a chassis of both unit construction and tubular steel. It won at Le Mans in 1955, 1956, and 1957, finishing

1958 XK150S six-cylinder; 3,442cc; twin ohc; three carburettors giving 250bhp @ 5500rpm and 132mph in fixed-head form; disc brakes.

first, second, third, fourth, and sixth
in the last year.

The XK140, replacing the XK120, was
Jaguar's production sports car for 1955 to
mid-1957. The body featured a narrower but
bolder grille and subtle refinements. The
choices of weather protection remained the
same, though the convertible version had rear
seating for two small children. High-lift cams
were introduced, giving a power output of
190bhp. As before, special equipment models
were available with C type engines, giving
more than 130mph. A Borg-Warner automatic
transmission was optional on the coupés.

From mid-1957 the XK140 was succeeded
by the XK150. Five inches in the interior
width were gained by new body lines. The
grille and bonnet were widened and a curved
one-piece windscreen was adopted, along with
leather trim. The coupé bodies had two
occasional rear seats. A new standard cylinder
head, based on the C type's, produced 210bhp;
the optional special 'S' version of the 3½-litre
engine and, later, the 3.8-litre (as used in the
Mark VIII saloon) were rated up to 250bhp.

The saloons continued to account for a
major share of the firm's output. The Mark V
was phased out in 1961, following the

1959 MkIX six-cylinder; 3,781cc; 220bhp @
5500rpm; automatic gearbox; over 110mph.

introduction of the Mark VII the previous autumn. (No Mark VI was marketed.) On a chassis, little changed from the Mark Vs, was mounted an all-steel true six passenger four-door body with sliding roof, wedded to the XK120 engine to justify the slogan 'Grace . . . Space . . . Pace'. The grace was 1950s Bulbous; the space was indisputably there, for both passengers and luggage; the pace now exceeded 100mph, retarded smoothly and fairly well by hydraulic power brakes. The 190bhp high-lift cam engine became standard for 1955, followed by an optional automatic transmission that further boosted overseas sales.

The essentially similar Mark VIII followed in 1957, with a 225bhp 3.8-litre engine developed from the veteran 3½-litre power plant as standard, and with optional power steering. The Mark IX for 1959-61 offered further refinements and disc brakes.

The E type of 1961, modelled on the racing D type, is a man's car par excellence, from the profile with the top down to various other features, ranging from an interior with no space for oddments to a stubborn transmission and the need for watchful maintenance, as in keeping up with twenty-two greasing points and topping up the oil every 300 miles or so. In the early examples the performance was truly neck-snapping—zero to 60mph in six seconds, zero to 100 in eighteen. This potent motivation was furnished by a 3.8-litre engine tuned to yield 265bhp—a net figure in competition versions. Underneath was an all-independent suspension, rack-and-pinion steering and disc brakes, all eminently effective up to the maximum speed of 150mph plus. The centre of gravity was low, as it had to be on a car with a raised-top height of 4 feet, yet the road clearance was 5½ inches.

Besides the open two-seater with optional hardtop, a fixed head coupé was available. Later versions had a 4.2-litre six and a 5.4-litre V12 engine with an optional automatic transmission.

E type 4.2 six-cylinder; 4,235cc; three carburettors; 265bhp @ 5400rpm; 150mph.

Jensen

Joining the old West Bromwich coachbuilding firm of W. J. Smith & Co in 1930, Allan and Richard Jensen designed sports bodies for modified Standard, Wolseley and Ford chassis. One of the latter was ordered by Clark Gable in 1936. Soon the brothers took charge of the firm, which in 1934 became Jensen Motors. Their S series of 1937, powered by a 3.6-litre Ford V8, incorporated the American-built Columbia dual ratio rear axle as used on Auburn eights and V12s, giving six forward speeds.

The Jensen brothers modified the Ford engines by fitting English SU carburettors and magneto ignition, claiming a power output of 120bhp, which was good enough for a top speed of 85mph and fuel consumption of over 20mpg. At a price of around £700, it sold moderately well, although a cheaper version powered by the 22hp Ford V8s was not very popular.

In 1939 Jensen came up with a very fine car, the H series, which was powered by the straight eight American Nash 4.3-litre overhead valve engine. With twin ignition and nine main bearings, this was a smooth and powerful engine which could propel the saloon version at a comfortable 90mph, although at £895 it was a trifle expensive for the type of cross-bred car which was later to be known by purists as an 'Anglo-American sports bastard'.

Hardly common, but more familiar, are the Interceptor four-seater cabriolet of 1949-58 and the companion sports saloon of 1953-8, powered by a modified A135 Austin 4-litre six and capable of 95mph. Both body styles were priced at £1,700 plus purchase tax, in 1953. This tribute appeared in an advertisement for a used 1950 cabriolet (from *Motor Sport*, September 1954): 'The qualitative products of this noted stable have been sufficiently commented upon in the motoring press not to need further remarking and the cognoscenti will, no doubt, be well aware of the wealth of data already available on the subject of design and performance. There are very few remotely comparable home-produced marques of this calibre.'

In 1953 the Interceptor was joined by the lighter and even faster fibreglass bodied 541 saloon. Like the Interceptor, it was powered by the 4-litre Austin engine. The somewhat costlier 541R series of 1957-60 had four-wheel disc brakes. The last 541s, the S series of 1961-3, were equipped with Rolls-Royce Hydramatic transmissions.

Later, Jensen was to achieve world-wide fame by producing the Jensen FF, powered by the V8 Chrysler engine and using the four-wheel drive system developed by the tractor millionaire Harry Ferguson, but relatively few of these cars were produced.

541 six-cylinder; 3,993cc with ohv based on Austin Princess; four-speed gearbox with overdrive optional; 110mph.

Jordan

Edward S. Jordan became a journalist while still at Wisconsin Unversity, 'learned salesmanship with Nat. Cash Register Co', to quote his *Who's Who* biography, and worked for the Jeffrey motor company before he founded the Jordan Motor Car Company of Cleveland in 1916. His evocative advertising copy set new standards. In his 'Somewhere West of Laramie' masterpiece, the Playboy roadster was said to be 'for the lass whose face is brown with the sun when day is done of revel and romp and race'. In another ad, males could share in this 'spirited companion for a wonderful girl and a wonderful boy . . . It revels along with the wandering wind and roars like a Caproni biplane. It's a car for a man's man—that's certain. Or for a girl that loves the out-of-doors. It's true—there's some of the tang of that rare old English ale that was brewed from the smiles of youth and of old boxing-gloves.'

Both advertisements alluded to the sporty Jordan of 1922-4, beautifully proportioned externally and powered by a 5-litre Continental six. The straight eights of the middle 1920s, the most popular models, were smooth and understated. The marque had record sales of 11,000 in 1926, but the 'Little Custom' six of 1927 sold poorly at a basic price near $2,000 when an Oldsmobile, for example, was $1,200.

The 1929-30 line was flamboyant yet tasteful. The rumble seat roadster and the companion phaeton, both Murray-bodied, are coveted types, along with convertibles. Some examples were equipped with natural finish wood wheels. The 4.4-litre straight eight engine developed 85bhp and gave a top speed of 95mph. The Playboy model went out of production in 1929, by which time it had the 90bhp Continental straight eight engine and cost $2,525. It was succeeded by the Speedway Ace with a 114bhp version of the Continental engine.

Asked in a magazine survey why the 1931 line was outstanding, Ned Jordan replied 'Because it's a Jordan.' Even he could have been more specific about his swan song, the 5.3-litre straight eight 114bhp $5,000 Speedway saloon, a rare car in every respect.

Playboy straight-8 Continental engine, 4,380cc; 65bhp @ 3200rpm; 80mph.

Jowett

1951 Javelin four-cylinder horizontally opposed engine; 1,485cc; ohv giving 52.5bhp @ 4500rpm; 80mph and 27mpg.

Jowett Cars of Bradford, Yorkshire, set the world's record for the longest lived power unit; their 7bhp 'little engine with the big pull' flat-twin was first built in prototype form in 1905, and was still powering the Company's Bradford vans in the early 1950s.

Jowett's first post-war car, the four-door Javelin saloon of 1947 to 1954, was a total breakaway from the company's staid image. The flat four light alloy engine was placed far forward along with the four-speed transmission, affording maximum passenger space; suspension was independent in front, with torsion bar suspension front and rear; body and frame formed a unit; the shape was

aerodynamic, inspired by the Lincoln Zephyr; with 50bhp, the car weighed only 2,128lb and could attain 80mph.

If the Javelin was advanced, the Jupiter three-seater convertible introduced in 1950 was revolutionary, especially in its space frame chassis designed by Eberan von Eberhorst of English Racing Automobiles and formerly of Auto Union. The aluminium-bodied car weighed 1,568lb and in sports versions could exceed 90mph with its modified Javelin engine. The front wings as well as the bonnet lifted in one unit, to make the front suspension and rack and pinion steering accessible. One of the first Jupiters won its class—and set a new 1½-litre record—in the 1950 Le Mans 24 hours.

Sadly, Jowett failed in 1954, after building 30,000 Javelins and 1,200 Jupiters.

1952 Jupiter four-cylinder; 1,485cc; 63bhp @ 4750rpm; two carburettors; 88mph and 24mpg.

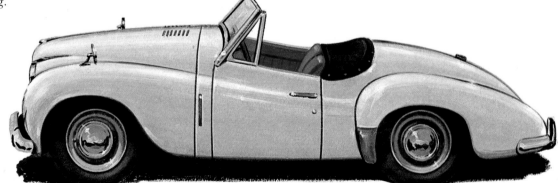

Kissel

The Kissel Kar of 1906-18 belied its childish name; during that period the Kissel Motor Co. of Hartford, Wisconsin, built sturdy, high-quality vehicles, most of them equipped with six-cylinder engines of its own manufacture, though a short-lived V12 appeared around 1914. It is best known for sport speedsters, originating with the Silver Special of 1917, which was first designed as the personal car of Conover T. Silver, the Kissel distributor in New York. The Silver Specials featured very attractive body lines, with rounded-top radiators and bullet headlamps. Three models were available—the Speedster, the Tourer and the seven-seater touring car.

Beginning with the improved 1919 version (when all Kissel Kars became just Kissels), the speedsters were called Gold Bugs, from their standard bright yellow finish. In early models, two extra passengers could be precariously accommodated on foldaway seats that could be pulled out in front of the rear bumpers. The steering wheel could be pushed upward to facilitate entry from the driver's side, which for a time lacked a door.

Much needed four-wheel brakes became standard in 1924; though these were the unsatisfactory American-type external contracting pattern. In truth, the rakish speedsters were faster in appearance than in performance, even when powered by modified Lycoming straight eights which were optional from 1924 and which superseded the Kissel-built sixes in 1928. The Lycoming was available in 3-, 4- and 4.9-litre capacities and the distinctive round-topped radiator was dropped in favour of a flat topped design. The round-top radiator had remained in production since the early Silver Special of 1917.

The final series of cars was known as the White Eagle and there was still a sporting model catalogued, the White Eagle 126 Speedster which was in production from 1929 to 1931. This was usually powered by the 4.9-litre engine, capable of 95mph.

Unfortunately, the Depression affected Kissel badly and sales plummeted from 1,071 in 1929 to a mere 16 in 1931, the year that the Kissel went out of production.

1925 Speedster straight 8; 4,712cc; SV; 75-80mph.

Lagonda

1939 LG6 Drophead Coupé six-cylinder; 4,453cc; 150bhp; redesigned chassis by W. O. Bentley with i.f. suspension; more than 95mph.

Like Herbert Austin, Wilbur Gunn of Springfield, Ohio, learnt engineering building sheep-shearing machinery. In the late 1890s Gunn settled in England and began building motorcycles in the greenhouse of his home in Staines, Middlesex. He called the machine 'Lagonda', after a creek near the Great Lakes, where he had played as a child. The first Lagonda tricar appeared in 1904, and Gunn developed his first car, a 20hp four-cylinder model, in 1906.

His reliable big sixes—one won the 1910 Moscow-St Petersburg Trial—were exported in quantity to Russia from 1910 to World War I, while the 1913 light four pioneered unit steel body and chassis construction, anti-roll bars and fly off handbrakes, and was continued for a decade.

Lagonda went for high performance with the 1,954cc 14/60 of 1926—developed into the Speed model in 1927—featuring twin camshafts set high in the block and operating the valves in hemispherical combustion chambers via long angled rockers; in 1930 a supercharger was optional. Contemporary with the fours, which were available both as open and enclosed types, was the 2.7-litre 16/65hp pushrod six.

In 1934, after production of the 2-litre fours had ceased, the highly developed

1937 LG45 six-cylinder; 4,453cc of Meadows design; 140bhp @ 3800rpm; four-speed gearbox; 95mph.

Lagonda Rapier four of only 1,104cc appeared. It was dropped the next year but was continued by Rapier Cars of London until 1940, by which time 300 had been produced.

Up for sale in 1935, Lagonda was rescued by Alan Good, a London lawyer. He continued to manufacture the impressive 4½-litre Lagondas which had been introduced in 1934, powered by a Meadows ohv engine of the type used by Invicta. Astutely, Good hired W. O. Bentley as technical director. Bentley soon modified the M45s (one of which had unexpectedly won the 1935 Le Mans). The resultant LG45 of 1936-7 had 140bhp, along with improved comfort and drivability. The LG6 of 1938-40, also with a modified Meadows 4½-litre engine, incorporated a new Bentley-designed chassis that featured independent torsion bar front suspension and adjustable hydraulic shock absorbers. Into the LG6 chassis was also fitted a V12 4½-litre ohc power unit designed by Bentley; it promised to be his masterpiece, but its performance potential had not been developed to the full when World War II halted all car production. Even so, V12 Rapides were third and fourth in the 1939 Le Mans 24 Hour race after Bugatti and Delage.

During the war, Lagonda was employed in a variety of military projects, including conversion of the V12 engine for use in patrol craft. The first post-war cars, powered by a Bentley-designed 2.6-litre twin overhead camshaft six, came into full production in 1948 after David Brown had acquired Aston Martin and Lagonda and transferred the manufacture of both marques to Newport Pagnell. This engine also powered the early DB Aston Martins, which offered out and out sporting qualities compared with Lagonda's fast but luxurious cruising. The restyled 3-litre Lagonda of 1954-8 retained the 2.6's cruciform frame and all independent suspension.

The last production Lagonda until the announcement of the futuristic 1977 model was the four door Rapide saloon of 1961-3, introduced after a three-year hiatus. Using an Aston Martin DB5 engine of 3,996cc, it was rated at 236bhp and advertised as being capable of 125mph. It had four-wheel disc brakes, independent front suspension and a De Dion back axle. At a basic price of £3,600 to £3,800, production was limited.

1957 3-litre Drophead Coupé six-cylinder; 2,922cc; ohc; 140bhp @ 5000rpm; independent suspension all round; 100mph.

Lanchester

Frederick W. Lanchester (1868-1946) of Birmingham made contributions to aeronautical theory before the Wrights left the ground. Also outside the automotive field, he was a poet, musicologist, and radio manufacturer. His prototype car, an air-cooled single cylinder model constructed in 1895, was the first in the world not influenced by stationary engine practice. Production Lanchesters of 1900-1903 had engines with two air-cooled cylinders, each with its own crankshaft and flywheel assembly for smooth running, mounted amidships. A single valve per cylinder served for both intake and exhaust. The three speed final drive was via worm gear. The first water-cooled series appeared in 1902 and the first four, of only 2½ litres, in 1904. From that year, nearly all Lanchesters had overhead valves instead of the old combined inlet/exhaust valve. When F. W. Lanchester left the firm in the charge of his brother George in 1912, the cars were fours and sixes of relatively conventional appearance, except that the engine's location beside the front seat gave a stubby effect. Two years later, George's sporting L-head Model Forty with six cylinder engine had an orthodox bonnet.

The Lanchester's most glorious decade was the 1920s. The impressive overhead cam 6.2-litre Forty of 1919-28 was favoured by the Duke of York, later King George VI. The equally exclusive Twenty-One, originally of 3.1 and later of 3.3 litres, was marketed from 1923 to 1931. The advanced 4.4-litre straight eight Thirty and an ohv Forty appeared in 1928.

The British Small Arms company, which had owned Daimler since 1910, acquired Lanchester in 1931 and moved its operations to Coventry. Soon, most Lanchesters were in effect junior Daimlers—ohv fours and sixes of 1.3 to 2½ litres. From 1946, beginning with the 1.3-litre four cylinder Ten saloon, only the grille retained a vestigial resemblance to the old line. In 1951 came the somewhat smartened 2-litre Fourteen four cylinder saloon with torsion bar independent front suspension, automatic chassis lubrication, and the traditional Daimler preselector transmission with fluid flywheel. Variants of 1952 were the Vega export saloon and a four seater convertible coupé, both with all steel bodies. None of them sold well, and the last production Lanchester, the 1.6-litre Sprite, appeared in 1956.

1952 Convertible four-cylinder; 1,968cc; ohv; 60bhp @ 4200rpm; pre-selector gearbox; hydraulic operation of hood mechanism.

Lancia

Vincenzo Lancia of Turin switched from accountancy to cars in 1898, at seventeen. Within two years he had become chief inspector and star racing driver for the newly formed F.I.A.T. company. In 1906 he founded his own firm in Turin, and the 2½-litre bi-block Lancia Alfa made its debut in 1907. The marque made rapid progress in the Greek alphabet with the monobloc 3.1-litre Beta, 3.5-litre Gamma, 1.4-litre Delta (also built as the Di-Delta), 4.1-litre Epsilon and Zeta and 5.1-litre-Eta fours of 1909-13. The lance and flag emblem designed by Count Carlo Biscaretti di Ruffia in 1911 has continued as an identifying symbol for Lancia through many changes in appearance.

In late 1913, the Eta was replaced by the 4,951cc Theta, the first European car with a standard electric lighting and starting set: 1,696 were sold.

The end of hostilities saw a short-lived narrow angle 6-litre V12, but the first post-war production model was the Kappa, a development of the Theta. The faster and smarter overhead valve Dikappa of 1921 was joined by the 1922 Trikappa, powered by Vincenzo Lancia's first V8, a 4-litre overhead valve unit cast in a single block.

Vincenzo's masterpiece, the Lambda, was running in 1921, on exhibition in 1922 and on sale in 1923. It had a production run of 13,000 in nine series up to 1931. One of the most innovative cars of all time, it combined the narrow angle V4 engine, unitary body and frame construction, and independent front suspension with sliding pillars enclosing coil springs. Though not intended as sports cars, the open models have always been driven as such because of their exemplary handling. Starting at 2.1 litres and 71mph, volume and performance increased in stages to 2.6 litres and 80mph. To accommodate coachbuilt bodies, a separate chassis was available from 1927, as were wheelbases longer than the original 10ft 2in.

The Dilambda of 1929-33 differed in concept. It was a larger and heavier luxury car. A hypoid rear axle enabled the separate frame to be lowered. The greatest contrast was in the engine, which was a 4.1-litre 100bhp V8. Starting in the early 1930s, Lancias were named after the highways of Imperial Rome. The Astura V8, first of 2.6 and then of 3 litres, headed the Lancia line from 1931 to 1940. Besides the factory built saloon bodies, many handsome creations, both formal and sporting, graced its long chassis.

The more utilitarian Augusta of 1932-7

1925 Lambda four-cylinder; 2,120cc; independent front-wheel suspension and unusual chassis construction made this a fore-runner of modern design.

was a lightweight four-door saloon with a V4 engine, unitary all steel construction, and four wheel hydraulic brakes.

Vincenzo Lancia's last car, the innovative Aprilia of 1937-50, appeared a few weeks after his death. Its aluminium V4 engine, of 1.35 and, from 1939, 1½ litres, with chain driven overhead camshaft, gave a top speed of 80mph. The rear as well as the front wheels had independent suspension. The attractively streamlined four-door saloon dispensed with centre pillars. Spyders (sports roadsters) by Zagato were also available.

The first all-new post-war Lancia, the Aurelia of 1950-9, was worthy of the founder. Designed by Vincenzo's son Gianni and Vittorio Jano, this 60 degree V6 had a longer wheelbase and a simpler rear suspension than the Aprilia's. The engine was also simpler, with overhead valves actuated by pushrods. Starting at 1.8 litres and 56bhp, it was soon offered with 2 litres and 70bhp. The latter version, modified to give 80bhp, powered the Pininfarina-bodied Aurelia B20 GT coupé. The B24 Aurelias of 2½ litres followed in the mid-1950s. A B20 finished second in the 1951 Mille Miglia, first in their class in the 1951 and 1952 Le Mans race, and first in the 1952 Targa Florio and the 1954 Monte Carlo Rally.

Encouraged by such victories, Gianni Lancia and Jano embarked on an ambitious racing programme, using the D23 3-litre sports/racer, derived from the Aurelia, and its successor, the D24 3.3-litre; Jano also developed the D50 2½-litre V8 GP car. The effort brought considerable glory—1-2-3 in the Carrera Panamericana of 1953, first in the Targa Florio and Mille Miglia of 1954—but racing costs were so high that the firm was nearly bankrupted. Control passed to the Pesenti cement interests, the GP cars were sold to Ferrari, and Gianni Lancia resigned in 1956.

The Aurelia was joined by the 2½-litre and 2.8-litre V6 Flaminia of 1957-70 with coil spring front suspension by Antonio Fessia. His Flavia of the 1960s, derived from his 1948 CEMSA-Caproni, had a flat four engine and front wheel drive, with transverse leaf springing in front and a live axle at the rear on semi-elliptic leaf springs. Output was raised from 1½ to 1.8 litres and then to 2 litres. Both the Flaminia and the Flavia appeared with distinguished bodies by Pininfarina and Zagato.

In 1969, control of Lancia passed to Fiat.

1952 Aurelia six-cylinder; 1,991cc; two carburettors; 74bhp @ 5000rpm; independent suspension; 100mph.

La Salle

1927 V8; 4,967cc; three-speed gearbox; 80mph.

The first La Salle, Cadillac's junior marque launched in 1927, was not designed by a committee; its body was the creation of General Motors' young stylist Harley Earl under the inspiration of Hispano-Suiza. La Salle equalled Cadillac in quality and was far smarter until the senior line emulated its offspring in 1928. Until 1933, prices were gradually lowered from $2,650 to $2,245, a few hundred dollars less than the similarly powered Cadillac V8s. From 1931 to 1933 they shared a 115bhp 5.8 litre engine.

In 1934, everything about La Salle changed except its name. The Depression years forced economies and the car lost its quality. The engine was now an Oldsmobile-type straight eight of 4 litres and 90bhp; the wheelbase shrank from 130 or 136 to 119 inches, the weight from 4,855 to 3,995 pounds, and the basic price to $1,595. The new body, by Jules Agramonte and Earl, was successful in its own right but lost all identification with Cadillac, featuring a tall, narrow grille backed by a row of holes on the bonnet. It was the first GM car with a solid steel roof.

The 1937 model marked a return to a powerful V8, this time of 5.3 litres and 123 bhp. The vertical grille was retained, but the styling once more gave the image of scaled down luxury rather than what it actually was —an upgrading of an Olds-Buick body shell. Subsequent La Salles were even better, but they were discontinued in 1940, crowded out by Cadillac and Buick.

1940 V8; 5,277cc; 125bhp @ 3400rpm; 90mph.

Lincoln

After guiding Cadillac to greatness in 1917, the perfectionist Henry M. Leland and his son Wilfred founded the Lincoln Motor Company in Detroit. For the next two years they built the V12 Liberty aircraft engine. Left with a plant without a product after World War I, Leland resolved to build America's finest car. He named it after Abraham Lincoln, for whom he had cast his vote back in 1864. Because of delays in factory conversion, the Lincoln, a 5.8-litre V8 with full pressure lubrication, did not appear until late in 1920. By that time, the post-war deflation had shrunk the market for a car priced at $4,300 for a touring car and $6,000 for a four door saloon. Also, the government was demanding from the firm more than $5.7 million in taxes which it claimed were due on wartime profits. In February 1933 Henry Ford bought the bankrupt firm for $8 million and later paid suppliers' bills totalling $4 million. The Lelands, still nominally in charge, could not agree with Ford's policies and were evicted in June. They had received only $369,000 for their shares.

The Lincoln of 1920-1930, the Model L, was powered by a side valve V8 angled at 60 degrees. The original engine capacity of 5.8 litres was increased in 1928 to 6.3 litres, when power went up from 81 to 90bhp. A top speed of more than 70mph with no loss in dignity was more than adequate for the time.

Early Lincoln coachwork was stodgy and ponderous. The production bodies' styling improved under Edsel Ford, to whom his father gave free rein at Lincoln. Naturally, coachbuilt examples are the most highly prized. Such firms as Locke, Le Baron, Judkins, Waterhouse, Brunn, and Willoughby created unique designs, many of which were duplicated in fair numbers at the plant or by outside coachbuilders. For a styling refinement, the famous greyhound radiator ornament became available in 1925.

The series K for 1931 carried on with the 6.3 litre engine. Various refinements increased the power rating to 120bhp. The then fashionable freewheel was incorporated. More importantly, the wheelbase was increased from 11ft 4in to 12ft 1in, giving more scope for coachbuilt designs.

For 1932, all Lincolns had vacuum-assisted brakes. The old 'short' wheelbase was used for the KA series, the last of the V8s. Reflecting the Depression, standard-bodied KAs were priced as low as $3,200 against $4,700 for the longer but otherwise similar Ks of 1931. Like most other American luxury marques of the time, Lincoln also introduced a V12. The 7.4-litre L-head unit of this KB series, angled

1932 KB Sedan V12; 7,238cc; 150bhp; three-speed gearbox; 100mph.

1936 Zephyr V12; 4,378cc; 110bhp @
3900rpm; 90mph and 17mpg.

at 65 degrees and equipped with aluminium
cylinder heads, developed 150bhp and gave a
top gear range of 2 to 98mph—remarkable
for a car weighing about 6,000lb. Standard-
bodied saloons listing at around $4,600 hardly
did justice to the engineering they concealed.

The KB continued essentially unchanged for
1933 except for a raked grille. That year
marked the introduction of a 6.3-litre, 67
degree V12 engine, still an L-head, that was
used on the 11ft 4in wheelbase KA series.
Increased to 6.8 litres for 1934, it powered
both the KA (short) and KB (long) series
from then on. Although its power and
performance equalled the 1932-3 KBs',
cost cutting design features represented a departure
from H. M. Leland's standards.

Even with such deviation from perfection,
Lincoln ranked fairly well in quality with
its American competitors. Always conservative,
the cars changed only slightly and gradually:
engine and passengers were moved forward in
1935, and two years later came wing-mounted
headlamps and superior streamlining.

The big Lincolns nearly always lost money
for Ford, and production never exceeded 9,000
in any year. By the late 1930s, hardly any
could be sold at $5,000 and more, and the
line ended in 1940. Foreseeing that a medium-

priced car would be needed to keep the
Lincoln name alive, as early as 1933 Edsel
Ford engaged John Tjaarda to modify a
rear-engined streamliner he had designed for
the Briggs body firm. With additional design
work by Eugene T. Gregorie, the new car,
the world's first medium-priced V12, was
ready for the 1936 model year. The flowing
unit construction body—expensive to repair
when rusted—featured integrated headlights
and an alligator bonnet. The shape, especially
that of subsequent three-window coupés (only
saloons were made at first), won wide acclaim.
Not so the 4.4-litre, 110bhp engine (later of
4.8 litres and 120bhp), a hastily conceived
unit prone to breakdowns.

The original Lincoln Continental was based
on standard Zephyr mechanical components,
including the 4.8-litre V12. When Edsel Ford
outlined to Gregorie what he wanted in a
personal car for use in Florida, the designer
developed a prototype, completed in March
1939. It drew such favourable attention that
Ford was encouraged to have the design
modified for limited production. From
October 1939 through the 1940 model year,
425 cabriolets (convertibles) and 54 coupés
appeared as special edition Zephyrs. Then,
with improved suspension and many

1941 **Continental** V12; 4,378cc; 120bhp @ 3600rpm; wide range of power-operated operations included in specification.

refinements, the new cars were marketed as Continentals, starting in the 1941 model year. The 1940-41s are more pleasing aesthetically than the heavier looking chrome-fronted 1942 and 1946-8 series. Total production was 5,322.

The V8s that succeeded the Continental—Mercury-bodied Lincolns and ponderous Cosmopolitans—were not material for legend.

The Continental Mark II of 1954-7 is a different proposition. Priced at $8,800 without air conditioning, it was avowedly a 'modern formal' Classic. William Clay Ford, Edsel's youngest son, was in charge of the project, and John M. Rinehart was chief stylist. The 6-litre engine was the same as in the $4,500 class Premiers, re-assembled and tested, but most other components were unique.

1955 **Continental MkII** V8; 6,075cc; 285bhp @ 4000rpm; three-speed gearbox; automatic transmission; 115mph.

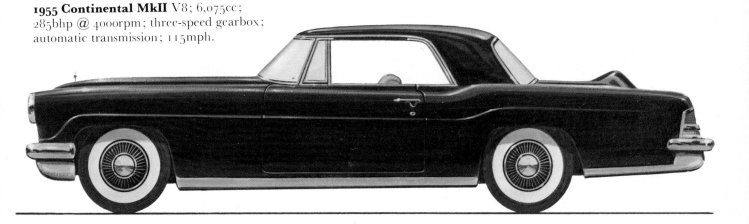

Locomobile

After building about 5,000 steam buggies between 1899 and 1903, Locomobile sold back their patent rights to the Stanley brothers—creators of the original design—and turned to the manufacture of high-quality petrol-engined cars in Bridgeport, Connecticut. These creations of Andrew L. Riker, with inspiration from Panhard, appeared in several sizes. They were among the first in America to use a front-mounted vertical four-cylinder engine, heat-treated steel alloys, a cellular radiator, and (from 1905) a four-speed gearbox. The legendary 'Number 16' of 1906, whose 16.2-litre engine had nearly three times the capacity of the largest standard model, won the 1908 Vanderbilt Cup.

Chain drive was succeeded by shaft drive in 1909, and 1911 marked the début of Riker's durable masterpiece, the Model 48, first selling for $4,800 and nearly trebling that figure by 1929. This massive six-cylinder T-head, first of 8 and then 8½ litres, had cylinders cast in three pairs. The crankcase and transmission case were of bronze. Even the factory bodies, in a comprehensive range of types, were in effect custom built. The Gunboat and Sportif styles were lower-built on the standard 11ft 10in wheelbase than other 48s, which were designed to appeal to the conservative rather than to the sporty rich typified by the proud Sportif owner Sidney Smith, creator of the 'Andy Gump' comic strip.

In 1922 Locomobile, having survived financial troubles which forced a merger with Crane-Simplex and Mercer in 1920, became the prestige marque of W. C. Durant's motor empire, which was just beginning its meteoric rise, but due to end in total collapse within a decade. Under his regime, the 6-litre L-head Model 90, in other respects very like the 48, was introduced in 1924, followed by the conventional 3½-litre Junior Eight of 1925-7. When the factory closed in the spring of 1929, only the redoubtable 48 and the 4.9 litre Lycoming-powered Model 88 straight eight were still in production. The 48 was available with a choice of no less than five body styles but the ageing design had lost its appeal, especially at its list price of $12,500 which was a great deal of money in the early days of the Depression.

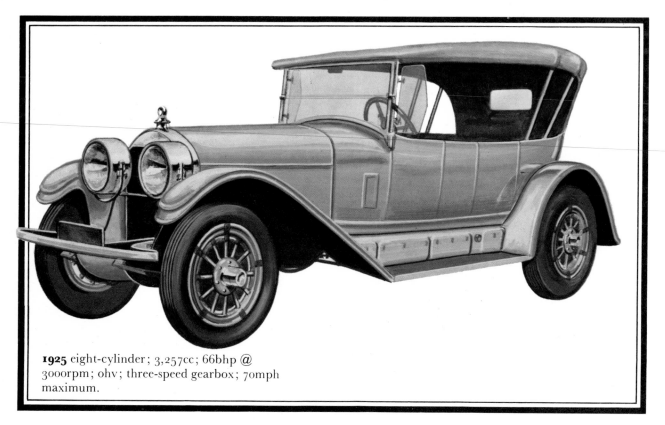

1925 eight-cylinder; 3,257cc; 66bhp @ 3000rpm; ohv; three-speed gearbox; 70mph maximum.

Lotus

1959 Elite four cylinder; 1,216cc; ohc;
75bhp @ 6100rpm; independent suspension;
114mph and 34mpg.

Colin Chapman, himself a racing driver, designed and built lightweight competition cars during the early 1950s at a small factory in London. His first production model, the open two-seater Mark 6 of 1953-5 was powered by a variety of engines, including the 1,172cc side valve Ford 10 Anglia Prefect unit. Like all Lotus's of the period, it had a minimal aluminium body and an ingenious space frame of small diameter tubing that kept the total weight to under 750lb.

After a two year interval, the Mark 6 was succeeded by the similar Seven. With the Ford 100E side valve engine, in 1957 it cost £1,036 including purchase tax, but was more commonly sold in kit form at £526. The purchaser-assembler earned the difference, since the components came in a big pile and frequently needed to be modified, while by law no instructions could be furnished. Once assembled correctly, the finished car gratified many a hardy young enthusiast with its incredible acceleration and handling. From 1961 into the 1970s, various overhead valve engines from Coventry-Climax and Ford were installed, the larger ones boosting the original top speed of about 80 to over 100mph. Many young racing drivers cut their teeth on the Lotus 7.

Moving to larger quarters in Cheshunt, Hertfordshire in 1959, Lotus put the 1956-designed Elite into production at last. This sleekly streamlined two seater coupé was in marked contrast to the Seven. Its body and chassis were of fibreglass reinforced plastics into which the few steel members were bonded; most stress points had thicker fibreglass but the steel components tended to work loose. Suspension was independent all round by Chapman struts. In kit form, it listed at £1,299 in 1961. The Coventry-Climax engine, of only 1,216cc, wafted this 1,400lb car to more than 110mph in standard form, and tuned versions excelled in Grand Touring events. Production ceased in 1963, after a total run of 988.

Later Lotus's included the Elan coupé and convertible of 1964-73 with steel backbone, the Lotus Cortina of 1965-6, the radically bodied Europa of 1966, and many racing types, notably the 1962 Lotus 25, the first Grand Prix car with a stressed-skin hull. The Lotus 38, piloted by Jim Clark, won the 1965 Indianapolis 500, and the Lotus 49, with the then new Ford-Cosworth DFV engine, won its first ever GP race, again driven by Jim Clark, at Zandvoort in 1967.

Marmon

Unlike many early cars, the Marmon did not represent a changeover from carriages or bicycles but supplemented the milling machinery that Nordyke and Marmon of Indianapolis had been making since 1851. As a member of a partner's family, mechanical engineer Howard Marmon had a free hand and ample funds for experimentation. His first prototype car, of 1902, was an air-cooled V2 with pressure-fed engine lubrication, a planetary transmission, and two three-suspension-point frames, one for the engine and transmission and the other for the body. The first Marmons to be marketed, the Models B, C, D and F V4s of 1904-7, continued these features and were also notable for an extensive use of aluminium in body components. Sales were modest: only 25 Marmons were built in 1905.

The model 32 of 1908-15, in a somewhat higher price bracket, was comparatively conventional. The engine was an in-line T-head four cylinder cast in pairs with detachable cylinder heads; the transmission was of the sliding gear type; water cooling was used

exclusively from 1909 after being offered as an option in 1908; and the double frame was discontinued. Aluminium was used for the crankcase and sump as well as in the body. A pioneering V8 Model 60 of 1907 was abortive commercially. Sales of the fours, however, shot up, following the many racing successes of special sixes based on the 32, most notably the narrow single-seater 'Wasp's' victory at the first Indianapolis 500 in 1911.

For his creative achievements in 1913 Howard Marmon became the only American ever to become an honorary member of the British Society of Automotive Engineers.

The 5.5-litre overhead valve six cylinder Model 34 of 1916-23 is the archetypal Marmon, even though much of the design was the work of Fred Moscovics and Alanson P. Brush. Thanks to a light frame and a lavish use of aluminium, it weighed far less than its competitors in the luxury field. Its more conventional successors, the Series 74 and 75 sixes of 1924-7, had a cast-iron engine block (already adopted for the 34 in 1920) and a heavier frame, while the bodies were less

1921 Model 34 six-cylinder; 4,945cc; ohv; 74bhp @ 2450rpm.

rounded and less distinctive. They incorporated such mid-1920s features as balloon tyres, four wheel brakes, and a belt line around the body.

With Howard Marmon relegated to the background, management of the renamed Marmon Motor Car Co. introduced a Little Marmon 3-litre straight eight in 1927 and went over to that engine type entirely in 1928, in a wide range of capacity classes. In 1929 a light car, the L-head Roosevelt (priced at $995) was the first straight eight ever offered for under $1,000. It was continued as the Marmon Model R in 1930, along with the L-head 3-litre Model 69 and two big four-speed overhead valve models of 4.9 and 5.2 litres. All these cars were worthy but not outstanding in their respective classes, which robbed the marque of its prestigious image.

The foundering company regained prestige but not profit with the aluminium block Marmon V16 of 1931, which Howard Marmon had been developing almost in secret for five years. This masterpiece ranks high among American classics. With superb styling by Walter Dorwin Teague Senior and Junior as executed by Le Baron, it surpassed even the Cadillac V16 in the rarified $5,000 market. Although the massive chassis frame and leaf spring suspension were not exceptional, the engine was a huge 8-litre V16 unit made entirely from aluminium apart from the wet liners. A power output of 200bhp at 3,400rpm was claimed and, even with the weight of steel saloon bodies, the car could do 105mph on the highest of its three gears. With its 12ft 1in wheelbase and total weight approaching 5,000lb it could still accelerate rapidly and was the only real challenger to the Duesenberg. It was originally designed to sell for $4,775 but, by the time production was under way, the price had risen $1,000.

Unfortunately, the Marmon was not ready for a full year after its G.M. counterpart, whose own sales plunged precipitously as the Depression deepened. Of the Marmon V16's total production of 850 before the firm went into bankruptcy in 1933, only about sixty survive.

1931 V16 sixteen-cylinder in two banks of eight; 9,100cc; ohv; 200bhp @ 3400rpm; servo-assisted brakes.

Maserati

Alfieri Maserati was one of six brothers, the others being Bindo, Carlo, Ernesto, Ettore and Mario. Alfieri established a tuning workshop in Bologna, Italy, in 1914, after working with Isotta-Fraschini. Carlo, the eldest brother, had died in 1910 after working for Fiat, Bianchi and Junior, Mario became an artist and Ettore and Bindo joined Alfieri during World War I to manufacture spark plugs. In 1922 Alfieri built a special racing car using one bank of cylinders from an Hispaño-Suiza V8 aero engine, then became closely involved with Diatto, first developing a racing 3-litre, then working on two blown straight eights. When Diatto withdrew from racing in 1926, the *fratelli* Maserati took over the straight eights, reducing their swept volume to $1\frac{1}{2}$ litres to comply with the current regulations. The emblem of the new Maserati was the trident of the city of Bologna. This first Maserati racing car, driven by Alfieri, led the $1\frac{1}{2}$-litre class in the 1926 Targa Florio, and more cars were built for private owners. In 1929 came the 16-cylinder 4-litre Tipo V4, with two straight eight blocks mounted in parallel, with the crankshafts geared together. Alfieri died in 1932 and Ernesto, the youngest Maserati, took over. Six years later the three surviving brothers sold the enterprise to an industrial combine headed by Adolfo Orsi and his enthusiast son Omer, who moved operations to a plant in Modena. The Maseratis stayed on as designers, and their 8CTF, a supercharged 3-litre V8, won the 1939 and 1940 Indianapolis 500 mile race for Wilbur Shaw.

The Maseratis returned to Bologna in 1947 and founded the Osca concern, whose racing and sports cars gained prominence during the next two decades. Their last design for Orsi was the $1\frac{1}{2}$-litre A6G sports car of 1947. Aided by light weight—2,100 to 2,300lb—and an ingenious coil spring suspension, its $1\frac{1}{2}$-litre overhead cam, six cylinder engine of only 65bhp propelled it to 100mph. With a 100bhp 2-litre engine available from 1948, the streamlined coupés were faster still. The 2-litre open A6GCS of 1954, developed by Gioacchino Colombo, weighed only 1,540lb. With three carburettors and double overhead camshafts it developed 160bhp at 7,000rpm. The Pininfarina coupé is the 'commonest' type from a time when Maserati production was under 100 cars a year.

The $2\frac{1}{2}$-litre Formula 1 Type 250 single seater, derived from the A6GCM with a space frame chassis and De Dion back axle, won many events following its début in 1954, culminating three years later in the Constructors' Championship for Maserati and the Drivers' Championship for Juan Fangio. A 420bhp $4\frac{1}{2}$-litre V8 sports/racing

1952 A6 six-cylinder; 1,488cc; ohc; 65bhp @ 4700rpm; over 90mph.

car, for which Omer Orsi had high hopes, won at Sebring, Florida, and the Swedish GP in 1957, but it generally failed or crashed elsewhere. Discouraged, Orsi withdrew from factory sponsored racing and concentrated on Grand Touring instead of racing cars. For a time, private owners could compete, often successfully, in Types 60 and 61, 2-litre and 2.8-litre four cylinder cars dubbed 'Birdcage Maseratis' from their chassis, which were built from hundreds of small diameter tubes.

The 3500 GT of 1958-66 became so popular that the factory were building 20 cars a month. This straight six was available as a coupé or a convertible. The 3½-litre twin overhead camshaft engine was rated from 230 to 260hp, and the top speed was about 145mph. Triple carburettors were soon superseded by Lucas fuel injection, which raised power output to 270bhp. The chassis was of stout tubing, with coil springs in front and underslung semi-elliptics at the rear.

The 1959-64 500 GT V8 of 4.9 litres, with a claimed 170mph, and the 4.1-litre Quattroporte (four door) saloon of 1964-70, a V8 rated at 260bhp and 145mph, rank with the 3500 GT as collectors' items, despite the Quattroporte's rather pedestrian bodywork.

With their enforced absence from the racetracks because of financial problems, Maserati turned to building rather mundane if exotically styled touring cars, although the Sebring and Mistrale are now becoming sought after, largely because of their handsome coachwork.

The Ghibli model and the later, similar Indy, were breathtakingly styled and were capable of 170mph, but their rigid rear axles meant that their handling and steering left a lot to be desired.

More financial troubles led to a takeover by Citroën of France, who introduced the Citroën-Maserati and fitted a number of Citroën features into the cars, such as a 3-litre V6 engine, and the Citroën power braking and steering systems. These cars were not a great success, although the brutish looking mid-engined Bora, capable of 175mph, was favoured by wealthy enthusiasts for a while.

Citroën's own financial troubles caused them to withdraw from the firm, allowing the de Tomaso firm to take over and begin the rebuilding of the company fortunes.

1959 GT 3500 six-cylinder; 3,485cc; twin ohc; five-speed gearbox; fuel injection optional when 235bph was developed; with carburettors 220bhp @ 5800rpm.

Mercedes-Benz

It was an Austrian Consul who gave his daughter's Spanish Christian name to a German car to help its sales in France, and thereby created one of the great marques in motoring history—the Mercedes. Consul Emil Jellinek was the moving spirit behind the development of a new high performance model to replace the fast but dangerous Phönix-Daimler 24hp and, by agreeing to buy the first production series of the new 1900 model, was able to dictate that it be called Mercedes after one of his daughters (he also persuaded Austrian Daimler to produce a car called the Maja after daughter number two, but that failed to catch on).

Designed by Wilhelm Maybach, the Mercedes was 'the car of the day after tomorrow' to its contemporaries, for it combined all the most up-to-date features— channel steel chassis, gate gear change, honeycomb radiator, mechanically operated inlet valves—with a long low look that was to set the pattern for car design for many years to come. After a poor showing in the Pau automobile meeting in February 1901, the new model swept the board at the Nice Automobile Meeting in March that year. For the first time a car that was strongly built, faster than existing racing cars, with impeccable roadholding, steering and suspension, could also be used as a comfortable touring carriage: it was a revolutionary concept.

'We've entered the Mercedes era!' wrote a contemporary French journalist, and suddenly all other cars were old fashioned overnight.

The Mercedes became *the* car for the very wealthy, its name kept prominently in the public eye by competition success—victory in the 1903 Gordon Bennett Cup race, the 1908 Grand Prix, the 1914 Grand Prix—and by the outbreak of the First World War, the company was also prominent in aero engine manufacture. In fact, the Mercedes cars that formed the winning team in the 1914 Grand Prix had power units that owed more to aviation practice than to the company's road-going engines.

As early as 1915, Mercedes had begun experimenting with supercharging on its aero engines, using two-bladed Roots blowers and, after the war, the company began trials of a

1928 SSK six-cylinder; 7,020cc; ohc; supercharged; 200bhp.

supercharged car engine, at first using a sleeve-valve 10/30hp unit. This was successful enough to encourage them to persist, and the poppet-valve 6/25hp and 10/40hp models became, in 1921, the first ever supercharged cars offered as a standard model to the public.

It was a remarkably bold venture, especially since, at that period, tyres were only available through the black market in Germany, and what little fuel there was available had generally been 'acquired' from military dumps. Like the subsequent Mercedes superchargers, that pioneer installation didn't function all the time, but was clutched in when additional power was needed by flooring the throttle pedal, producing a Stuka-like howl as well as the extra horsepower.

Paul Daimler, whose idea the supercharged car had been, retired in 1922; his replacement as chief engineer was Dr Ferdinand Porsche, who had been working at the Austrian Daimler plant at Wiener Neustadt. The first new models to appear during Porsche's tenure of office were two supercharged six cylinder sports

models, the 4-litre 15/70/100 and the 6-litre 24/100/140. Mercedes described these cars as the 'Stradivarius of the road' but they were, in fact, rather ponderous vehicles—the 24/100/140 scaled 47cwt with a Weymann saloon

1937 540K eight cylinder; 5,401cc; supercharged; 180bhp; 110mph giving 10-12mpg; wide choice of body styles.

body, in which form it had a top speed with the blower engaged of just under 75mph. The problem was that on such vehicles the supercharger was of little practical use. The *Brooklands Gazette* tested a blown Mercedes in 1925, and discovered a major shortcoming in its design: 'To get the best results from the engine, one must get up to a fairly high speed in third gear, then change into top and allow the car to pick up speed still further before the supercharger is brought into engagement. In these conditions the benefits are apparent at once, but otherwise the engine is handicapped by having to work the blower, which is not working fast enough to exact any useful pressure on the carburettor.'

In 1924, towards the end of the shocking inflation that had brought Weimar Germany to a state of virtual collapse, Mercedes entered into an 'association of common interest' with Benz, followed by a complete amalgamation between the Daimler-Motoren-Gesellschaft and Benz & Cie in June 1926. The products of the new group were to be known as 'Mercedes-Benz' and their radiators carried the three-pointed star of Mercedes inside the laurel wreath of Benz.

During 1926, a development of the 6.2-litre supercharged six cylinder appeared, which

developed 110bhp unblown, 160hp blown. Because of its short wheelbase, this sports model was known to its makers as the 'K' (*Kurz* = 'short'), but contemporary motorists, apparently, called it the 'Death Trap'. Its roadholding and cornering at speed seemed to leave more than a little to be desired, and its four-wheel brakes recorded a stopping distance of 140 feet from 40mph during an *Autocar* road test.

But its successor, the 6.8-litre 'S' of 1927 was perhaps the finest of all the vintage Mercedes sports cars. With a considerably lower centre of gravity, achieved by a double-dropped chassis with underslung rear springs, it had the same 11ft 2in wheelbase as the 'K', and a more powerful supercharger was used, in conjunction with twin carburettors. It was said to have a top gear range from a walking pace to 103mph, and

1954 300SL six-cylinder; 2,996cc; ohc; 200bhp @ 5400rpm; independent suspension all round; 100mph.

the model scored 53 victories and 17 records during the 1928 season, including the German sports record of 110.4mph. A total of 155 examples of this model (known in Britain as the 36/220S) were built; it was succeeded in 1928 by the 7.1-litre SS (38/250SS) which, in short chassis form (9ft 8in wheelbase) was known as the 'SSK'. *Motor Sport* road-tested a 38/250 in 1929, and wrote: 'Words fail me—this is the most amazing motor car it has ever been our fortune to drive.'

But the ultimate development of the supercharged Mercedes sports car was the SSKL (Super Sports Kurz Leicht): this had a liberally drilled chassis, where even the dumbirons had been given the Gruyère treatment, which brought the weight down to 24cwt. The engine was highly tuned, with a lightened crankshaft, special valves and a high-lift camshaft, raised compression ratio and,

since the very few SSKLs that were built were all works team racers, a very special oversize supercharger known as the 'elephant blower'. Among the events won by SSKLs, which developed almost 300bhp with the blower engaged, were the 1931 Mille Miglia and German Grand Prix, driven by the man whose name is virtually synonymous with the supercharged Mercedes sports car—Rudolph Caracciola. The ultimate speed for this model was 156mph, achieved by Manfred von Brauchitsch with a specially streamlined car on the Berlin Avus track.

The year 1930 had seen the introduction of the 7,655cc 42/280 model, which weighed 36cwt and had a wheelbase of 12ft 4in; not unnaturally, this monstrous machine was known as the 'Grosser Mercedes'. In its original form, it had had an entirely orthodox chassis, but in 1938 it was totally redesigned, acquiring

a low-built tubular chassis, independent suspension all round by coil springs, with swing axles at the rear and a five-speed gearbox. Its straight-eight engine developed 150bhp normally aspirated, and 200bhp when a supercharger was fitted. In all, there were 117 of the earlier version, 88 of the later version, built. The original model didn't lack for distinguished owners: King Zog of Albania, King Gustav of Sweden, the King of Siam, ex-Kaiser Wilhelm, General Franco, Field-Marshal von Hindenburg and Emperor . Hirohito of Japan, who ordered seven of them (all armour plated) in 1932. Stalin and Mussolini were recipients of the second version.

A new sporting Mercedes, the 3.8-litre supercharged eight cylinder 90/120bhp, appeared in 1933. This model had independent suspension all round by coil springs, with double wishbones at the front and swing axles at the rear; it was developed in 1934 into the 5-litre 100/160hp 500K and ultimately into the 5.4-litre 540K.

Unlike their predecessors, these were fast tourers rather than sports/racers, for of course by this time Mercedes' racing laurels were being gathered by the Nazi-sponsored Grand Prix cars. Nevertheless, the 540K was a handsome machine, usually endowed with the fashionable sporting cabriolet bodywork that was so popular in Third Reich Germany. Its catalogued maximum speed without the

supercharger engaged was 88mph; with the blower clutched in, the 540K could achieve over 105mph. An even bigger-engined version, the 580K, appeared at the 1939 Berlin Show, but never went into production.

The war wrought vast damage at the Daimler-Benz factories: in 1945, reported the directors, the company 'had ceased to exist'. Of the company's factories, Unterturkheim had lost about 70 per cent of its plant, Sindelfingen about 85 per cent, Mannheim about 20 per cent, Gaggenau about 80 per cent and what remained at Marienfelde was completely pulled down.

Initially, the company concentrated on clearing the rubble and on repairing existing vehicles. Truck production then began, followed by limited output of pre-war models like the 170V 1.7-litre four cylinder. The first 'new' post war models were developments of the 170V, and then, in 1951, came two new six cylinder models, the 220 and the 300. The latter was a high quality touring car, complete with fittings such as electrically controlled auxiliary torsion bar suspension at the rear. It was joined in 1952 by a high performance version, the 300S, which had a raised compression ratio and triple downdraught carburettors, giving it a maximum speed of 110mph.

That same year, Mercedes-Benz produced their first sports car since the war—the

1956 190SL four-cylinder; 1,897cc; ohc; 120bhp @ 5700rpm; over 105mph.

300SL ('Sport-Light'). It had a tubular space frame, with the fuel-injected engine inclined to the left to give a low bonnet line. The 300SL went into full production in 1954, after early models had successfully established a competition record with victories at such events as the Swiss Grand Prix at Berne, the Le Mans 24 Hours, the German GP at the Nurburgring and the third Carrera Panamerica in Mexico.

With a power output of 215-240bhp, the 300SL had a top gear range of 15-166mph; unlike its pre-war ancestors, it could stop easily too, for it had automatically-adjusted hydraulic brakes and self-cooling turbo brake drums. The most characteristic version of the 300SL was the coupé, with its famous 'gull-wing' doors, though open two-seaters were also built.

Developed from this model was the 300SLR sports/racer, with a 3-litre straight-eight engine, with twin overhead camshafts operating desmodromic valves; it had a five-speed gearbox and could reach 185mph. It won its first race, the 1955 Mille Miglia, and its second, at the Nurburgring, and 300SLRs came in 1-2-3 in both the Tourist Trophy and the Targa Florio that year. Its power unit was similar in design to that of the 2.5-litre W196 grand prix racer which, driven by Fangio, took the world championship in both 1954 and 1955.

A less exotic sports model appeared in 1955.

This was the 1.9-litre 190SL, which its makers claimed was 'just as suitable for sporting events as it is for ordinary touring or even town purposes'. It had a four cylinder engine with twin sidedraught carburettors, developing 110bhp at 5,500rpm, giving a top speed of 118mph. Developed from the touring 180 and 220a models, the 190SL was the first integrally-constructed Mercedes sports car, with its engine carried on a separate sub-frame.

In 1961, Mercedes-Benz became the first motor manufacturer to be able to celebrate its 75th anniversary. To celebrate the occasion, a new fast tourer, the 220SE Coupé was announced; it was the first Mercedes to feature front disc brakes. And also to mark their Alabaster Jubilee, Mercedes-Benz opened a magnificent museum containing examples of all their major models since Gottlieb Daimler and Karl Benz, unknown to one another, had built the first two practical petrol cars in 1885-86.

1957 300S Cabriolet

Mercer

As a sideline to their lucrative wire rope enterprise, the Roebling family of Brooklyn Bridge fame built the Roebling Planche car from 1906 to 1909. The largest in the range, rated at 120bhp, cost $12,000. In 1910, F. W. Roebling, Jr, and C. W. Roebling introduced a single series 34hp marque, naming it Mercer after the New Jersey county where the factory was situated—in Trenton, the state capital. The 1910 Speedster was succeeded by the equally stark Type 35 Raceabout of 1911-4, listed at $2,250. Besides the engine and chassis, it had cycle wings, running boards and headlamps, all removable for racing, a big cylindrical fuel tank behind two bucket seats, and a 'monocle' windscreen for the driver.

This no-frills sports car, created by Finlay Robertson Porter, had a 5-litre, four-cylinder T-head engine with two spark plugs per cylinder, developing 55bhp at a lazy 1,650 to 1,800rpm. With a weight of only 2,610lb, that was enough to attain nearly 80mph in road trim—fast for the period. A smooth shifting, four-speed transmission adopted in 1912 made for rapid acceleration. Handling and roadholding, but not the brakes, were outstanding. Driven by such stars as Barney Oldfield and Ralph De Palma, the Type 35 and the similar 7.3-litre Type 45 figured prominently in American racing until 1915, often duelling with the somewhat burlier Stutz Bearcat.

Thanks to their satisfying appearance, functional design, and competitive tradition as well as their rarity, the two dozen or so Type 35s still existing are among the most coveted collectors' items in America.

For 1915, Mercer dropped the Type 35 in favour of the radically different Series 22. The engine, a 70bhp L-head four designed by Erik H. Delling, had a bore of 93mm and a stroke of no less than 148mm, requiring 15in connecting rods. All bodies, whether the short wheelbase new Raceabouts or the longer touring models, were smoothly streamlined and equipped with doors. Starting in 1919, the Raceabouts followed the other types with a full width windscreen and an optional cloth top. Steering was from the left instead of the right, and the gear lever for the four-speed transmission was centrally located. Although somewhat faster than the 35s, the L-heads never distinguished themselves in competition.

By 1920, production was down to about twenty cars a year. Celebrities such as Buster Keaton might have been enthusiastic, but not many people were willing to pay $4,000 or so for a four-cylinder car, however well made. Following reorganization after a receivership, the new management offered a Rochester-built 5½-litre overhead valve six as an alternative unit in 1922 and as the only engine in 1923. The move proved unavailing and the receivers in a second bankruptcy assembled the last Mercers in 1925.

1912 four-cylinder; 4,927cc; four-speed gearbox; SV; 58bhp @ 1700rpm.

Mercury

To compete with General Motors and other car makers in the lower medium priced field, Ford's Lincoln Division introduced the Mercury in 1939 under Edsel Ford's sponsorship. It followed the Ford's body lines and shared many of its components, although the side valve engine was larger at 3.9 litres, with an output of 95bhp. The new car reached eleventh place in sales among American makes in its first year, when more than 76,000 were sold.

For 1940 the line included a four door convertible with removeable side pillars. This and the wood trimmed 1946 Sportsman convertible are far more desirable than the saloons and coupés of Mercury's early years.

As with Ford the 1949 models represented a complete change of styling and running gear. Bodies, shared with the smaller Lincoln, were bulbous instead of angular; the archaic solid front axle gave way to independent coil sprung front suspension and the torque tube drive was dropped as well. For improved performance, the engine was enlarged to 4.2 litres and remained that size until 1953. It became a favourite among the hot rodding set for many years.

A major change for 1954 was the adoption of a short stroke overhead valve engine of almost the same size as the L-head, but developing 161 instead of 125bhp. Underneath, ball joints replaced king pins. The most interesting (but not the most comfortable because of the heat) body style was the Sun Valley, similar to the plastic roofed Ford Starliner. By 1956 Mercury was offered in four series, all powered by a 5.1 litre engine with varying power outputs, ranging from 210 to 260bhp.

Radical changes came in 1957. For the first time since 1951, the newly widened and lengthened bodyshell gave more passenger room than Ford. The wrap-round windscreen was more extreme than its 1955 forerunner —indeed the total glass area was greatly increased—and the rear quarters had sweeping concave curves at the top as though to outdo Chrysler's tail fins. As with Chrysler the automatic transmission had a push button selector panel. The re-designed chassis had optional air cushion front shackles on the rear springs. Lincoln's 6 litre V8, developing 290bhp was available on all automatic models. Heading the line was the Turnpike Cruiser hardtop pillarless saloon. Besides a tachometer and the then innovative quadruple headlights, it featured a steering wheel flattened at the top, fresh air intakes above a compound curve windscreen and a three piece rear screen, the central section of which could be lowered into the body electrically.

This formidable conveyance, derived from a 1956 dream car, foretold Mercury's transformation from its traditional image as just a somewhat larger Ford, while Ford itself would soon range through most of the marketing spectrum.

Despite all Mercury's changes in theme since World War II, it has never fallen below ninth best seller among American cars.

1957 Turnpike Cruiser V8; 6-litre; up to 290bhp.

159

MG

In the early 1920s, many British enthusiasts rebodied and tuned numerous standard cars to try and extract more performance. Cecil Kimber, then manager of Morris Garages, Morris's agency in Oxford, decided to cater for this demand with modified versions of the Bullnose Morris with sporting bodywork. Six Cowley-based two seaters emerged in 1923, followed by the Oxford-based side valve 1.8-litre Super Sports 14/40 of 1924-9.

At the Olympia motor show in October 1928, Kimber exhibited two new series along with the 14/40. The larger of these, the 18/80, was a 2½-litre overhead cam six capable of almost 80mph. MG's destiny, however, lay with small sporting creations such as Kimber's other offering of 1928, the M-type Midget. The facilities of the third and ultimate MG factory completed at Abingdon, six miles south of Oxford, in 1929 were initially devoted largely to its production. This diminutive 847cc 20bhp two seater, introduced at £175, was based on the original Morris Minor but at 65mph was more than 10mph faster, thanks to Kimber's revision of the advanced little overhead cam engine originally intended for a Wolseley. It was only 10ft 5in long and weighed 1,120lb when clad in the original fabric-covered plywood body. Before the M-type was discontinued in mid 1932, it had undergone many running changes; improved brakes, a redesigned camshaft giving 27bhp, doors

hinged at the front, and optional metal bodies, four speed transmission, and, for £245, a smart Sportsman's Coupé version. One of the 3,234 units was bought by Edsel Ford and it is now on view at the Henry Ford Museum in Dearborn.

Development continued with the C-type Montlhéry sports racer of 1931-2, reduced to 746cc so as to be eligible for 750cc events. In standard and supercharged form, these and subsequent J and P-type Midgets won renown on many circuits even after the factory had discontinued its racing programme in 1935. It was the J2 open two seater of 1932-3, with its vertical slab fuel tank and cutaway doors, that set the definitive style for MG and many other British sports cars until the mid-1950s.

Concurrent with the early Midgets were two main types of light overhead camshaft sixes, the 1,087cc Magnas of 1931-4 and the longer Magnettes of 1932-6, with both 1,087cc and 1,286cc engines. The open two seaters won many important competitions: two supercharged 1,087cc K3 Magnettes were first and second in their class in the 1933 Mille Miglia and another K3, driven by Tazio Nuvolari, won that year's Ulster Tourist Trophy.

Successive generations of purists have bemoaned the passing of cherished MGs, then learned to endure and eventually to embrace the models that took their place. This was true of the TA two seater of 1936-9, which was powered by a two-carburettor version of the Morris Ten's 1,292cc pushrod overhead valve engine, instead of the inherently more sophisticated but less reliable overhead cam types that had prevailed since 1928. But the TA marked no lapse in styling and performance and had the boon of hydraulic brakes; as might have been predicted, it became the best selling British sports car of its time.

The 1,250cc TB of 1939 had a shorter stroke, higher compression and better performance but the war halted its production after only a few months. Its famous post-war successor, the TC, was identical except for a wider cockpit and synchromesh on the three upper gears. This thoroughbred, with the long

1929 Midget four-cylinder; 847cc; ohc; engine based on the Morris Minor.

bonnet, 1930 vintage 19-inch wire wheels, and walnut dashboard, was a great success in America from the time of its arrival in 1946. In fact, the TC can be said to have re-introduced America to the sports car. Granted that the top speed obtainable from 54bhp was a rackety 75mph, the fun lay in getting there.

Amid initial groans, the TD of 1950-3 made such concessions to modernity as 15-inch steel wheels and stiffer chassis with independent front suspension. Bumpers, too, became standard equipment. Top speed was around 80mph; zero to 60mph at a shade under 20 seconds represented a measurable improvement over the TC's performance.

The last vintage style MG, the TF of 1954-5, incorporated styling changes, notably faired-in headlamps, that elicited an ambivalent response from enthusiasts. The standard engine was the 1,250cc unit. To satisfy a demand for greater performance, an optional 1,466cc engine was introduced for 1955, giving 65bhp and 85mph.

The MGA 1500 of 1956-9 broke from the marque's styling tradition with the choice of coupé or open bodies and only a nostalgic MG grille. It was powered by a 1,498cc ohv four like the one used on revised Magnette saloons (actually restyled Wolseley 4-44s) from 1953 to 1961. The A's aerodynamic shape enabled it to go much faster than the TF, but with less excitement. Including the fragile 1600 twin cams of 1959-62, some 100,000 As were sold. They were replaced by the MGB.

1933 Magnette six-cylinder; 1,286cc; ohc; twin SU carburettors; pre-selector four-speed gearbox; 80mph and 25mpg.

Minerva

Sylvain de Jong, a cycle and motorcycle manufacturer in Antwerp, built a number of prototypes before marketing a line of two-, three-and four-cylinder Minervas in 1904. These were soon joined by a well made single-cylinder voiturette of 636cc; and none other than the Hon. C. S. Rolls was London agent for Minerva in 1905, before he became totally involved with the Rolls-Royce. Starting in 1909, Minerva was one of the first two companies to use sleeve valve engines under Knight patents. All of the wide range of fours were exceptionally smooth and quiet, whether used as taxis or for transporting royalty—King Albert of Belgium had a 37hp model in 1910—and the firm also made a good showing in road races and reliability trials with sleeve valve cars, in 1911-4.

Production was halted during the four year German occupation of Belgium, but Minerva was able to introduce a new luxury four and six hardly a year after the Armistice. They carried Minerva's distinctive compound curve radiator shell, first used on the pre-war TT cars, which in turn was soon graced by a mascot in the form of the helmeted head of the goddess Minerva. The 5.3-litre 30CV six of 1920 typifies 'The Goddess of Automobiles'. It was supplemented by the 1927 6-litre AK six on a 12ft 6in wheelbase, then by the similarly gigantic 1930 6.6-litre AL straight eight. These and more modest models sold well abroad, especially in France and Britain, until the Depression and economic nationalism took their toll. Symbolic of changed conditions was the 2-litre M4 four of 1934. Late the next year, Minerva merged with Imperia, the only other surviving Belgian manufacturer.

Until the end, in 1939, only Minerva-Imperias, four-cylinder front-wheel drive machines based on the Adler Trumf, were offered.

1930 40hp eight-cylinder; 6,616cc; sleeve-valves.

Morgan

Today the sole survivor among traditional British sports cars, the Morgan began in 1918 as the tiller steered single seater three wheeler runabout that motor agent W. F. S. Morgan designed for his own use. It aroused so much interest that he put the design into production. An advanced feature was independent front suspension using sliding pillars and coil springs, a system retained to this day on its four wheeled descendants. With its light weight, good road holding, and potent V twin motorcycle engine hung out in front, the Morgan soon proved its worth in competitive events. Originally, Morgans just had two forward speeds, provided by a simple chain-and-dog transmission, and perfectly adequate with the torquey V twins by JAP, Anzani and MAG that were normal equipment. But brakes on the classic Morgans—the Aero and the Grand Prix—were on the rear wheel only, and of the most minimal kind. Front-wheel brakes appeared in 1927, and the 1930 M-type had a three-speed and reverse transmission and detachable wheels too. Somehow it took some of the edge off the Morgan, even though

the Super Sports M-type was clocked at more than 100mph with tuned versions of its JAP, Matchless, and other engines. The F4 with water-cooled four-cylinder engine dating from 1934 to 1950 was powered at first by the 933cc Ford Y then by the 1,172cc Ford C-Type engine which was fitted under a conventional bonnet. About 40,000 three wheelers were built over the years.

Starting in 1936, Morgan finally built a four wheeled model with conventional drive to the rear axle and a four-speed gearbox. It was called the 4/4, denoting four wheels and four cylinders. The engines came from Coventry-Climax and these were succeeded in 1939 by a special Standard 1,267cc ohv unit. In 1950, a larger Standard Vanguard engine installed in a strengthened 4/4 body and frame improved performance significantly. Called the Plus Four, it was the only Morgan until 1955, when a companion Series 2 4/4 was announced with the side valve Ford 1,172cc engine. These two series have been

1934 Three-wheeler fitted with a choice of engines by JAP or Matchless, both air and water cooled, two or four cylinders; a very successful competition vehicle.

163

continued, the 4/4 with ohv Ford units and the Plus Four with modified versions of the Triumph TR engines, until the Rover V8 took their place, providing the car with a top speed of 125mph. In the mid-1950s, along with front disc brakes, they took on their present appearance with what for Morgan was a radical restyling: the headlamps were faired into the body, while the grille canted rearward and diminished vertically.

Almost unbelievably, the Morgan of today still has the same basic chassis layout as its pre-war predecessors, only strengthening members being added to cope with the increased power outputs, while restyling has been made largely to cover the ever increasing tyre sizes needed with the Rover V8 engine. The

body is still made from aluminium over an ash frame, using the same tools as in the 1920s and very often by the same men.

With its Spartan appointments, lack of creature comforts and an extremely hard ride the Morgan is hardly designed for the 1980s, but as it has passed all the current European safety tests there seems little reason why it should not carry on for many years to come.

1936 4/4 four-cylinder; 1,122cc; ohv; four-speed gearbox; more than 75mph; 35mpg.

Morris

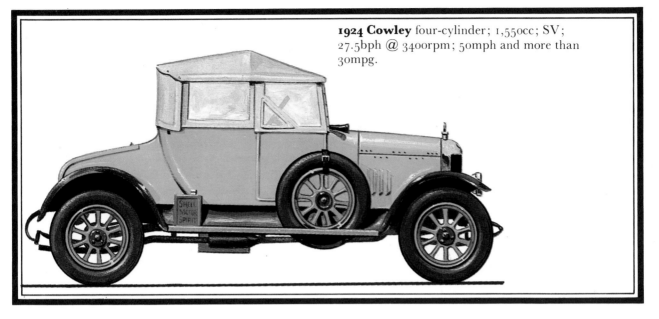

1924 Cowley four-cylinder; 1,550cc; SV; 27.5bph @ 3400rpm; 50mph and more than 30mpg.

William R. Morris's first car was the 1-litre White & Poppe-engined T-head two-seater Oxford four of 1913. It was followed in 1915 by the 1½-litre L-head Cowley two and four seaters, named after the town near Oxford where the cars were assembled. The Cowley, built largely from American components during the War, had a power unit by Continental Motors, an American firm which provided power units for scores of makes.

After concentrating on munitions production during World War I, Morris was able to sell his light cars on such a scale that he became known, with some exaggeration, as the British Henry Ford. Soon he was able to gain

1925 Bullnose four-cylinder; 1,550cc; SV; 27.5bph @ 3400rpm; 50mph and more than 30mpg.

control of Hotchkiss of Coventry, which made the 1½-litre engine then used in both the Oxford and Cowley.

The last 'Bullnose' (so called because of the radiator shape) Oxfords of 1923-6, had a 1.8-litre engine and, latterly, four-wheel brakes, but like the Cowleys they retained magneto ignition and an oil-bath clutch plate.

Good value was a factor in both cars' popularity. The 1913 Oxford sold for £165 but the 1919 Cowley, reflecting post-war inflation and shortages, cost £465. This was reduced in frequent stages to £225 by late 1922 and, almost full circle despite the depreciated pound, to £170 in 1926. By the time the annual output of Morris's had reached 50,000, then a record for Europe.

Oxfords and Cowleys of 1927-31 had an angular radiator which was used with little modification on a long line of MGs. More subtly styled sixes, beginning with the simply named Morris Six of 1928-39, were current throughout the 1930s. Some of them had a symbiotic relationship with contemporary Wolseleys.

Wolseley design, too, was evident in the 847cc overhead camshaft Minor of 1928-34. This baby car's engine reflected the fact that Wolseley had built Hispaño-Suiza aero-engines during World War I, but it was designed to compete with the even smaller Austin Seven. It was available as a conventional or fabric-bodied two-door saloon and as a two-seater roadster. The Minor was succeeded by the Eight of 1935-9, a 918cc L-head four with smartened appearance, hydraulic brakes, and marginally improved performance with a top speed of 50mph. The Series E Eight introduced in 1939 had faired-in headlamps, a waterfall grille, and, more importantly, a four-speed gearbox. Equipped with hydraulic brakes, it served as a stopgap bread-and-butter model when Morris resumed car production after World War II. Paralleling the Minor and the Eights from 1933 to 1948 were somewhat larger and faster Tens, first with L-head and then with overhead valve engines, with speeds in the middle sixties.

Besides controlling MG, William Morris acquired Wolseley in 1927 and Riley in 1938. In that year he was created Viscount Nuffield and his holdings were renamed the Nuffield Group.

The Morris Eights and Tens were superseded late in 1948 by a trio designed by Chief Engineer, Alec Issigonis: the MM Minor, the MO Oxford, and the MS Six. All had similar rounded lines. torsion-bar front suspension, and integral construction. The Minor used the old Eight's side valve engine but had greatly improved roadholding.

1935 Tourer four-cylinder; 918cc; SV; three-speed gearbox; 60mph and 40mpg.

The post-war Minor was so successful—
a million had been sold by January 1961—
that it remained in production until 1971.
Following Nuffield's merger with Austin in
1952 to form the British Motor Corporation,
the Series II Minor of 1953-6 used the
Austin A30's 803cc overhead valve engine
which gave more flexible performance through
the gears. Similarly, the Minor 1000s of
1956-62 and 1963-71 shared ohv fours with the
948cc Austin A40 Farina I and the 1,098cc
Austin A40 Farina II 1100 respectively.
Starting with the Series II, the two-door
saloon and the convertible were joined by a
four door saloon and the sought-after
Traveller, a wood-trimmed estate car.

During 1959 came Issigonis's revolutionary
Mini-Minor with Morris and Austin
nameplates. For maximum interior space, its
848cc four-cylinder engine was mounted
transversely, driving the front wheels. The
engine, four-speed transmission, and front drive
made up an easily removable assembly with
a common oil supply. Even more novel was
the all independent suspension, using conical
rubber springs. Although the total length was
only 10 feet, there was room for four adults and
ample luggage space. Performance was brisk,
the ride was level, and cornering speeds
were superior to many sports cars. Only the
frequent failure of small components detracted
from the Mini's ranking as the world's best
small car. More powerful variants, notably
the Mini-Coopers, began to appear in
1961, along with the slightly longer and better-
trimmed Riley Elf and Wolseley Hornet.
Despite many detail changes the car remains
in production today.

1935 8 Saloon four-cylinder; 918cc; SV;
three-speed gearbox; 60mph and 40mpg.

Nash

1926 six-cylinder; 3,210cc or 3,473cc; ohv; three-speed gearbox.

Charles W. Nash was president of Buick from 1910 to 1916, and also of General Motors from 1912 to 1916. Then he founded Nash Motors, buying the Jeffery car factory in Kenosha, Wisconsin. The re-christened firm's first Nash-designed engine, a six installed in some 1917 models, followed Buick valve-in-head practice. A companion valve-in-head four was offered in 1921-5.

Nash's big sixes did well in the luxury market, and in 1925 all Nash series followed the competition by adding a belt line around the bodies. Only sixes of various capacities were offered in the late 1920s. Sales then exceeded 120,000 each year, thanks to a well earned reputation. The Light Six, a side valve model, succeeded the unsuccessful Ajax of 1925-6. The 400 series introduced in 1928 featured two spark plugs per cylinder and a seven bearing crankshaft.

As with many American makes, Nash built its finest cars during the Depression, just when affluent buyers were few—total Nash sales were about 18,000 in 1932 and 15,000 in 1933. Long-bodied and convertible models of the nine-bearing ohv Twin-Ignition eights introduced in 1930 vie with other American classics among collectors. Nash pioneered steel saloon car roofs in 1933, a year ahead of G.M.'s La Salle. Along with the rest of the American industry, Nash adopted tentative streamlining in 1934 and went all the way in 1935, with the result that the cars lost much of their distinction.

In 1941 Nash went over to unitized welded body construction, a method still used by its successor firm, American Motors. Nashes of 1946-8 were merely revamped 1941 models. All were sixes and no more eights were produced until 1955.

Nash lost its remaining identity in the Airflyte bathtub body design of 1949-51. American Motors, formed by the merger of Nash and Hudson in 1954, dropped both senior marques and concentrated on the Rambler.

1932 straight-8; 4,834cc; ohv; dual ignition; 115bhp @ 3600rpm.

Nash-Healey six-cylinder; 3,848cc; ohv; 125bhp @ 4000rpm; engine by Nash fitted with two SU carburettors and fitted into chassis by Donald Healey.

Nash President George Mason was the moving spirit behind the three-seater Nash-Healey sports roadster and coupé of 1950-4. Their engine and torque-tube drive train were slightly modified from the 3.8-litre Nash Ambassador six, the aluminium bodies were British-built at first, then hand made by Pininfarina in Italy. The chassis was based on Donald Healey's Silverstone two-seater and the cars were assembled at the Healey works in Warwick. A Nash-Healey finished fourth at Le Mans in 1950, and another finished third in 1952. At $6,400 in 1954 the Nash-Healey could not compete against Jaguar and only 506 were built.

Another Mason inspired car was marketed successfully from 1954 to 1961, after four years' gestation. This was an inexpensive three seater first known as the Nash Metropolitan, then from 1957 simply as the Metropolitan. It, too, was available in both open and hardtop forms and was assembled in England by Austin. Although the body styling, soft suspension, and three-speed transmission followed contemporary Nash practice, the car was entirely of British manufacture; the engine was successively the 1.2-litre Austin A40 and the 1½-litre Austin A50.

Metropolitan four-cylinder; 1,489cc; ohv; of Austin origin developing 47bhp @ 4100rpm; three-speed gearbox; better than 75mph and more than 30mpg.

Oldsmobile

Ransom E. Olds had built several steam and petrol-engined buggies before the Olds Motor Vehicle Company was formed in 1896, but serious production only began with the famous Curved Dash model, designed by Olds in 1900 but not marketed until 1901 because of a fire in his Detroit works. A new factory at Lansing, Michigan, turned out 425 examples of this simple machine ('Nothing to watch but the road') in 1901, 2,500 in 1902, nearly 4,000 in 1903, and 5,508 in 1904, accounting for more than a third of all US car production during the two latter years. It was the first mass-produced car, pioneering assembly-line techniques.

The one-cylinder engine located under the buggy-like body, gave a cruising speed of 14mph. The engine was started by a cranking handle—like that of a clockwork gramophone —beneath the driver's right hand, and steering was by tiller. Among the many components bought from outside firms, engines supplied by the Dodge brothers yielded 3hp; those from Leland & Faulconer gave 3.7hp, thanks to the precision methods that Henry M. Leland later carried over to Cadillac and Lincoln. Leland & Faulconer also was the source of most of the two-speed transmissions. The car weighed 700lb and was priced at $650

1916 six-cylinder; 3,154cc or eight-cylinder 4,043cc; ohv; three-speed gearbox.

without such optional amenities as headlamps.

Ransom Olds left to found Reo in 1904 because his backers at Olds wanted to build large cars. The Curved Dash, however, was retained until 1905 and far outsold the new two and four-cylinder front-engined models. That year's total production figure of 6,500 was not exceeded until 1915. In the interval, in 1908, William Crapo Durant acquired Oldsmobile for his fledgling General Motors

1932 six-cylinder or eight-cylinder.

Company and made it his flagship car. The 11.6-litre Oldsmobile Limited of 1910-2, with six cylinders and four forward speeds, could reach 70mph. It was the largest capacity Oldsmobile ever, as well as being the loftiest, with its 42in wheels and two step running boards. In real money terms, at $4,600 to $5,000 it was also the costliest. At that time, G.M.'s Cadillac was less than $2,000.

In 1915, under new G.M. management following the expansive Durant's first ousting, the Oldsmobile became a modest 30bhp four. This was succeeded in 1916 by an advanced aluminium-pistoned 58bhp V8 that was continued until 1921, and by a long lived 40bhp six in 1917. The eight, redesigned for 1922 to produce 64bhp, was discontinued the next year. To cover the low-medium field, a Chevrolet engined 2.8-litre four was also available in 1921-3. Then, in 1924, output was standardized on the 2.8-litre six. The various 1916-24 cars were similar in appearance, with a rounded nickel-plated radiator shell and short, louvred bonnet.

For the 1925-7 models, the frontal appearance was changed by the adoption of a shouldered, Buick-like radiator shell and bonnet. The 1926 series pioneered chromium plating for the radiator shell. The staple cars among these sixes were enclosed types selling at under $1,000. Though yielding only 40bhp and a top speed of 72mph,

Oldsmobile touring cars set records for the Pike's Peak climb in 1926 and 1927.

Further changes in styling identity came in 1928 and 1930, with respective La Salle and Buick influences. Sales topped 100,000 in 1929. This figure includes the La Salle-like 4.3-litre Viking V8 with chain-driven camshaft, launched that year and dropped the next. For 1932, when all G.M. bonnets sported little doors instead of louvres, a 3.9-litre straight eight supplemented the six. All these cars except the $1,595 Viking continued to be listed at under $1,000 for standard equipped models.

From 1933 until 1947, Oldsmobile sixes and straight eights incorporated such evolutionary changes as independent front suspension and solid steel roofs. In the late 1930s, Oldsmobile was the first American car to offer an automatic transmission.

Sensational Futuramic styling appeared in 1948. Of more importance was the overhead valve V8 Rocket engine of 5 litres, introduced at 135bhp in 1949 and climbing upwards during the 1950s. This efficient and durable unit made Oldsmobile a strong contender in stock-car races and brought the marque as high as fourth position in the production race. The six (outclassed even at 105bhp in its final incarnation) was dropped in 1950.

1957 Starfire 98 V8; 6,080cc; 277bhp @ 4400rpm; hydramatic automatic transmission.

Packard

Long the most honoured name in American
motoring and the most popular American car
among collectors, Packard was started in
November 1899 by James Ward Packard with
single cylinder models that soon proved their
merit. A Model C Packard crossed the
United States in 61 days in 1903. Under
the leadership of Henry B. Joy, who moved
operations from Warren, Ohio, to Detroit in
1903, production was soon concentrated on
larger and more luxurious types. The Model

1915 Twin-Six twelve-cylinder; 6,914cc; SV;
3-70mph in top gear.

L four of 1904 was the first to bear the
shouldered radiator shell and bonnet that were
a Packard hallmark for four decades and made
for continuity of styling. Thus the L's successor,
the 60bhp 30, was continued with little
outward change from 1907 until 1911. The next
series, the 7.25-litre 48 of 1912-5, a massive six
of baroque but tasteful splendour, gave Packard

1932 straight-8; 5,342cc or 6,318cc; SV;
110bhp and 135bhp respectively; adjustable
ride control.

1940 Darrin eight-cylinder; 5,837cc; ohv; 180bhp @ 3500rpm.

undisputed leadership among America's fine cars. Also available at that time was a somewhat smaller Series, the 38.

Even the 48 was eclipsed by the Twin Six of 1915-23, designed by Jesse G. Vincent. Its flexible performance and lighter weight, typified by the use of aluminium pistons, compensated for a reduction in swept volume to 6,950cc compared with the 48's $7\frac{1}{4}$ litres. The engine, two banks of six cylinders in a 60 degree vee, was an awe-inspiring innovation in 1915. Refinements such as detachable cylinder heads followed with the second series V12 during 1916, while the basic price increased to a still modest $3,050 from the initial $2,600. Annual production was in excess of 10,000 until in mid-1917 the firm concentrated on trucks and the Liberty aircraft engine, a V12 developed by Vincent and E. J. Hall. Just before and after America's participation in World War I, Ralph De Palma set road and track records in special Packards, notably a land speed record of 149.87mph at Daytona Beach, Florida, in 1919.

Under Alvan Macauley, Packard attained new heights in the 1920s. At the start of the

decade, a plain looking Single Six supplemented the thirsty Twin Six. The latter was superseded by an 84bhp straight eight— the prototype of all pre-World War II Packard eights—for 1924. The last sixes of the period, for 1924-7, shared the eights' smart new styling

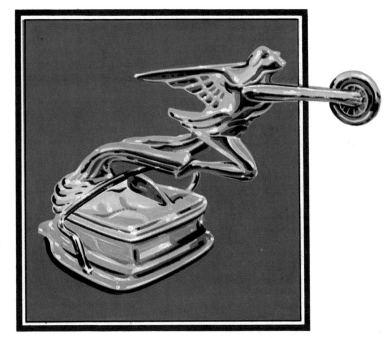

and played a major role in doubling Packard production to around 35,000 units. Only eights were made from 1928 to 1931, ranging from the 90bhp Standard series selling for as little as $2,535, to the 12ft 1in wheelbase Custom priced as high as $6,000.

Ranking with the eights, body style for body style, are the Twelves of 1932-9, Packard's splendid but unavailing answer to the multi-cylinder offerings with which Cadillac and other prestigious American marques were already trying to lure buyers in the declining luxury market. This mighty reincarnation of the Twin Six accounted for only 582 among 8,010 Packards in 1932, about average for its eight-year span. A 1939 Twelve phaeton with bulletproof glass was Franklin Roosevelt's favourite parade car.

Placing survival above tradition, manufacturing chief George T. Christopher introduced a car for the middle masses. The 120 straight eight of 1935 bore the Packard name and lines, and at less than $1,000 it boosted sales to above 50,000. When a companion Series 110 six, priced even lower,

was introduced in 1937, the total was 109,518, an all-time record for the firm. However, these cars lost prestige for the senior Packards, and Cadillac gained dominance of the luxury field. Widely blamed for harming instead of rescuing Packard, the junior sixes and eights were considered hardly collectable for many years but are now gaining favour.

Definitely classics are Howard Darrin's special Victories of 1940-1, based on the Senior Series 160 and 180 chassis.

Packard underwent many vicissitudes in the

1955 Caribbean V8; 6,138cc; 310bhp; push-button Ultramatic automatic transmission.

1940s. The decade began with the narrow bonnet 5.8-litre 180 as the top line, a cut below previous senior Packards. The 1941 junior sixes and eights, renamed Packard Clipper, underwent a graceful restyling. The firm then turned to engines for aircraft—like Ford of Britain, they built the Rolls-Royce Merlin—emerging in a solid financial position in 1945. The Clippers were reintroduced as a stopgap for 1946-7. The management made a serious misjudgment for the 1948-50 range. Styling deteriorated badly, with the traditional Packard lines only vestigially visible in the grille. The three series of straight eights of 135 to 160bhp were hardly distinguishable except in length and price—the top-line Custom cost more than the imposing Cadillac 60S. Even these misconceived vehicles sold well until 1950 marked the end of post-war shortages, but Packard never recovered its reputation.

The 1951 body shell was a new design from the inside out, with notable improvements in seating and boot space as well as in appearance. Sales held up well until 1954 when the old L-head straight eight engines had become anachronisms. Super salesman James J. Nance, president of Packard since 1952 and of the newly merged Studebaker-Packard in 1954, embarked on a costly comeback programme that ended two years later in a $34 million deficit. Among his positive accomplishments were the striking Caribbean

convertibles of 1953-6 and a sturdy overhead valve 260bhp V8 Packard engine for 1955-6 bodies, derived from 1951 dies with an unpredictable and complex 'Torsion Level' suspension. The medium price brackets were served by five series of less garish Clippers (without the 'Packard'), some with scaled down 225bhp versions of the senior engine.

The so-called Packard Clippers of 1957-8 were stretched-out Studebakers with special trim. A supercharger gave the 1957 saloon and station wagon 275bhp. The 1958 line consisted of an unsupercharged 225bhp saloon and the Packard Hawk, a fibreglass nosed version of the Studebaker Golden Hawk. All were of limited production and the Packard name died for good soon afterwards.

1958 Hawk V8; ohv; 5,322cc; 275bhp @ 4800rpm; power steering; last of the line.

Panhard

1957 two-cylinder horizontally-opposed engine; 850cc; ohv; 42bhp @ 5000rpm; front-wheel-drive.

Panhard et Levassor, of Paris, began the manufacture of cars in 1891, under an arrangement with Gottlieb Daimler. The first cars were rear-engined, but soon Panhard had the engine—a Daimler V twin—in front, the transmission amidships, and rear wheel drive, all in a frame designed for a car instead of a carriage. Panhard built the first vertical four-cylinder engine for their 1896 racers, although it was another two years before the general public could buy a four-cylinder Panhard. The marque tied with Peugeot in the first reliability trial, the Paris-Rouen trial of 1894, won the 1895 Paris-Bordeaux-Paris race, but was really past its competitive peak when 15.4 litre-Panhards were victorious in the 1904 Vanderbilt Cup and Circuit des Ardennes. From 1900 to 1904 its London agent was the Hon. C. S. Rolls, just before his association with Henry Royce.

Panhard then settled down to produce conservative fine cars, including some of the largest and costliest. From 1911 to 1939, most of them featured Knight-based sleeve valve engines. The 1937-9 Dynamic coupé was far from conservative: it had a backbone chassis and worm-gear drive, all-round torsion-bar suspension, convoluted wheel covers, and initially, a central driving position.

Unlike many French luxury car makers, Panhard met the challenge of post-war austerity. Its various Dyna series of 1946-67 were all based on a flat-twin, air-cooled design by J. A. Gregoire. Whatever the engine size, from the 1946 610cc to later 750 and 850cc, they combined modest and thrifty performance with very capacious bodies: the bulbous saloon of 1955-64, the Dyna 54, accommodated six passengers and 17 cu.ft of luggage, and attained 80mph. The 1955 and later Dynas of more attractive appearance and the higher performance 1961 Tigre and 1964 24 CT coupés, had front wheel drive.

Panhard won the 1961 Monte Carlo Rally and the Index of Performance from 1950-3 and 1963, as did the Panhard-based D.B. in 1954, 1956, and 1959-61. Citroën acquired an interest in Panhard in 1955 and took over in 1965, halting production in 1967.

Peugeot

Like Panhard, the French ironmongery and cycle firm of Peugeot began regular production of petrol-engined cars in 1891, though they had built a steamer as early as 1889. Peugeot went on to make a number of fine cars.
In 1912, its designer Ernest Henry's lightweight twin overhead camshaft four cylinder engine, with four inclined valves in each hemispherical combustion chamber, made previous ponderous racing cars obsolete. Peugeots won the French Grand Prix of 1912 and 1913, the Indianapolis 500 of 1913, 1916 and 1919, and the Vanderbilt Cup of 1915 and 1916.

Certainly no racer, with its 35mph top speed, was the 856cc Bébé Peugeot of 1912. This Ettore Bugatti creation had space for only two passengers but was a fine car in miniature. Its successor, the 668cc Quadrilette of 1920-9, was more like a cycle car.

During the 1920s, Peugeot made conventional fours and some sleeve valve sixes. The 1,100cc Series 201 four of 1930-7 was a capacious successor to the Quadrilette. Along with its larger companions, the 301 and 401, it acquired independent front suspension in 1932. For 1934-5, Peugeot offered coupés with electrically actuated hardtops. The 2.1-litre 402 of 1936-9 and 1946 had close-set headlamps behind the grille of its aerodynamic body.

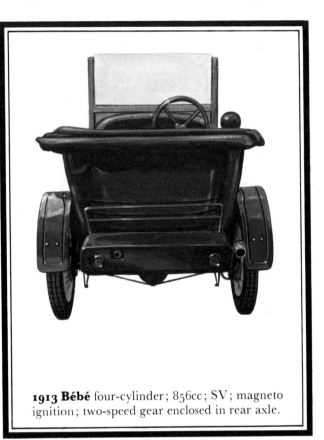

1913 Bébé four-cylinder; 856cc; SV; magneto ignition; two-speed gear enclosed in rear axle.

Post-war Peugeots gained a reputation for ruggedness and reliability, cars like the 203, 403, 404 and 504 being especially popular with farmers.

1958 403 four-cylinder; 1,468cc; ohv; 58bhp @ 4900rpm; 80mph and 30mpg.

Pierce-Arrow

Starting in 1901 with a one cylinder 2¾ horsepower model, the George N. Pierce Co, former builders of birdcages, of Buffalo, New York, had progressed to the four cylinder 28hp Great Arrow by 1904. Great Arrows, conservatively rated at 32 to 60hp and advancing to six cylinders, won acclaim by finishing first in the Glidden Tour Reliability trials for five successive years from 1905 to 1909. During the latter year, the cars became Pierce-Arrows and the firm was renamed the Pierce-Arrow Motor Car Co.

Only sixes were available from 1910. Three sizes were offered from 1914 until 1918: the 38, the 48 and the 66. (These numbers denoted taxable horsepower, based on the bore.) The 100hp 66 had a capacity of 12.7 litres, compared with the Packard Twin Six's 6.9. In 1917 a 66 cost $6,400 to $8,000, as much

as two good houses. The 38 started at $4,800, the 48 at $5,400. All three looked much alike, with respective wheelbases of 11ft 2in., 11ft 10in, and 12ft 3½in. The engines had twin ignition (by magneto and jump spark) and were cast in three pairs of cylinders. A T-head configuration was used. The crankshaft had seven bearings. Body panels, the crankcase, and the housing of the four speed gearbox were of aluminium. Headlamps faired into the wings, a Pierce-Arrow hallmark, were introduced in 1913.

A policy of limited production for people of unlimited means was successful until the early 1920s, when sales began to fall. In belated steps toward modernisation, in 1919 the 66 was dropped and the other engines acquired four valves per cylinder; left-hand steering was adopted for 1921 and monobloc engines were

1915 48B3 six-cylinder; 48hp.

introduced for 1922. These large Dual Valve sixes were continued throughout most of the decade.

For 1925, Pierce-Arrow introduced a companion Series 80 starting at under $3,000. This 4.7 litre L-head six delivered 70bhp and had a wheelbase of 10ft 10in. Sales of the 80 and its successor, the 75bhp 81 of 1928, were comparatively high at about 5,000 units a year, but still the firm incurred heavy losses. The management gladly agreed to merge with Studebaker in 1928, whilst still retaining its autonomy. For 1929 both series of sixes were superseded by a 6 litre straight eight. Eight-cylinder cars of 5.3 and 6.3 litres were added for 1930-31, the large 132bhp Model A being designed to appeal to the Dual Valve clientele. These and later eights approach their forerunners in distinction.

V12s of 1932-38 constituted Pierce-Arrow's last splendid gesture. Although sales were destined never again to approach even 1932's 2,692 units, for that year two series of twelves were offered, initially of 5.5 and 7 litres, then of 6 and 7.6 litres. Nothing helped, not even publicity engendered by the veteran driver Ab Jenkins's record breaking twenty four hour runs on the Bonneville Salt Flats in Utah or the futuristically styled $10,000 Silver Arrow of 1933. A Buffalo group took over after Studebaker went into receivership that year, and presented revamped models for 1935. Three years later the firm's assets were auctioned off at $40,000—less than one prime example of the marque would fetch today.

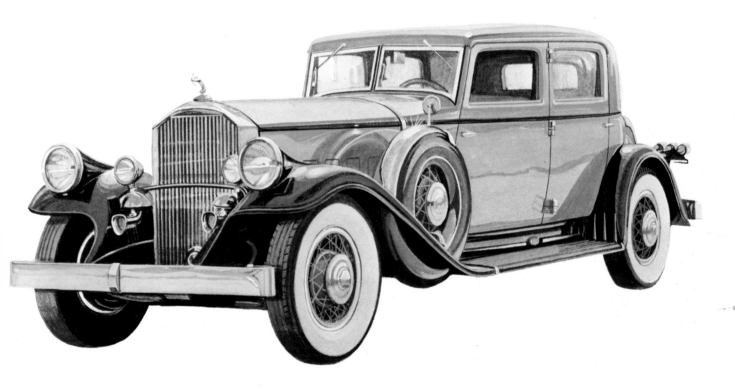

1931 41 Custom Club Sedan eight-cylinder; 132hp.

Plymouth

With almost the fanfare that had introduced the Model A Ford less than a year earlier, in July 1928 Walter Chrysler unveiled the Plymouth which would soon challenge Ford and Chevrolet. Actually, this successor to the Chrysler four—its 45hp engine was practically identical—was more expensive, at an average of $700, than its entrenched rivals. But it offered more, too: pressure-fed engine lubrication, aluminium alloy pistons, four-wheel hydraulic brakes and smooth Chrysler styling. The attractive ribbon radiator models of 1928-30 found fewer buyers than did the corporation's recently acquired Dodge line and not many more than the Chrysler itself, but they carved out the needed niche. Over 100,000 were sold in the model's first year.

Their redesigned successors, bigger and burlier, advanced Plymouth from eighth to an admittedly distant third place in total production, with 105,000 units in 1931 and 121,000 in 1932. Chrysler, Dodge and De Soto dealers now handled the Plymouth, thus broadening the market, and the price was

1929 four-cylinder; 2,794cc; SV; 45bhp @ 2800rpm; hydraulic brakes.

lowered to the $600 range. Positive factors in the car itself were the then popular freewheeling clutch, successive increases in horsepower, and 'Floating Power' three-point engine mounting, which made Plymouth's four cylinder engine less vibration-prone than Chevrolet's cast-iron six.

Except for the re-tooling year of 1945, Plymouth held on to third place until 1954,

1931 four-cylinder; 3,218cc; SV; 56bhp @ 2800rpm; free-wheel incorporated in transmission.

frequently topping the 500,000 mark and reaching 662,000 in 1953; evidently the public heeded the Chrysler Corporation's advice to 'look at all three' low priced cars. In tune with trends in the industry, the boot was enclosed in 1935, all-steel roofs soon succeeded fabric types, steering column gear change was adopted in 1939, when a power-operated convertible was introduced, and running boards were dropped in 1941. A semi-automatic transmission (Hy-Drive) became available in 1953. The L-head six-cylinder engine underwent breathing modifications and enlargement until it was rated at 100bhp in 1953 against 70bhp on its début in 1933. Throughout, the conservative Plymouths were noted for reliability and good riding qualities, but only the convertible models are of special interest.

The 1954 models, with 110bhp, did not differ greatly from the 1949 models and the old, high bodies looked stodgy. Production sagged to 400,000 and Plymouth sank to fifth place in US sales. Virgil Exner's 'Forward Look' styling of 1955, along with optional 4.2-

and 4.4-litre engines, started a recovery and Exner's 'Flight Sweep' styling of 1957 brought Plymouth back up to third place in the sales race.

Torsion bar sprung front suspension was fitted on the 1957 models and in 1960 the venerable L-head six was at last replaced by the slant-six overhead valve unit. This engine was fitted in the Valiant model in 1960, this car being Plymouth's version of the small economy car, known as the 'compact'.

The 'Forward Look' marked Plymouth's departure from its previous image of low price and low power and, with ever more powerful V8 engines and makes like Plymouth Fury, they moved into a different sector of the market.

1939 six-cylinder; 3,299cc; SV; 70bhp @ 3600rpm; 75mph.

Porsche

In 1948, after half a century in the motor industry, the brilliant designer Ferdinand Porsche built a car that bore his name and was worthy of it. The Porsche bore little resemblance to the Löhners, Austro-Daimlers, and Mercedes of his early and middle years, with his brutal Auto-Union racers that won prestige for the Nazi regime, or with his Tiger tanks of World War II. Instead, it was a modified version of his utilitarian Volkswagen.

No other machine could have served him so well as the basis for the very special car he had in mind. At seventy four and in poor health after nearly two years of imprisonment by the French, Porsche lacked the time and energy to start from a blank sheet. Also, post-war Central Europe was not a likely market for exotic sports cars or mighty road cars, and in any event he lacked capital.

With his pre-war headquarters in Stuttgart occupied by American forces, Ferdinand joined his son Ferry and his long-time associate, Karl Rabe, in the village of Gmund in his native Austria. In a small factory there, they abandoned a mid-engined prototype and, with Ferry in charge, built the first fifty 356 Porsches and exhibited one at the Geneva Show in March 1949. The engine had the VW's displacement of 1,131cc, but its output

A1600S four-cylinder horizontally-opposed rear engine; 1,488cc; 70bhp @ 5000rpm; over 100mph.

was increased from 25 to 40bhp by revised overhead valves, crankshaft and connecting rods. Aluminium alloy replaced steel in the engine, and the two-seater coupé bodies by Reutter had aluminium panels.

In 1950, operations were transferred to a fine new factory in Stuttgart, where the 500th Porsche was completed just two months after Ferdinand Porsche's death. The small new car won the 1,100cc class at Le Mans in 1951 and 1952 and, with a 1½-litre engine, won its class in the 1952 Mille Miglia.

With a 1½-litre engine available from 1952, the 356 developed 50 to 70hp and could exceed 100mph in the Super version, thanks to a weight of less than 1,800lb. Before the 356s were discontinued at the end of 1955, a claustrophobic convertible supplemented the coupé, braking was improved, and the four-speed gearbox had acquired synchromesh. The combined production of 1.3 and 1.5-litre types (the 1.1-litre was phased out in 1954) had risen to more than 2,000 annually.

A 1.6-litre engine was the most popular engine in the 356A of 1956-9, the 356B of 1960-3, and the 356C of 1964-5—the final development of the original Porsche design. The 1.3 and 1.5-litre were dropped in the late 1950s. At the other end of the scale, a potent 2-litre four was optional in 1962-4, and a 2-litre six—still of the opposed configuration inherited from the Volkswagen—came in 1965. In all, some 76,000 of the 356s were built.

Railton

1937 eight-cylinder; 4,168cc; SV; 130bhp @ 3800rpm; 85mph and 17mpg.

Reid Railton and Noel Macklin, co-designers of the Invicta, assembled the similarly sporting Railton at the Invicta works in Cobham, Surrey, from 1933 to 1940. Most Railtons were based on the Terraplane straight eight of 4 and then 4.2 litres and established a pattern for fast, sporting machines known as Anglo-American hybrids. The engines were modified to increase horsepower, the chassis was lowered, the steering was given more direct gearing and lightweight bodies in the Invicta tradition were fitted. Top speeds of 85 to 100mph compared well with the Invicta's 95mph, and at around £600 the Railton cost little more than a third as much. Also, it was an individual car: of the 1,460 examples hardly any two Railtons were alike.

The ultimate Railton was the Light Sports, which appeared in 1935. This car, fitted with a light four-seater body, was capable of a top speed of 107mph and acceleration figures of 0-50mph in 6.4 seconds and 0-80mph in 80 seconds. By the standards of the day this was rapid indeed, but the price of £878 kept sales to a very small number, as cars like the SS Jaguar were on the market at less than half the price.

Sales tapered off after the mid 1930s, when the annual British car tax was increased to 25 shillings per taxable horsepower—quite an expense for the 4.2-litre eight with its rating of 29hp. For 1937-40 the eight was supplemented by Hudson sixes of smaller capacity, but the drop in performance negated the appeal of a cheaper licence. Then too, starting in 1938, cars like the Railton and the similar but more extensively modified Hudson-based Brough Superior were outclassed by the even more reasonably priced, all-British 3.5-litre Jaguar SS 100. Still, Railtons appeared in dwindling numbers until early in 1940, when war halted all private car production in Britain, and a few were assembled in London in the late 1940s.

Fifty Railtons of 1938-40 were powered—if that is the word—by the Standard four cylinder Ten engine of 33bhp, giving a top speed of 68mph. Symbolically, Standard also supplied engines for the first SS cars by Jaguar. Reid Railton also designed the Napier-Railtons that set world land speed records in 1938, 1939, and 1947; the final record of 394.2mph, stood until 1963.

Renault

1922 six-cylinder; 9,123cc; SV; four-speed gearbox; 140bhp @ 3000rpm; servo-assisted four-wheel brakes; 90mph maximum.

Through many vicissitudes, Louis Renault became the leading French car manufacturer, triumphing over André Citroën during the 1920s. As early as 1900, Renaults had adopted a sloping 'coal scuttle' bonnet which became a distinguishing mark of the company's products. The engines ranged from a 1.1-litre two-cylinder through a quartet of fours of 2.1 to 7.4 litres, followed in 1908 by a 9.5-litre six. Except for the taxi-orientated twins, the emphasis was on prestige until World War I.

Following that war, Renault offered three updated fours, accounting for most of the firm's production, and a big-block six, the F1. Its successors, the legendary 9.1-litre '45' of 1921-9 and the 4.8-litre JY introduced in 1923,

1954 4CV four-cylinder; 748cc; ohv; three-speed gearbox; more than 80mph.

retained integral heads, with the cylinders cast in threes. At weights in the 5,000-6,000lb range, top speed—not a prime consideration for this class of car at the time—was about 75mph for the 4.8-litre and 90mph for the 45. Renaults of the 1930s gained in sales but lost distinction both mechanically and visually. Radiators were moved to the front, behind grilles imitative of those on contemporary Buicks and Chryslers. All the bodies were roomy for their respective price classes. In 1931 full sized models included a 2.4-litre four, a 3.2-litre six, and two straight eights, the 4.2-litre Nervastella and the 7.1-litre Reinastella. The latter replaced the 45 but lacked its panache.

During the Depression decade, Renault also made small cars. The last of these was the 1 litre Juvaquatre four of 1937-40, a four-seater, four-door saloon resembling a scaled-down 1936 Ford. A slightly revised version was the newly nationalized firm's only passenger car just after World War II. It was succeeded in 1947 by the ingenious 4CV, a car just right for its time. This 760cc (later 750cc) four had been developed in secret during the war; then, before the design was made final, a distinguished prisoner named Ferdinand Porsche was coopted as a consultant. Like his Volkswagen, the 4CV was a rear-engined four but was liquid cooled. Among its features

were replaceable cylinder liners, independent suspension all around with swing axles at the rear, an aluminium cylinder head, and hydraulic brakes. Fuel consumption was better than 40mpg and it carried four in comfort to its maximum of 60mph. More than a million were sold before production was discontinued in 1961.

The 2-litre (later 2.1-litre) Frégate of 1951-7 was a front-engined family saloon and convertible noted for quick but uncertain handling. Of more importance commercially, was the 845cc Dauphine of 1957-68, somewhat faster and more spacious than the 4CV. Its limited cornering abilities and thin bodywork did not endear it to owners. Worthier of consideration by collectors, even though based on the Dauphine, are the sporty Floride coupé and convertible introduced in 1959, later renamed Caravelle.

1960 Caravelle four-cylinder; 845cc; 40bhp @ 5000rpm; three-speed gearbox; over 80mph.

Riley

The Riley Cycle Co, later Riley (Coventry) Limited, built an experimental car in the late 1890s, introduced motors and tricycles in 1900 and V-twin four wheelers in 1907. Their patented demountable wire wheels were far more popular than the cars themselves, being sold to 183 makers over the years. A 2.9-litre side valve four-cylinder car of 1913 was succeeded after the war by a 1½-litre 11hp four. Its sporting version, the Redwinger of 1923-6, was quite dashing with its polished aluminium body and red wings.

In 1926 came the first of the Nines, with an admirable overhead valve engine by Percy and Stanley Riley. Its efficient layout, with hemispherical combustion chambers and twin camshafts mounted high on the block, was retained on all Rileys until 1957. The 9hp engine had a capacity of 1,087cc and in single carburettor form it developed 26bhp, while with twin carburettors it gave 41bhp. By 1931 four-speed gearboxes with central gear levers were standard, and although the engine had only a two-bearing crankshaft it would rev to 5,000rpm with ease. This was obviously the basis for a small sporting machine and Riley were set for a long string of successes in racing, although many of their road cars were fitted with heavy bodywork which stifled performance.

The famous Brooklands Riley four of 1928-32 evolved from the work of J. G. Parry Thomas and Reid Railton on the Nine. After Parry Thomas died in 1927 while attempting to set his fourth land speed record, Railton continued its development with twin carburettors, higher compression, and special camshafts. With the centre of gravity lowered, shortened wheelbase, and radical lightening, the Brooklands had a top speed of around 100mph. It won its class in the Northern Ireland Tourist Trophy in 1929, 1930 and 1931 and was the outright winner in 1932.

Nines also led the light car class in the 1931 Monte Carlo Rally and won the 1934 Le Mans Index of Performance. Freddy Dixon further developed the Riley engine to give high specific outputs and the engine was adopted as the basis of the successful ERA single-seater racing cars. The 1929-35 Kestrel and the 1928 fabric-bodied Monaco saloon bodies on the Nine, designed by Stanley Riley, were highly innovative: the Kestrel was an aerodynamic fastback, while the

1934 Lynx 9 four-cylinder; 1,089cc; ohc; four-speed gearbox; 65mph and 30mpg.

squarer Monaco featured between the axles seating, a dropped floor, and an integral luggage compartment. The Kestrel and Monaco designations were also borne by enclosed 1½-litre fours of 1934-9, when there was a 1,725cc Kestrel six as well. Also powered by the large four and the six were the striking Falcon saloons of 1934-9; they had a less pronounced fastback than the Kestrel's.

Among numerous open versions of the 1½-litre in the late 1930s were the sporting Lynx and Sprite two seater. The racing 1½-litre finished fourth at Le Mans in 1933, second and third in 1934, and first in the 1935 and 1936 TTs.

An outstandingly attractive Nine was the two-seater Imp of 1934-5, with optional pre-selector transmission.

The first Riley six of 1929-34 had a capacity of 1,633cc, as did the Stelvio and Alpine, introduced somewhat later. The 1934-8 Lynx, Falcon, Adelphi, and Kestrel sixes were of 1,726cc, and the 12/6 of 1935 had only 1,458cc. The MPH six was perhaps the handsomest of all Rileys, with its long bonnet and flared wings.

With such a bewildering range (some fours and a V8 haven't been mentioned) it is not surprising that financial failure overtook the Riley family firm. In 1938 it merged with Morris, MG, and Wolseley to form the Nuffield Group. Soon the line was pared to two engine sizes, both of them fours: the 1½-litre and 2½-litre introduced in 1937. In 1948, production of Rileys was moved to the MG works in Abingdon, while the Coventry factory made components for all Nuffield marques. Except for a three seater 2½-litre roadster and convertible of 1948-50, only Riley saloons were produced after World War II. Equipped for some time with true Riley engines, they were worthy of their name. After Nuffield's merger with Austin in 1952 to form the British Motor Corporation, rationalization proceeded apace. The 100mph 2.6 litre Pathfinder of 1954-7 had a Riley engine with a Wolseley 6/90 body/chassis. After that, Rileys were minimally sporting versions of Wolseley and Morris. The name disappeared when the Riley Elf Minis were dropped in 1970.

1947 1½ litre four-cylinder; 1,496cc; ohc; 56bhp @ 4500rpm; 75mph and 27mpg.

Rolls-Royce

'Whatever is rightly done, however humble, is noble.' That was the philosophy which led Henry Royce, a self-made electrical engineer, to move into motor manufacture in 1904. He bought a secondhand Decauville, one of the better light cars of its day and, after some experiments, decided to improve on the design and to build a car which met his own exacting requirements. The 10hp Royce car, which first ran on April 1, 1904, was a refined, silent, well-engineered vehicle which attracted the attention of young Charles Rolls, son of Lord Llangatock. Rolls had owned a car as early as 1894, when he was only 17; now, wealthy, charming and an experienced amateur engineer and racing driver, he had recently set up as a motor dealer, importing many of the better Continental makes.

An agreement was made whereby Rolls took the entire output of Royce Limited, whose works were then in Manchester. The cars became known as 'Rolls-Royce', and the classic radiator design which was to become synonymous with the marque was adopted. A four-model range was laid down: the 10hp twin, of which an initial batch of 20 went into immediate production, a 15hp three cylinder, a 20hp four (one of these came second in the 1905 Tourist Trophy race in the Isle of Man) and a 30hp six.

But the model which really set the seal on the success of the Rolls-Royce company was the 40/50hp six cylinder which made its début in 1906, and was named the 'Silver Ghost' after the 13th car of the type, which successfully covered a 15,000 mile run under observation by the Royal Automobile Club with only one voluntary stop, when the petrol tap vibrated shut after 629 miles.

The cost of new parts to bring the car back to its original condition after the trial—the equivalent of three years' normal service—was just £2 2s 7d, and the running costs, including tyres, were calculated at 4½d per mile. In 1908 it was decided to adopt a one model policy, and this was adhered to until after the Great War. The Silver Ghost was to remain in production for 19 years and set the pattern for the Phantom I and II which were its immediate successors.

By 1909, Rolls-Royce could claim to be one of the leading marques in Britain, and proved this convincingly soon afterwards, by beating the performance of a 65hp Napier in a top-gear-only run from London to Edinburgh, followed by a speed test at Brooklands track. The 7.4-litre Rolls-Royce achieved 24.32mpg against the Napier's 19.35mpg, and 78.26mph against its rival's 76.42mph maximum; this car, which differed from standard in having a raised compression ratio, bigger carburettor, taper bonnet and cantilever rear springing, became the basis of perhaps the finest of all the Silver Ghost variants, the 'London-Edinburgh'.

Charles Rolls was killed in a flying accident in 1910, and Henry Royce's health broke down a year later, so that he was to spend the rest of his life a semi-invalid, living in Sussex in the summer and the south

1923 20hp six-cylinder; 3,127cc; SV; three-speed gearbox; 60mph.

1920 Silver Ghost six-cylinder; 7,428cc; SV;
four-speed gearbox; 70mph and 10-12mpg.

1925 Phantom I six-cylinder; 7,668cc; SV;
four-speed gearbox; 75mph.

of France in the winter for most of that
period. But the fortunes of Rolls-Royce
continued to prosper under the careful
guidance of the firm's commercial managing
director, Claude Johnson, while a picked team
of draughtsmen and assistants worked with
Royce at his retirement homes.

Rolls-Royce gained fresh honours during

World War I, not only for their magnificent
aero-engines but also for the remarkable
performance of their cars under battle conditions, especially those converted into
armoured cars which, among their many
achievements, ensured the success of Lawrence
of Arabia's desert campaign.

Post-war Ghosts had alloy pistons, electric

1929 20/25 six-cylinder; 3,699cc; four-speed
gearbox; 75mph.

lighting and starting and other concessions to modernity, but otherwise were firmly rooted in pre-war practice: it was not until November 1923, for example, that four-wheel brakes were standardized. When the Ghost finally went out of production in 1925, a total of 6,220 had been made.

In 1922, a new 'baby' Rolls-Royce was introduced with a six cylinder, 3,127cc engine rated at 20hp, it was the first Rolls-Royce to have a detachable cylinder head, and, initially, broke with tradition in having a central gear lever and three-speed gearbox. From November 1925, however, the Twenty adopted a four-speed gearbox with right-hand change, then considered the hallmark of a 'quality' car.

Meanwhile, Rolls-Royce had expanded into overseas manufacture with the establishment, in November 1919, of an American manufacturing company at Springfield, Massachusetts, where Silver Ghosts were built with the aim of beating the high tariffs on imported cars which were restricting sales in the United States. Right from the start, these Springfield Rolls-Royces were almost entirely made from American-manufactured

components, but it was not until 1923 that the company provided for the American habit of driving on the wrong side of the road by offering left-hand steering and central controls. However, styling was always indisputably 'American' in taste—impeccably so, of course.

The successor to the Silver Ghost appeared in 1925; appropriately, it was called the New Phantom. It differed mainly from the earlier car in the design of its engine, which was a 7,668cc long stroke unit with detachable cylinder heads (one to each block of three cylinders) and pushrod overhead valves. The New Phantom proved to be a transitional model and lasted only four years before it was supplanted by the Phantom II, which took many of its design features from the 20hp (which was itself to grow up that year of 1929 into the 20/25, with a 3,699cc engine).

Engine and gearbox were in unit on the Phantom II, which also had underslung semi-elliptic rear springs instead of cantilevers, and Hotchkiss drive instead of a torque tube. Springfield practice was followed in the provision of a centralized chassis lubrication

1929 Springfield identical specification to the Phantom I, but optional wheelbase sizes available.

system, which fed all the moving chassis parts with oil from a pedal-operated foot pump. It was a definite advance on pre-war Ghosts, which had 99 lubrication points needing weekly attention.

Springfield was slow in changing over to the new model, which proved costly to introduce; sales collapsed rapidly after the 1928 peak of 400 cars, dropping to 200 in 1929, and 100 in 1930. Springfield production was halted in 1931, though for a while the factory struggled on, selling left-hand-drive chassis built in the British Rolls-Royce works at Derby. The Massachusetts works was finally closed down in August 1935.

Meanwhile, Rolls-Royce had acquired a subsidiary of very different character, in the shape of Bentley, and before long the 'silent sports car' came on the market, using a modified 20/25hp engine with improved gas flow; a $4\frac{1}{4}$-litre Bentley appeared in 1936.

Sir Henry Royce, who had been made a baronet for his work on the Rolls-Royce 'R' aero engine which ensured Britain's victory in the Schneider Trophy contests, died in 1933;

coincidentally perhaps, the red 'RR' on the radiator badge was changed to sombre black.

The first new model to be produced after Royce's death appeared in 1935; this Phantom III proved to be a radical change from previous Rolls-Royce practice, for it had a V12 engine of 7,340cc, with dual coil ignition and hydraulic tappets, set in a chassis with independent front suspension. In keeping with Rolls-Royce tradition of improving on the best designs available—the four-wheel servo brakes on the Ghost had been based on those of the Hispaño-Suiza—the Phantom III followed General Motors' practice of adopting independent front suspension. Its improved GM type layout used short parallel arms controlled by coil springs enclosed in oil-filled cylinders which also enclosed the telescopic dampers, and gave the Phantom III excellent cornering and roadholding which, in a $2\frac{1}{2}$-ton car capable of virtually 100mph, were essential qualities. Exceptionally light steering was another characteristic of this magnificent car; the only drawback was that it could prove extremely expensive to maintain if the maker's

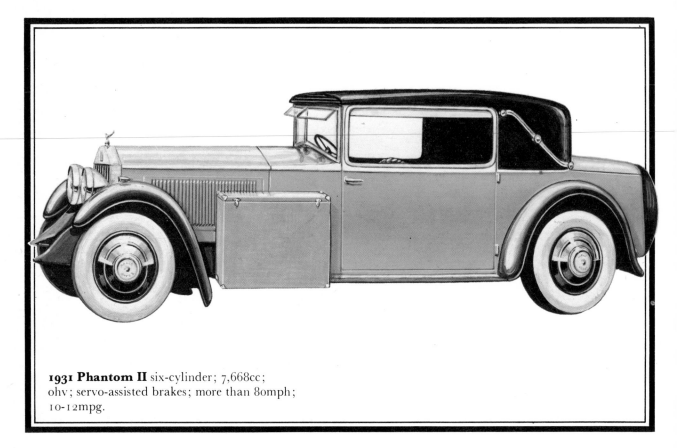

1931 Phantom II six-cylinder; 7,668cc; ohv; servo-assisted brakes; more than 80mph; 10-12mpg.

instructions were neglected, and dirty oil could play costly havoc with the hydraulic tappets and engine bearings.

Shortly after the Phantom III, Rolls-Royce introduced the 25/30, which was capable of speeds in the 80mph range, although independent front suspension did not become available on the smaller models until the advent of the Wraith in 1938. This had a completely redesigned engine which had little but its swept volume of 5,257cc in common with the 25/30.

During the war, of course, Rolls-Royce aero engines played a vital role in ensuring Britain's victory; and the tremendous development of this side of the company's activities meant that when car production again became possible in 1946, it had to be transferred to Rolls-Royce's factory at Crewe, for the facilities at Derby were now fully occupied.

The post-war Silver Wraith of 1947 adopted an F-head inlet-over-exhaust engine. While this may have seemed a retrograde step—it had been used on the original Royce cars of 1903—it enabled larger valves to be used, and gave adequate water cooling space round the valve area. Another major change in specification was the adoption of belt drive for the water pump and dynamo instead of a train of gears. The final development of this six-cylinder power unit came in 1955, when the bore was increased in diameter to give a swept volume of 4,887cc, after an intermediate uprating in 1951 to 4,566cc; any further increase in bore size would have been impossible.

The Silver Wraith was in production until 1959. Produced in parallel with it, from 1949 to 1955, was the Silver Dawn, of similar dimensions, but normally available with series-produced steel bodywork and initially produced for export only. It was the first Rolls-Royce with pressed-steel coachwork although it was finished to the traditional standards of excellence.

In 1950 Rolls-Royce introduced their first post-war big car: this was the straight-eight Phantom IV, whose F-head engine was a 5,675cc development of the Wraith power unit.

Phantom III twelve-cylinder; 7,340cc; hydraulically operated ohv; independent front suspension; more than 90mph; 10mpg.

Although this model was in production until 1956, it was only built to bespoke order for royalty and heads of state, and just 16 were made.

A new six-cylinder model appeared in 1955; this was the Silver Cloud I, and like the ultimate Wraiths, it had automatic transmission as standard without the option of a manual gearbox. It also shared the same bodyshell as the new SI Bentley, which differed only in radiator shell and trim, and was succeeded in 1959 by the Silver Cloud II (and Bentley S2) of similar external appearance, but now endowed with a 90 degree V8 power unit of 6,230cc. A similar engine was used on the limited production Phantom III, which was designed for the services of the custom coachbuilders like Park Ward and James Young. Incidentally, these 1959 models were the first to abandon the centralized pedal-operated chassis lubrication system adopted in the 1920s and, as service intervals were 12,000 miles, there was little inconvenience in this. Surprisingly enough, it had been found that a large number of post-war owners didn't bother to use the 'one-shot' pedal, and that as a consequence their cars were suffering from prolonged neglect.

The final variant of the Silver Cloud, the Silver Cloud III, appeared in 1962: it attracted not a little criticism for its four headlamp arrangement, which many thought looked out of place with the classic Palladian lines of the traditional Rolls-Royce radiator. But in retrospect, the Silver Cloud III seems quite a conservative vehicle, for it was succeeded in 1965 by the Silver Shadow, which was a total departure from Rolls-Royce engineering tradition, for it had integral body/chassis construction, independent suspension all round and four-wheel hydraulic disc brakes instead of the Rolls-Royce friction servo. There was, too, automatic hydraulic height control incorporated in the suspension system.

Against this advanced specification, Rolls-Royce continued to cater for the traditional bespoke market; in 1968 came the Phantom VI, which cost around £13,000 for the seven seater enclosed limousine by H. J. Mulliner Park Ward, and could be had with twin air conditioning units, one for the front seats, one for the back, so that chauffeur and passengers could ride in different climatic conditions.

Silver Wraith six-cylinder; 4,257cc to 1951-52, then 4,566cc; shared engine with Bentley range; 90mph and 16mpg.

Rover

The Coventry firm of Rover added motorcycles to its well-established bicycle and tricycle lines in 1903, then a year later supplemented all three with a one-cylinder four-wheeler that was continued for eight years. This 1,327cc 8hp model was short and light, with a 6ft 6in wheelbase and a weight of only about 1,000lb. Advanced in specification, it had shaft drive, steering column gearchange, and—a world's first—a central tubular backbone chassis with no side framing. A similar but even lighter 6hp model was in production from 1906 to 1912. Knight sleeve valve engines were offered on the single cylinder and 12hp twin in 1911-2. Side valve fours of various capacities rounded off the line from 1906 to 1914. The first of these, the 3.1-litre 16/20, won the Tourist Trophy in 1907.

After World War I, the gracefully styled and popular 12/14 28hp four designed by Owen Clegg and introduced back in 1911 was continued to 1925. It was well streamlined for its time and, thanks to worm drive, strikingly low built. The two-cylinder 13hp Eight of 1920-4 upheld the traditions of the light pre-war Rovers, with improved road holding and a top speed of 40mph. This air-cooled Rover was built in Birmingham.

A wide variety of other models, nearly all

1921 8hp twin-cylinder, horizontally-opposed air-cooled engine; 998cc; 14bhp @ 2000rpm; three-speed gearbox; over 40mph; 40mpg.

1948 P3 four-cylinder, 1,595cc, 60bhp; or six-cylinder, 2,100cc, 72bhp @ 4000rpm; freewheel fitted; 75mph and 25mpg.

with overhead valves, appeared between the wars. Notable among them were the worm drive, four cylinder Nine of 1924-7, and the similar Ten of 1928-33. Of larger and more powerful types, the Light Six of 1930, and the Meteor and Pilot sixes of 1931-3 were especially attractive.

Most Rovers were restyled in 1937, with an outside boot. From 1939-45, Rover was engaged in military projects, including the production of engines for jet aircraft. This experience was utilized to develop promising but abortive experimental gas turbine cars in the 1950s. Fitted in BRM racing chassis, the turbine engine performed well at Le Mans. The Coventry facilities were bombed and post-war car production was transferred to Solihull where the government had built a large aircraft engine plant. The cars of 1945-8, two fours and two sixes, retained the 1937 body lines. Except for a tourer in the 1½-litre Twelve model, only saloons were offered. During 1948 came the P3 range of only two models, the 1.6-litre 60 four and the 2.1-litre

75. Although differing little externally from early post-war models, they incorporated fundamental changes: a new chassis with independent front suspension, and F-head engines (overhead inlet valves and side exhaust valves) with hemispherical combustion chambers, a configuration continued into the 1960s.

Representing a radical restyling by Rover standards was the P4 75bhp six of 1950, with a bulbous full-width body whose life-span was conterminous with the F-head engines. The new Seventy-Five was the only model until 1954 when it was bracketed by a 2-litre 60bhp four and a 2.6-litre 90bhp six. These and later variants, including the statelier P5 3-litre saloon and coupé of 1958-67, enjoyed wide acceptance at home and abroad among doctors and other professionals who valued an aura of understated respectability.

Later, Rover became more adventurous with the advanced 2000 and 3500, followed by the 'new' 3500 of 1977.

1956 90 six-cylinder; 2,638cc; oh inlet; side exhaust valves; 93bhp @ 4500rpm; more than 80mph; 23mpg.

Saab

1958 Model 93 750 GT three-cylinder; 748cc; 50bhp; up to 100mph.

The Svenska Aeroplan Aktiebolaget (Swedish Aircraft Corporation) of Linkoping and Trollhattan embarked on automobile production with the 1950 Model 92. The car's unitized body was streamlined in accordance with wind-tunnel tests and underwent little change in shape until the late 1960s. To this day, all Saabs have front wheel drive and, until 1967, all engines were either two or three cylinder two strokes developed from the unit fitted to the German DKW. Dispensing with valve gear, such engines draw in fuel through transfer ports on the down stroke and get their compression and exhaust on the upward stroke, with the exhaust gases escaping through another port. The 764cc, twin cylinder Saab engine of 1950-55 had only five moving parts: pistons, connecting rods, and crankshaft. Suspension was by torsion bars, and the top speed was about 65mph from a modest 25bhp.

With one more cylinder, the Model 93 introduced in 1955 had seven moving parts. With 748cc, it developed 37.5bhp and had a top speed of 75mph. Suspension was by coil springs and telescopic shock absorbers with a dead rear axle. The first Saab exported in quantity, the 93 was continued with little change for the rest of the decade. Despite its rough and burbly two stroke idle, limited rear vision, and the problems of mixing oil with the petrol, the 93 and its variants were popular.

The cars performed well in international rallies.

The handsome two seater Sonett convertible of 1956-57 hardly went beyond the experimental stage, but the sports minded were happy with the 750 GT of 1958-61. In appearance hardly distinguishable from the standard saloon, it had such features as racing tyres, larger front brakes, racing seats, a tachometer, and a Halda average-speed meter. The engine yielded 50bhp and another 10mph. The 1962-67 GT850 of 841cc, based on the 96 saloon of 1960, adopted a wrap-round rear window and automatic oil-fuel mixing.

The Sonett coupe of 1966-67, lighter than the GT850, had 70bhp and a top speed of 105mph. The two stroke engine was abandoned first in favour of a V4 Ford engine then a 2 litre in-line four derived from the Triumph Dolomite engine.

1966 Sonett coupé version of Model 93; three cylinder; 748cc.

Salmson

Famous for its radial aircraft engines of World War I, the Société des Moteurs Salmson of Billancourt near Paris built GN cyclecars under licence in 1919, followed by their own design of cyclecar in 1921. The first of these was a blend of the bizarre and the primitive: the 1.1-litre four cylinder engine had unique combination pull and pushrods and a camshaft within the block, there was no differential or starter and no front shock absorbers, and only the right rear brake on the solid rear axle (there was none at the front) was operated by the pedal, the left one being actuated by a hand lever. As early as 1922, however, twin overhead camshaft units were fitted to racing Salmsons. Sporting, pointed tail Salmsons often won in the cyclecar class at Le Mans and elsewhere from 1922 to 1928.

After the cheaper and better MG Midget rendered such cars unsaleable, the French firm specialized in small touring models with a touch of luxury. The twin cam SC 1.2-litre four-cylinder saloons of 1929-32 had smart bodies, some of them of the fashionable fabric-covered type by Weymann. The even more refined S4C of 1933-4 was the basis for the four-cylinder British Salmsons of 1934-8, built in London and marketed as a separate line of saloons and sports cars. Continuing the trend to luxury, the French Salmson S4D 1.6-litre introduced in 1935 had transverse leaf spring independent front suspension and an electrically operated transmission by Cotal. This delightful gearbox offered fingertip gear selection by means of a tiny lever mounted on the steering column, which eliminated the need for the clutch pedal.

A 2.3-litre four with 70bhp joined the 1.6-litre in 1939, and both sizes were continued after World War II. In 1951 came a restyled coupé the Randonnée, with an aluminium 2.2-litre engine and Cotal electrically selected gearbox, and in 1953 came the G72 version with revised rear suspension and wire wheels. The latter offerings, with handmade bodies and Cotal transmissions, found few takers despite smooth 105mph performance.

Renault took over in 1955 and soon phased out the Salmson.

1954 E-72 four-cylinder; 2,328cc; ohc; 105bhp @ 5000rpm; Cotal electric four-speed gearbox.

198

Simca

Founded in 1935, the impressively named Société Industrielle de Mécanique et Carrosserie Automobile of Nanterre, near Paris, produced small Fiats under licence until the fateful year of 1940. Both before and after World War II, until 1951, special Simcas prepared by Amédée Gordini won many rallies and races. Simca's first non-Fiat design for mass production, the four-cylinder, overhead valve, 1.3-litre Aronde (Swallow) sedan, appeared in 1951 and was continued until 1964 with periodic restyling and additional body types.

Of more interest to collectors are Simca's sports coupés and convertibles. A coupé, with a body designed by Pininfarina and executed by Facel Metallon, was among the ten cars exhibited as works of art at the Museum of Modern Art in 1951. The even smarter 80bhp V8 coupé of 1953-4 by Facel entered the luxury class at around £2,000. Unassuming but desirable fours based on the Aronde included the Weekend and Plein Ciel coupés and the Océane convertible of the late 1950s and early 1960s, followed in 1963 by a rear engined coupé with body by Bertone.

With the acquisition of French Ford in 1954 Simca inherited a 2.2-litre side valve V8 engine that was designed in 1935 for the European market. As used in senior Simcas from 1956 to 1961, capacity and output were increased in stages to 2.35 litres and 84bhp. Chrysler took a minority share in Simca in 1958 and gained absolute control in 1963.

1956 Weekend

1959 Vedette

Simplex

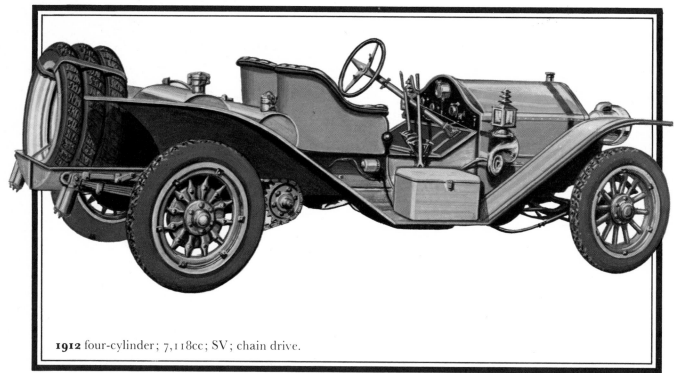

1912 four-cylinder; 7,118cc; SV; chain drive.

Cars built by Smith & Mabley of New York from 1904 to 1907, close copies of the contemporary Mercedes, were named Simplex, after the German firm's senior models. When Smith & Mabley went bankrupt, an enthusiastic Simplex owner, Herman Broesel, Snr, acquired the assets and continued operations. Among these assets was Edward Franquist, whose four cylinder T-head engines were masterpieces of design. His rugged and massive cars of 1908-14, ranging up to 10 litres and 90hp, were nearly all chain driven, and Krupp chrome-nickel steel was employed wherever possible, including the frames. The famous 50hp 10-litre Model 50 cost about $5,000 in chassis form and not much more with stark roadster and touring bodies. An 80mph example in the Smithsonian Institution is typical of Simplexes that won many of what were then factually called stock car races, in which standard factory-built cars were raced against each other.

In 1915, after Broesel's death, the Simplex Automobile Co was acquired by the Crane Motor Car Co of Bayonne, New Jersey, which had been making the $8,000 Crane since 1912. With Henry M. Crane in charge at Simplex headquarters in the former Broesel foundry in New Brunswick, New Jersey, a breed of Simplex altogether different from the Franquist types emerged. This Crane-Simplex was a 46hp, 9.2-litre L-head six on an 11ft 11½in wheelbase. The left-hand steering and shaft drive were standard. The chassis cost $5,000 with a lifetime guarantee. Coachbuilt bodies were still being fitted in the early 1920s, after the last chassis had been completed. Perhaps the most desirable Crane-Simplex is the Holbrook-bodied land yacht which now resides in the Harrah Museum in Reno, Nevada. In 1917 the firm took up the manufacture of Hispaño-Suiza aircraft engines and floundered into bankruptcy during the post-war depression.

Singer

George Singer, three times Mayor of Coventry, had built cycles in that city under his own name since 1875; his company began manufacturing the Perks & Birch Motor Wheel in 1901, fitting this early 'power pack' to cycles and tricycles. Their first proper car came in 1905, a curious three-cylinder model. Outstanding was the bi-block 1,100cc Ten of 1912, which was still in production in the 1920s. The Junior and Nine series, starting in 1927 and hovering around 1 litre, also sold well to a thrifty clientele.

In 1933 Singer introduced a sports model with twin carburettors, remote control gearbox and hydraulic brakes. A standard version ran at Le Mans, finishing 13th, and the company ran a team again in 1934 and 1935. The Le Mans road model began to do well in smaller competitions, and for a time threatened MG's position. But a series of crashes in the 1935 Tourist Trophy race caused the factory to withdraw from racing and the sporting image faded.

The Nine Roadster of 1939, Singer's semi-sporting venture in this range, was reintroduced after World War II with the original 1,074cc overhead camshaft four-cylinder engine and traditionally British cutaway body, nominally a four seater. It had a basic price of £450, slightly higher than for the MG TC and the same as for the four seater Morgan 4/4; although a game little car capable of 65mph from its 36bhp high revving sewing machine-like engine, it had little to offer the sporting motorist and was handicapped by a three-speed transmission.

In 1948 the engine was enlarged to 1,497cc giving 78mph. Independent front suspension and a four-speed gearbox were adopted. The roadster had a modest success and it remained in production until 1955, a few months before the Rootes Group took over Singer and gave the Singer name to modified Hillmans.

1948 Roadster four-cylinder; ohc; 1,074cc; 36bhp @ 5000rpm; three-speed gearbox; 65mph and 30mpg.

Standard

When this Coventry firm began operations in 1903, the primary meaning of 'standard' was 'having a recognized and permanent value'. That well described all the Edwardian types, from the original single-cylinder model to the impressive sixes used as state vehicles at George V's durbar as Emperor of India in 1911.

After a four year concentration by Standard on airframes and aircraft engines, in 1919 the 1.1-litre Rhyl roadster was reincarnated with a dickey seat; a tourer and a coupé were also available. In 1921 came the SLO 1.6-litre overhead valve-engined version, faster at 46mph.

More modern in appearance was the 52mph Fourteen of 1923-7, with a 1.9-litre ohv engine. At a time when saloon bodies were increasingly popular, the Pall Mall version introduced in 1925 sold for about £450. Standards of the late 1920s and early 1930s, starting with a 2.2-litre Eighteen, had a more rounded look. That six was the last ohv until 1947. The companion Nine, Little Nine, and Big Nine fours of 1928-34, ranging from 1 to 1.3 litres, were of the L-head type. So were the 65mph Ensign and 75mph Envoy sixes, successors to the Eighteen. During this period, the traditional shouldered radiator design was dropped. So were Standard's prices, which for 1931 started at

£195 for the Nine and ascended only to £385 for the Envoy. Standard engines of 1, 2, 2½ and 2.6 litres were used in the SS cars of the 1930s. Standard itself boasted sporty roadsters and coupés with special Avon bodies.

The radically restyled fastback Flying Standards were introduced in 1936, starting with the 1.6 litre Light Twelve four and soon augmented by other fours and sixes from 1.1 to 2.6 litres. The last between-wars type was the diminutive Eight of 1939, only 10ft 8in long, which was available as a roadster, tourer, and saloon. It and two larger fours, the Twelve and the Fourteen, were continued from 1945 to 1948 with a slightly notched roofline.

In 1948, Standard adopted a single model policy with the bulbous 2.1-litre ohv Vanguard four cylinder saloon. It was rugged and capacious and deceptively fast—the engine was used in the sporting Morgan Plus Four—but it lacked the character implied in the slogan 'All That's Best in Britain'. The last Vanguards, somewhat smartened, were 2-litre sixes introduced in 1961. The Triumph marque, a subsidiary of Standard since 1945, overtook it in popularity and the senior make was discontinued in 1963.

1936 **Flying 20** six-cylinder; SV; 2,664cc; four-speed gearbox; 75mph and 20mpg.

1954 **8** four-cylinder; ohv; 803cc; 26bhp @ 500rpm; 63mph and 44mpg.

Stanley

In the early years of the industry, steam-powered cars were competitive with the sluggish electrics and the noisy petrol engines. In 1897, the identical twins Freelan O. and Francis E. Stanley of Newton, Massachusetts, who had already made a fortune from a photographic dry plate process, built a buggy-like steam car that was soon selling at the rate of 200 a year, with long waiting lists. Two years later the twins made another fortune by selling the patent rights to Locomobile. Then, to avoid patent infringement suits, they redesigned the car with the 8hp engine geared directly to the rear axle and the boiler in front. This remained the configuration of later and more powerful Stanleys from 1906-14.

These Stanleys were quieter and faster than most of their petrol-powered contemporaries, although they hardly approached the performance of the streamlined Stanley Rocket that in 1906 set a land speed record of 127.6mph at Ormond Beach, Florida. Contrary to a persistent rumour, none of them ever blew up in use, despite a pressure of 600psi. Other drawbacks limited their acceptance: the half-hour drill of bringing the kerosene-heated boiler to operating pressure from cold, and the short range of 50 miles before the water had to be replenished. Also, the pilot light under the boiler had to be kept alight in freezing weather.

Later, Stanleys stretched the range to 300 miles by the use of a condensing boiler, which recirculated the water instead of letting it escape as steam. Steam cars were doomed anyway by the universal adoption of the electric self-starter on petrol-engined cars, and the last of about 18,000 Stanleys appeared in 1927.

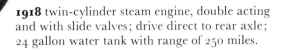

1918 twin-cylinder steam engine, double acting and with slide valves; drive direct to rear axle; 24 gallon water tank with range of 250 miles.

Stearns Knight

The Stearns, made from 1899 to 1930, was among the first and last of the many cars built in Cleveland. Its initial single-cylinder model was a typical gas buggy though, by 1901, its cylinder capacity was a hefty 4,083cc. In 1902 Stearns built a front-engined two cylinder of 5.5 litres. The even larger four of 1905, rated at 40hp, cost $4,000 with a canopy top at the rear but without a windscreen. This was followed by a colossal six of 13 litres and 90hp, with an 8.75-litre four also available at $4,600. They could reach 90 and 60mph respectively. In 1909 the slogan for Stearns was 'The car to keep', so as to obtain full value for a large initial outlay.

The Knight sleeve-valve engine and the Stearns-Knight name were adopted in 1912. By 1914, both four- and six-cylinder models had electric lighting and starting, and central gear change—three speeds in the four, four speeds in the six. Dignity rather than speed was emphasized all through the Knight era. The Knight engine enjoyed a brief vogue throughout the world in the 1910s and 1920s and, as well as Stearns, car makers such as Daimler in Britain, Panhard in France, Minerva in Belgium and Willys in America persevered with the sleeve-valve engine. Its advantages of smoothness and silence were somewhat negated by mechanical complexity and the haze of blue smoke which tended to trail behind it.

List prices for 1917 ranged from $1,585 to $3,200 for the 5-litre four, $2,375 to $3,785 for the 5.4-litre V8 that replaced the six for a few years. The upper figures were for landaulette broughams, a cut above limousines. Such types were coach-built by Baker; Rauch & Lang of Cleveland; Phillips of Warren, Ohio; Brunn of Buffalo, New York.

In 1925 the firm was taken over by Willys, which soon dropped the fours as not in keeping with an image of prestige. Sixes of Classic quality and low production, starting in the low $2,000s, were joined in 1929 by a much costlier 6.3-litre V8 on a 14ft 1in wheelbase. Unfortunately, America's Depression years heralded the end of the road for many of America's quality cars and the Stearns was no exception. The factory doors finally closed late in 1930, although Willys carried the Knight engine for a while but, by 1932, with sales of Knight-engined cars down to 3,000, it was dropped.

The remaining stocks of chassis were sold to DuPont, who used them in their Model H, which featured a Continental engine and Franklin bodies. Not surprisingly, it soon died.

1930 eight-cylinder sleeve valve engine of Knight type; 6,292cc; three-speed gearbox; 75mph.

Studebaker

Henry and Clem Studebaker of South Bend, Indiana, constructed their first wagon in 1852. Six years later a third brother, John, bought Henry's interest in their rapidly expanding firm. With the participation of two other brothers, Peter E. and Jacob F., Studebaker Brothers Manufacturing Co became the largest vehicle works in the world by 1875. Its vast dealer organization facilitated the firm's entry into the automotive field, at first with electric cars in 1902, then in 1904 and 1905 with two- and four-cylinder petrol-engined cars. Starting in 1908, however, the Everitt-Metzger-Flanders Co. of Detroit built four-cylinder Flanders and EMF cars to Studebaker designs, and then sold them to such good effect that their cars ranked between second and fourth among US makes from 1909 to 1912: 28,000 units were built in the latter year, in spite of detractors' appellations like 'Every Mechanical Fault' for the EMF, though it *was* that marque's last year.

For 1913, Studebaker launched its own immediately successful four- and six-cylinder models. Both series established an enviable reputation for ruggedness and ease of maintenance. A line of trucks was added in 1915, the year that Albert Russel Erskine succeeded John M. Studebaker as president.

In keeping with the times, the wagons which had done much to open up the West and had seen service in the Civil, Spanish-American, Boer, and Great wars, were discontinued by 1921. In 1920 a Light Six (renamed Standard Six in 1924) supplemented the larger Special and Bix Sixes; the four was dropped in 1920. Production for 1923 reached 143,000, a figure not surpassed for a quarter of a century.

Acclaim went hand in hand with prosperity. Ab Jenkins set 1926 and 1927 transcontinental records in Studebakers, and other drivers did similar endurance runs with a 1927 Big Six and its successor, the 100bhp President straight eight. Another President climbed Pike's Peak for a 1929 record that stood for a decade. The President of 1931 was equal in many respects to the luxurious Pierce-Arrow, acquired by Studebaker in 1928. A more powerful variant, the Speedway Eight, had an output of 165bhp.

Dizzy with success, Erskine began to make wrong guesses. Two small companion sixes, the Erskine of 1927-9 and the Rockne of 1931-3, were failures, and the Pierce-Arrow association was a drain until its termination in 1933. In 1931, when production at 49,000 units was well below the break even point, Erskine paid out $2.8 million in dividends. In July 1933, two months after Studebaker

1923 six-cylinder; 3,347cc; SV; more than 55mph; 25mpg.

went into a two-year receivership, he committed suicide.

The firm was luckier when another Light Six, the Champion, designed by Raymond Loewy, helped boost annual sales to more than 100,000 from 1939 to 1941. The 'glass house' bodies ('Which way is it going?') of 1947, by Loewy and Virgil Exner, made for all-time record sales in 1948-50—268,000 in the latter year.

Retrograde changes in styling and a refusal to plough profits into product improvement found Studebaker slumping again in its centennial year. Then it surprised the industry with the Loewy studio's 1953 long wheelbase Commander coupé, a masterpiece in styling but cursed with indifferent handling and poor brakes. Its engine, a V8 introduced in 1951, was as heavy as the Cadillac's but developed only 120bhp against 210bhp. An even more attractive car, the Starliner coupé, was designed in 1953 by Bob Bourke from the Loewy studio. Various delays frustrated buyers who went elsewhere and in 1954 Studebaker was forced to merge with Packhard, which prevented the adoption of exciting plans such as an all-independently sprung car powered by a V6 engine designed by Porsche.

The Starliner was restyled and renamed the Hawk for 1956. It was available in a variety of guises with engines ranging from the small six-cylinder of the Champion right up to the ponderous Packard V8, which was 100lb heavier than Studebaker's own V8. The Golden Hawk, illustrated here with the Packard engine, was capable of 125mph, but the handling did not match this velocity.

1953 Commander V8; 3,812cc; ohv; 120bhp @ 4000rpm; automatic; 97mph and 16mpg.

From 1957 to 1964 the V8 Hawks were fitted with Studebaker engines, with the 1957 model having the option of a supercharger. The 1962-4 models styled by Brooks Stevens were particularly attractive.

Studebaker made a sensible move in producing the Lark in 1959. This was the first of the so-called compact cars, which was achieved simply by cutting the nose and tail off a standard saloon model. That year Studebaker earned $29 million but it was the last really profitable year.

Of other Studebakers made in the declining years, the Daytona convertibles and coupés are pleasing in appearance; most of these were made in Hamilton, Ontario, Canada, where the company moved its car production facilities in 1964.

Studebaker bravely tried to introduce technical novelties and attractive styling, very often anticipating industry trends, but the more conventional machinery from rivals always seemed to sell better. Disc brakes were introduced on the front wheels of several models in 1964, well ahead of American rivals, but only 26,073 Studebakers were registered in the USA in 1964, hardly enough to keep its 450 dealers fully employed.

The final fling for the beleagured company was the Avanti, conceived by the firm's President Sherwood Egbert and designed by Raymond Loewy. Little money was available for chassis development so it used a near-standard Hawk chassis with the choice of a 4.7- or 5-litre V8. The largest engine could be specified with a supercharger which was claimed to endow the unit with over 300bhp.

The car was clothed in a sleek four-seater body made from fibreglass reinforced plastics, the low build of which enabled a top speed of 130mph to be reached with the blown engine. Unfortunately, the body fit and finish left a lot to be desired and handling was none too brilliant. Only 1,000 were built in the first year and when Studebaker moved to Canada they dropped the Avanti.

Car production ceased in 1966.

1956 Golden Hawk V8; 4,741cc; ohv; supercharged; 275bhp @ 4800rpm; three-speed plus overdrive or automatic transmission.

Stutz

'The Car That Made Good in a Day', ran the slogan. The day was May 30, 1911. The car was the first one that axle and transmission maker Harry C. Stutz had built to bear his own name (though his first gas buggy appeared in 1899, and he had later designed the 1907 American Underslung) which appeared in its first race. It made good by finishing eleventh, with no mechanical failures, in the first Indianapolis 500 mile race. Stutz racers proceeded to finish fourth and sixth in their home town's classic race in 1912, and third in 1913, behind Peugeot and Mercer.

The most famous of the Stutz cars, the Bearcat, introduced in 1914, was in effect a racing car equipped with wings, running boards and headlamps, resembling its equally stark rival, the Mercer Raceabout. Most were powered by a 6.4-litre T-head four-cylinder Wisconsin engine that developed 60bhp at 1,500rpm. At 4,500lb, the car was heavier than the Mercer and, at $2,000, cheaper.

The equally rare but not quite so legendary Bearcats of 1917 had a streamlined bonnet and scuttle, a windscreen, an enclosed fuel tank, and inboard gear lever. The engine had a capacity of 6 litres with a long stroke of 150mm. Right hand drive and Harry Stutz's original combination differential and three-speed transmission were retained. Thanks to a reduction in weight to about 3,000lb, these cars were somewhat faster, at 80mph. Other models, including a roadster, Bulldog touring cars, and even enclosed types, were available; these were all comparatively sybaritic, with doors and weather protection. Stutz underwent mechanical but not thematic changes until 1925, six years after Stutz himself left the firm.

With losses piling up and production at about 300 cars a year, it was time for a change. Stutz's new president, Frederick E. Moscowitz, brought in Belgian engineer, Paul Bastion, late of Metallurgique, whose Vertical Eight Stutz, introduced in 1926, stressed safety and luxury but had performance in abundance. To quote an advertisement, 'The safest car in America has the right to be the fastest'. It featured safety glass, a double-dropped frame, and worm drive, along with an advanced 4.7-litre engine (soon enlarged to 4.9 litres) with overhead camshaft and dual ignition. Sales leapt to 5,000 a year.

Bearcat four-cylinder; 6,400cc; three-speed gearbox; 80mph.

1928 eight-cylinder; 4,811cc; ohc; 125bhp; 100mph.

The lighter and more powerful (125 against 115bhp) Black Hawk tapered back speedster joined the Safety Stutz in 1927 and bested Auburn as the fastest stock car in America, then finished second in the 1928 Le Mans race. For 1931, the Bearcat name was revived for the boat-tailed speedsters in the new line of DV32 Stutz eights, so called from the 32 valves, actuated by double overhead camshafts in the redesigned head. The shorter wheelbase Super Bearcat exceeded even the new Bearcat's guaranteed 100mph. Such cars were not targeted at a Depression market, and 1935 marked the end.

1932 DV 32 Bearcat eight-cylinder; 5,277cc; dohc and four valves per cylinder; 100mph.

Sunbeam

1951 90 four-cylinder; 2,267cc; ohv; 70bhp @ 4000rpm.

Sunbeam of Wolverhampton built its first cars in 1899 and seemed to make them in every size and guise—including the eccentric Sunbeam-Mabley of 1901-4, with its wheels in diamond formation—and won many important races before World War I. In 1920 Sunbeam merged with Talbot and Darracq to form the STD combine and continued its racing successes with standard and special versions. With special V12 racing cars, Sunbeam set

1953 Alpine MkIII four-cylinder; 2,267cc; ohv; 80bhp @ 4200rpm; 95mph and 24mpg.

five land speed records between 1922 and 1927, the last with Major H. O. D. Segrave's 203mph.

During the 1920s, Sunbeam built a wide range of fours, sixes and eights, most of which put refinement before performance, although the twin camshaft 3-litre six-cylinder sports model of 1925-30 was 'too fast for its chassis'. Sunbeam continued to build cars in great variety but in diminishing numbers until the mid-1930s, when the STD combine collapsed and was taken over by the Rootes Group. This takeover meant the end of Sunbeam as a separate marque until 1954.

From 1938, the cars were called Sunbeam-Talbots and were merely faster versions of Rootes' Hillman and Humber models. The more distinctive 1944cc 64bhp four-cylinder overhead valve Sunbeam-Talbot 90 appeared in 1948, followed late in 1950 by the more commanding Mark II with independent front suspension and a 2,267cc engine of 70bhp, shown here as a four-seater convertible, but more familiar as a four-door saloon. These cars were well suited for rallies—they won the

Manufacturers' Team Prize in the Alpine Rally in 1948 and 1952. Weighing about 2,700lb they could hardly exceed 80mph in standard form, but they were flexible, responsive and vice free throughout, with excellent braking and cornering.

In 1953, production was transferred to the Hillman works in Coventry and for two years the line was augmented by the Sunbeam Alpine (minus the 'Talbot'), an export-directed two-seater convertible based on the 90 but reinforced in nearly every respect and capable of 90mph. Its appearance was exceptionally clean and functional: the top, when not in use, was stowed invisibly behind the seats, while rear wheel spats were abandoned.

The Sunbeam Mark III saloon (also without the 'Talbot') was introduced in 1954. It retained the early 1950s appearance of the 90, but now the veteran 2,267cc engine gave 80bhp and was capable of more than 90mph. In 1956 the Mark III was joined by the much smaller Hillman-based Sunbeam Rapier, which superseded it the following year.

Mk III Saloon four-cylinder; 2,267cc; ohv; 80bhp @ 4,200rpm; 95mph and 24mpg.

Talbot

105 six-cylinder; ohv; 2,969cc; 100bhp @ 4500rpm; Wilson-type epicyclic gearbox; 95mph and 16mpg.

The firm of Clément-Talbot, Ltd, financed by the Earl of Shrewsbury and Talbot, was formed in 1903 to import French Clément cars into Britain, but gradually its wide range of models dropped the French connection. Among the solid side valve types of just before World War 1—a six and four fours—the big 4½-litre 25 four did well in competition: racing against time on the Brooklands course in 1913, a specially prepared 25 was the first car to cover 100 miles in an hour.

Clément-Talbot merged with Darracq in 1919 and Sunbeam joined the group to form the Sunbeam-Talbot-Darracq combine in 1920. The pre-war side valve types were succeeded in 1922 by a 967cc overhead valve 8/18 Talbot, actually a Darracq design. It was soon redesigned by chief engineer Georges Roesch to incorporate a 100cc engine and a longer chassis to take four-seater coachwork. Talbot fortunes were low when Roesch revived them in 1926, with the 14/45, a 1,666cc precision-made six noted for silence and efficiency, rather than for its 65mph maximum; it remained a Talbot mainstay for a decade. Roesch's advanced creations of 1930-6, refined and enlarged versions of the 14/45, won enduring prestige for the marque. Against more powerful specialized machines, the

1935 Model 105 sports-saloon coachwork; up to 100mph.

1937/9 Figoni & Falaschi six-cylinder;
ohv; 3,996cc; Cotal electric gearbox; 95mph.

2.3-litre 90 finished third and fourth in the
1930 Le Mans 24-hour race, followed by the
3-litre 105's third places there in 1931 and 1932.
The STD combine collapsed in 1935, after
financial trouble in many of its branches. The
Rootes group took over Sunbeam and Talbot,
and the last British Talbots were side valve
types in another tradition: the Hillman 1.2-litre
Minx of 1936-9 and the Humber Snipe 3-litre
of 1937-8.

Talbot-Darracq, of Suresnes near Paris, was
acquired by Major Tony Largo, a talented
Italian engineer. His superb luxury cars were
known as Talbots, Lago Talbots, or Talbot
Lagos, with a capacity of 4½ litres from the
late 1930s. One of these won at Le Mans
in 1950 and another led for 23 hours in 1952,
driven single-handed by Pierre Levegh. They
are even more renowned as works of art,
with curvaceous coachwork by such masters
as Saoutchik and Figoni & Falaschi. Talbot
Lago survived until lack of demand forced
the firm's sale to Simca in 1959. The last
body-type, the America Grand Touring coupé
by Henri Chapron, was generally powered by a
2.6-litre BMW V8.

1957 Rapide V8; 2,580cc or 3,200cc; 125bhp
@ 5000rpm or 140bhp @ 6200rpm respectively.

Triumph

The Triumph Cycle Company of Coventry began building cars in 1923. Renamed Triumph Motor Co in 1930, the car and motorcycle sides of the business became separate companies in 1936, and the car company went bankrupt in 1939. The most famous Triumphs of the 1930s were the Dolomites and Glorias. The first Dolomites of 1935 were Alfa Romeos in all but name; later series were more conventional. Triumph was taken over in 1939 by the Sheffield steel firm of Thos. W. Ward, but war frustrated production plans. In 1944 the Triumph name was acquired by the Standard Motor Co. Triumph's first postwar car was the razor-edged 1800 four-door saloon of 1946-8. It used the Standard 14's four cylinder overhead valve engine of 1,776cc and then continued from 1949 to 1955 as the more luxurious Renown, with the 2,088cc Standard Vanguard engine.

Quite different in character but using the 1,776cc unit (also supplied to Jaguar) was the 1800 sports tourer of 1946-8, featuring a four-speed gearbox (the Renown's was three-speed) and a tubular chassis. Its uniquely styled aluminium body had pontoon front wings of steel. There was seating for three in front. Aft, a flip-up windscreen afforded a degree of protection to the two occupants of a dickey seat. The similar but heavier 2000 model sports of 1948-9 used the 2,088cc engine.

Appearing with the Renown in 1949 was a very junior but equally refined partner, the two-door Mayflower saloon. Seating four within its overall length of 14ft 10in, the Mayflower had a 38bhp L-head engine which could propel it in excess of 65mph.

Continuing to build unusual cars from unremarkable components, in 1953 Standard unveiled the pace-setting Triumph TR2 two seater sports car, derived from the 1937 Standard 10 chassis, using the Mayflower's suspension, and the 2,088cc Standard Vanguard engine tuned and scaled down to 1,991cc for eligibility in the 2-litre category. The body, however, with its grille-less nose and its front wings blending smoothly into the bonnet, then sloping downward to meet the rear wings, bore no resemblance to its pedestrian relatives; neither did its astonishing maximum speed of 105mph. It was immediately popular with enthusiasts on both sides of the ocean—more were sold in America than in Britain—and became the mainstay of Standard-Triumph. In 1955 it was succeeded by the TR3, with 10 more horsepower than the TR2's 90 and with a discreet grille veiling the nose. Standard-Triumph merged with Leyland Motors in 1961. In 1962 they announced the TR4, endowed with 2,138cc and wind-up windows. Independent rear suspension arrived with the TR4A, minor cosmetic modifications with the TR5 and fuel injection with the TR6.

The radically restyled TR7 used the Triumph Dolomite 2-litre engine.

1950 Mayflower four-cylinder; SV; 1,247cc; 38bhp @ 4200rpm; three-speed gearbox; 65mph and 33mpg.

1952 TR2 four-cylinder; ohv; 1,991cc; based on Standard Vanguard; developed to give 90bhp @ 4800rpm; overdrive; more than 100mph; 32mpg.

1948 1800 Roadster four-cylinder; ohv; 1,776cc; 63bhp @ 4500rpm (Standard Vanguard based); 75mph and 28mpg.

Vauxhall

In 1903 the Vauxhall Iron Works constructed 43 1-litre single-cylinder cars with chain drive, tiller steering, and two forward speeds. In 1905 came a 1.8-litre three-cylinder and a 2.4-litre four-cylinder model.

The company moved to Luton in 1905 and in 1907 changed its name to Vauxhall Motors Limited. From 1906, Vauxhalls sported fluting on the radiator shell and bonnet which remained a Vauxhall hallmark for more than half a century. In 1908 Lawrence H. Pomeroy designed the L-head 20hp with a 40bhp output, which won the 1908 RAC 2,000 Miles' Trial.

In 1910 came Pomeroy's famous 3-litre

C Type, which performed so well in the Prinz-Heinrich-Fahrt in Germany that it was named—*anglicé*—'Prince Henry'. It was soon enlarged to 4 litres and these pointed-nose masterpieces were capable of a smooth 75mph in standard form.

Pomeroy surpassed even the Prince Henry with his E-type 30/98, again a side valve four but enlarged to $4\frac{1}{2}$ litres and capable of 80mph. All but thirteen 30/98s date from after 1918. During the war, Vauxhall's output was limited to conventional Model 25 4-litre tourers for use as staff cars. The Type OE 30/98 of 1922-7 had a 4.2-litre overhead valve engine rated at 112bhp and capable of nearly 90mph. Both series' engineering was matched in excellence by the timeless elegance of the best-known body style, the four-seater Velox, supplemented from 1924 by fabric covered Wensum coachwork. Only about 270 Es and 310 OEs were built.

Despite the desirability of the 30/98s and 2.3-litre 14/40, announced in 1922, Vauxhall failed to prosper and the total annual

1922 30/98 four-cylinder; ohv; 4,250cc; 100bhp; two-wheel brakes; better than 80mph.

production was only 1,400. In 1925 General Motors took over and soon supplanted Pomeroy's classics with transatlantic-type light and medium-sized cars for the family trade. Various ohv sixes were produced until 1936. The smallest of these was the 2-litre Cadet of 1931-3, with a top speed of 60mph and an attractive price of £280. The 1932 version has the distinction of being the first 'British' car with synchromesh.

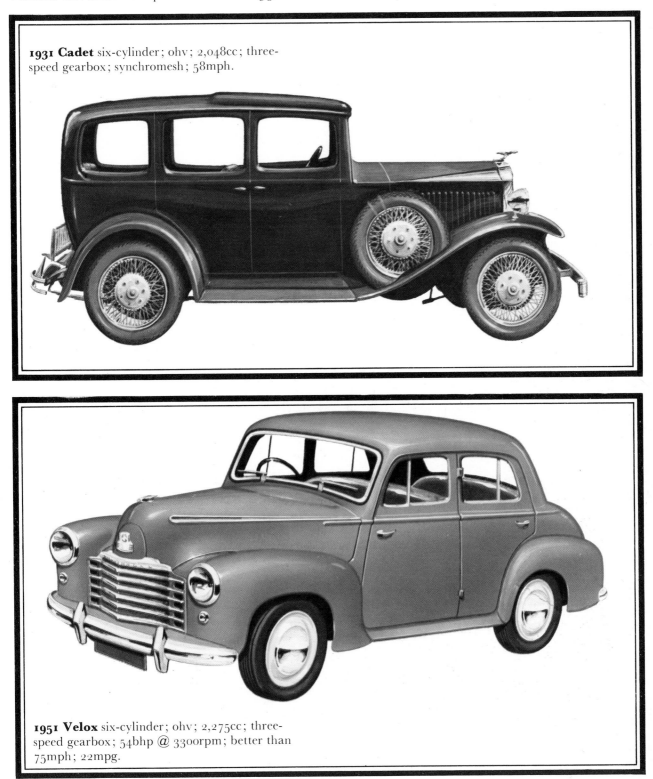

1931 Cadet six-cylinder; ohv; 2,048cc; three-speed gearbox; synchromesh; 58mph.

1951 Velox six-cylinder; ohv; 2,275cc; three-speed gearbox; 54bhp @ 3300rpm; better than 75mph; 22mpg.

Voisin

1924 Type C1 four cylinder; 4-litre; up to 90bhp and 80mph.

For Gabriel Voisin, engineering was not a profession but a passion. A pioneer in aviation, he built a successful biplane which flew in 1907, and by the end of the Great War had built some 10,000 aircraft. But peacetime killed the demand for areoplanes, and Voisin's factory at Issy-les-Moulineaux turned to car manufacture.

During the next two decades, all the strikingly original cars from the Voisin factory reflected their creator's very personal engineering beliefs. Their engines were of the Knight sleeve-valve type developed for lightness and durability. The 4-litre C1 four of 1919-26 was capable of 80mph. Rudolph Valentino bought the car shown here in 1924

and attached his cobra mascot.

V12s such as the C12 4.8-litre Diane of 1930-8 represented the height of functional luxury. These V12s and sixes ranging from 2.3 to 5.8 litres were most eye-catching when clad in lightweight bodies of Voisin's own design. Note the strutted wings on the 1934 3.8-litre Aero Sport. This had a two-speed rear axle, giving six forward speeds.

Voisin's magnum opus was the C23 straight twelve of 1936, using two 3-litre sixes in line. It never progressed beyond the prototype stage, but could achieve 125mph. In 1937 Voisin lost control to a group that, until 1939, made pseudo Voisins powered by 3.6-litre side-valve Graham engines.

1934 Aero Sport

Wills Sainte Claire

C(hilde) Harold Wills, commercial artist and draughtsman turned metallurgist, worked with Henry Ford as early as 1902, sometimes without pay, and helped develop every model from the first A to the T. Rewarded with a 10 per cent share of Ford's own dividends, he was truly rich by 1919, when he resigned, with a severance payment of $1.6 million, to build his own car.

His first priority was an ideal settlement for his workers, at Marysville, Michigan near Lake Sainte Claire, where he bought 4,400 acres and spent a fortune on worker housing and amenities before the first cars appeared in March 1921, amid a severe depression. This Series A-68 was advanced and distinctive, powered by a 6-litre 65bhp at 2,700rpm twin overhead camshaft 60 degree angle V8, unique in America and featuring myriad innovations, notably in the use of molybdenum steel wherever applicable, and of aluminium in the engine block. The chassis design was not particularly notable but the running gear was meticulously designed to the highest standards. As well as the aluminium block, even the connecting rods were of light alloy, which was a rare innovation for 1921. Another unusual feature for the '20s was the cooling fan which could be engaged or disengaged by means of a clutch, so that engine power was not wasted in driving the fan when it was not needed. The styling was clean and smart, with a hint of Hispaño-Suiza.

A smoother eight, the B-68, followed in 1924, and a 66bhp overhead camshaft six in 1925. The American public of the '20s were clamouring for bigger, faster and flashier cars and the new six met the first two demands, but Wills did not go in for exotic bodywork. The 4.5-litre engine was fitted into the larger wheelbase V8 chassis and although performance suffered, the engine gave a power output of 66bhp at 3,000rpm and excellent torque at low speeds. In 1925 and 1926, the six set trans-continental speed records with no mechanical difficulties. The best known record was the San Francisco to New York run in 1926 which took 83 hours 12 minutes, a quite outstanding record on the poorly surfaced roads of the era. For all its sterling qualities, the Wills went out of production early in 1927, the victim of Wills' costly striving for perfection—he sank $13 million and ended penniless. Fewer than a hundred of his 16,000 or so cars survive.

1926 six-cylinder; ohc; 4,480cc; 66bhp @ 3000rpm; four-speed gearbox; 70mph and 15mpg.

Willys

1916 Overland four-cylinder; 3,685cc; SV;
three-speed gearbox combined with rear axle.

In 1907 John N. Willys, a dynamic car dealer in Elmira, New York, gained control of the struggling Indianapolis firm of Overland which had progressed from a single cylinder runabout of 1902 to a 1.3-litre twin in 1905. Willys introduced an 18bhp four in 1907, bought the large Pope-Toledo factory in Toledo, Ohio, in 1908 and concentrated car manufacture there. The Willys name was temporarily dropped in 1910; the following year four lines of sturdy fours, ranging from $775 to $1,600 for open models, blanketed the middle-range market.

The Willys-Knight marque with sleeve-valve power constituted the firm's senior line from 1914 until 1932, with the Overland name reserved for the firm's conventional L-head cars. Willys-Overland held second place in the American market behind Ford, from 1915 until 1918. In 1916, the peak year of that period, the combined output was 140,000 units. This 45hp six-cylinder Overland roadster, with a three-passenger 'cloverleaf' seating arrangement, had a special body and cost $1,250—$105 more than the standard model. As early as 1914, however, all Overlands had smoothly rounded bodies.

The big and expensive fours of 1912-4 were succeeded by a 4-litre four of 1916-9 that

cost only $1,125 at its introduction, though there was a 5-litre six in 1916 and a V8 in 1917-9. At a time when the horsepower race was unheard of, the 3.1-litre Willys-Knight sixes of 1920-6 developed the same 40bhp as the previous fours. Starting in 1922, the rounded body gave way to styling reminiscent of a scaled down Packard. These lines were continued with refinements until 1928, when three series of Willys-Knight sixes, ranging from $1,145 to $1,995 for basic closed models, were available, and 55,000 were sold. The last Willys-Knights, of 1929-32, included a smart senior series that cost up to $2,700 and vied with the satellite Stearns-Knight marque. Such cars were not in tune with the Depression, and in any event sleeve valves no longer offered sufficient advantages. Meanwhile, from 1919 to 1926, the 2.3-litre

1926 Knight six-cylinder sleeve-valve engine;
3,929cc; 60mph and 15mpg.

Overland four had a high and spindly look.
The L-head engine, developing first 27 and
then 30hp, was the ancestor of the unit used
in the Jeep of the 1940s. This model was
also produced by Willys-Overland-Crossley in
England; in 1924 the British version was
offered with a 1.8-litre Morris engine.

For 1927-30, the four- and six-cylinder
L-head cars, ranging from 30 to 53hp, were
known as Whippets. They were so popular
that in 1928 the firm's total output reached
an all time high of 315,000 units. By 1932,
when a 65bhp six and an 80bhp straight eight
made up the Overland line, the figure was
down to 27,000. During a trying receivership
from 1933 to 1936, only a few Model
77 four-cylinder saloons were made. Later
pre-war models, known successively as Willys,
Overland and Americar, were more attractive
and commodious. Many of the 1941-2 Americars
have been modified into V8 drag racers. Even
as they were being phased out, the firm was
winning acclaim and profit by building the Jeep.

With one exception, Willys-Overland's
only passenger vehicles from 1946 to 1952

were four- and six-cylinder two- and four-wheel
drive station wagons. The exception was the
similarly powered two-wheel drive Jeepster
four-seater tourer of 1948-50, endearing but a
money loser. The last Willys passenger cars
were the Aero fours and sixes of 1952-5,
nimble and high quality compacts born before
their time.

1936 4-77 four-cylinder; SV; 2,200cc;
48bhp @ 3200rpm; three-speed gearbox;
70mph and 25mpg.

Wolseley

Herbert Austin designed the prototype Wolseley car in 1896 when he was manager of the Wolseley Sheep-Shearing Machine Co. in Birmingham. Production began in 1899 with a 3½hp single-cylinder model of 1.3 litres. From then until he left to found his own firm in 1905, Austin also designed two-, three-, and four-cylinder types ranging from 1.6 to 11.9 litres, all with horizontal engines. The 1906-10 cars designed by J. D. Siddeley, vertical twos, fours and sixes from 2.3 to 15.7 litres, were marketed as Wolseley-Siddeleys. Shaft drive, introduced in 1907, had superseded chain drive by 1909. Evolutionary changes followed until 1914, when the firm became Wolseley Motors. The cars lost their angular Edwardian contours, and total production reached a pre-war peak of 3,000 units, making Wolseley second biggest producers on the British market.

After World War I, Wolseley continued its irrational myriad-model policy. Among interesting offerings of the early 1920s are the Ten, an overhead camshaft 1.3-litre four with worm drive and rear-mounted transmission, the diminutive two-cylinder flat twin 1-litre Seven and the 3.9-litre six. Rather predictably, the firm went bankrupt

and was acquired in 1927 by William Morris, later Viscount Nuffield. Wolseley influence on the Morris marque was strong and Wolseley type overhead camshaft engines were used on Morris and MG models after the merger.

The buzzing Hornets of 1931-4 were unique in their power plant, an overhead-cam six, the first mass-produced small engine of this type. With only 1.3 litres, it achieved 70mph from a power output of only 30bhp—a remarkable achievement. This engine had Wolseley's typical bevel drive overhead camshaft and four main bearings, which allowed performance tuning without the fear that the engine would fly apart. Consequently the Hornet sports models became popular with the less well-off enthusiasts. At £160 in 1932, it was very good value.

Gradually, the Wolseley design features disappeared as the Morris régime began its rationalization programme, but the illuminated oval radiator badge of the 1933 models was allowed to stay for many years.

In 1949 Wolseley operations were transferred to the Morris plant at Cowley, near Oxford. The 2.2-litre Six-Eighty of 1952, shown here, a handsomer twin of the Morris Six, typifies the police Wolseleys shown in old films.

1952 6/80 six-cylinder; ohc; 2,215cc; 72bhp @ 4600rpm; four-speed gearbox; 80mph and 22mpg.

Index

Acknowledgments
The publishers would like to thank the following organisations and individuals for their kind permission to reproduce the photographs in this book:
Bettmann Archive Inc. 15 above, 18 below, 26; Daimler-Benz AG, W. Germany 11 above, 11 below, 12 above, 12 below, 13 below, 14 above, 15 below; Mary Evans Picture Library 8 above, 9 below; Ford Archives/Henry Ford Museum, Dearborn, Michigan U.S.A. 19; Ford Motor Co. Ltd. 17 below, 20; General Motors Corporation 31; National Motor Museum 18 above, 25 below; Popperfoto 16 above; Cyril Posthumus 10 above, 10 below, 23; Radio Times Hulton Picture Library 13 above; Renault Ltd. 22; Roger-Viollet 14 below, 16 below, 21 above; Nicky Wright 21 below.

PDO 78/454